Cybernetics Today: Achievements, Challenges, Prospects

Editor
I. M. MAKAROV,

Corresponding Member
of the USSR Academy of Sciences

Compiled by V. D. Pekelis

Translated from the Russian
by Felix Palkin and Valerian Palkin

MIR PUBLISHERS MOSCOW

First published 1984

На английском языке

Cybernetics Today

Кибернетика на новом этапе

Под редакцией чл.—корр. АН СССР
И. М. МАКАРОВА

Составитель—В. Д. ПЕКЕЛИС

Издательство «Мир»
Москва

Contents

Preface

The publication of these articles on cybernetics appears to be both timely and necessary. The point is that cybernetics and especially its development are sometimes misinterpreted not only in popular books but also in scientific literature. Readers influenced by sensational publications often get a misleading impression that cybernetics is omnipotent and that its possibilities are unlimited. Take, for instance, all the talk about "thinking machines", about robots taking over from man, about the coming reign of "intelligent machines" over human beings, and so forth.

In order to orient the scientific community and the general public and to give them first-hand information about cybernetics, the USSR Academy of Sciences several years ago entrusted the Scientific Board on Complex Problems of Cybernetics with the task of publishing papers on cybernetics. These were to be written by leading experts in the field. The publication project was headed by a prominent Soviet scientist Academician A.I. Berg, the Chairman of the board on cybernetics.

The first collection of articles entitled *The Possible and the Impossible in Cybernetics* was published by the Academy of Sciences in 1963. It dealt with the problems then topical in the new science such as automation —life — consciousness, and discussed controversial ideas: whether machines can think or create, and what living organisms and cybernetic systems have in common.

The second book *Cybernetics Expected and Unexpected* appeared in 1968. It continued the discussion started in the first book and made prospects as to the future of cybernetics.

Both books were successful, and it was decided to launch a special series of books under the general title *Cybernetics: Unlimited Possibilities and Possible Limitations*. After the death of Academician Berg, the editorial board of the series was headed by Academician B.N. Petrov, a Vice-President of the USSR Academy of Sciences. In addition to the books already mentioned, several more books in the series were issued. Their titles: *Cybernetics: Review of Developments*, *Cybernetics: State of the Art*, *Cybernetics: New Horizons*, and *Cybernetics: Practical Aspects*, reflect their contents. The authors endeavoured to develop the ideas in the new science: from the early discussions to recent debates and the latest forecasts for the future; from excessive enthusiasm to serious doubts; from the claims of "extremists" who refused to see any limitation in principle to the "soberminded" people who regarded the radical views with a good measure of scepticism.

It is remarkable that at the time when the boundaries of cybernetics had yet to be clearly defined, some scientists had predicted the absolute superiority of informational machines to man's nervous system in the future, in the same way as mechanical power is absolutely superior to muscle power today.

Cybernetics tried, offhand, to invade a most intricate area of study—the workings of the human intellect — and so unlock the subtle secrets of the brain. Indeed, at the outset cybernetics succeeded in automating a considerable number of logical and arithmetic operations and in gaining a firm foothold for a deep penetration into the area of knowledge relating to information and control. It seemed that a single step needed to be taken and the last obstacle would be overcome, and then the dazzling prospects of limitless possibilities would open out. But real life applied its corrections to the expected progress of cybernetics. The value of this book is that it not only deals with the discussions of the past from a correct scientific standpoint, but also endeavours to show the reader what has been achieved and where cybernetics is heading.

The past, present, and future are analyzed by such prominent Soviet scientists as Academicians A.N. Kolmogorov, V.M. Glushkov, B.N. Petrov, and O.M. Belotserkovsky, Corresponding Members of the USSR Academy of Sciences I.M. Makarov, G.S. Pospelov, and I.S. Shklovsky and other leading experts in cybernetics, mathematics, and automation.

Despite the wide range of the topics offered and their careful treatment, this relatively small book cannot claim to have covered all the problems of cybernetics. It contains only some of the articles that have appeared in the different books in the series, namely, those that have stood the test of time and could be of interest to the reader.

I hope that the efforts made to popularize cybernetics on a solid scientific level will be fully appreciated.

Academician E.P. Velikhov,
Vice-President of the USSR Academy of Sciences.

Note from the Compiler

This book covers a wide range of problems relating to cybernetics. It has seven chapters, excluding the preface and the conclusion, arranged so that the reader, as he goes through the articles of different authors, can follow the development of ideas in cybernetics from the first debates to recent discussions and get a glimpse at the future of this new scientific discipline.

The first chapter, "Discussions from Different Years", opens with an article by Academician Kolmogorov which, with a fair degree of accuracy, can be regarded as a standard work. The article is published here in full for the seventh time, to say nothing of the number of times excerpts from it have been published and the article cited. The paper has drawn so much attention because the author, an outstanding Soviet mathematician, accurately and comprehensively showed the meaning and character of the discussions on cybernetics in the 1960s, summing up the initial stage of the debates. He also advanced hypotheses which are still valid today and raised several fundamental questions which still remain unanswered. Moreover, an approach to resolving the problems he raised has yet to be found.

Kolmogorov's article took the wind out of the sails of those who had pinned boundless hopes on cybernetics and computer technology, an attitude typical at the time. The absolute confidence that cybernetics could do everything was shaken, for the unreasonable hopes and undue predictions had been upset by the application of a genuinely scientific analysis to the problems in question.

Today, advances in cybernetics and computer science are considered more dispassionately. Of course, they have made an impact on modern science and technology. Cybernetic systems are used to simulate and control manufacturing processes; to plan production; to do business accounting, to operate vehicles on land, on sea, and in outer space; to control traffic; to solve intricate mathematical problems; to decipher puzzling texts; to solve strategic problems; and so on.

Cybernetics has been applied to biology and medicine for studying physiological (particularly genetic) phenomena; for replacing (during surgical operations or illness) natural organs with self-adjusting devices; and for implanting artificial organs. Cybernetics has branched out into the new scientific discipline of bionics. This field studies the possible use for technological purposes of the principles and methods of the information handling abilities found in living organisms. Finally, cybernetics supplies biology and the sciences studying the mind (pedagogy, psychology, psychiatry, gnoceology) with methods that help them to achieve stricter mathematical accuracy in research.

Cybernetics has a role to play in the social sciences too. Its methods are borrowed by political economy, law, linguistics, and logic. Cybernetics invades other areas of science and industry, agriculture, and even daily life. This is the result not only of theoretical advances in cybernetics but also of its technological advances as represented by high-level automatic devices, electronic computers, especially the mainframe and minicomputers; various electronic mathematical systems; and powerful information complexes.

The cybernetic devices of today are no longer mere computing machines; their practical use is much wider. The latest cybernetic products have caused a veritable revolution in science and technology. The speed and memory capacity of modern electronic computers have brought about qualitative changes in intellectual work and extended the creative power of man. They have given rise to peculiar man-machine systems which combine the rigid formal logic of the electronic computer and the flexibility of the human brain.

Some of these questions—the most important ones—are touched upon in the chapters "The State of the Art" and "On Specific Problems of Control".

One chapter is completely dedicated to the concept of artifical intelligence. It is presented in the form of a small discussion, entitled "Artificial Intelligence: Pros and Cons". It should be noted that the term "Artificial Intelligence" is somewhat misleading, although it is alluring and stirs the imagination. It fascinates many people (particularly those outside cybernetics) and promises fantastic potential and achievements, which will be realized soon, possibly tomorrow.

Such views are only natural, for even professionals, who say that artificial intelligence is the science of making a computer perform the tasks of an educated man, see an irresistible challenge in the theoretical solution and practical realization of this concept.

The relations between the creative process and cybernetics and the interaction between man and machine are treated in two consecutive chapters entitled "The Fine Arts and Cybernetics" and "From a New Angle".

The articles on artistic creativeness and ethical problems carry some elements of polemic. Formalizing ethical categories, even on the fairly limited scale that is possible, is not as easy as it might appear. The approach of cybernetics to purely human and social problems is interesting as such, although ethics is only part of the whole field of social relations. But to apply mathematics and cybernetics to moral values has proved very difficult indeed, and cybernetics has not really shown, as is claimed by its proponents, any ability to approach personal moral problems.

It seems opportune to caution the reader against extreme generalizations at excessively high levels of abstraction, which is the trend with some authors. For some reason, this trend often managed to escape criticism until recently. Attention should also be drawn to some of the controversies in terminology still found in cybernetics. This is largely the result of merely borrowing ready-made concepts and terms for the new science.

The chapter "Vision of the Future" requires some commentary. The article by the late Professor F.G. Staros, D. Sc. (Engineering) who was a prominent Soviet expert in electronic technology, is full of factual data which, although taken from the past, are still significant today. He sketched out a daring project, and taking the latest advances in microprocessor technology as his point of departure, endeavoured to look far ahead. We know that the large microelectronic memory circuits of today are still a far cry from the human brain, and that the main difference between the two is the method by which links between elements are formed and arranged. We have now grounds to believe that the brain, like the computer, or perhaps to a greater extent than the computer, processes the information stored in its memory and puts the results back in the memory.

Professor Staros's project induced other authors to put forward an even bolder proposal supported by calculations and going even farther than the project of the three-dimensional memory which had provided the principle of designing the "electronic brain". This new proposal, the "optical brain" project, is described in the article by V. M. Zakharchenko and G.V. Skrotsky, who are specialists in electronics and quantum physics.

The same chapter contains articles on the cybernetic double and on artificial intelligence in extraterrestrial civilizations. Since "superoptimistic" concepts are likely to give rise to various objections, it would be useful to support these extraordinary ideas with authoritative views. Thus, Academician Glushkov wrote: "I have long been preoccupied with the problem of developing a cybernetic double. Today, most of the leading scientists seem to believe that it is a necessary and feasible task. The core of the problem is the transfer of personality and consciousness from a human being to his double. If this problem can be solved, a cybernetic double will have been created".*

But with this problem solved, another may arise. Man is not likely to end up producing accurate models of real personalities, but may want to create new ones, which could exist, think, and act on their own, without him.

Corresponding member of the USSR Academy of Sciences I.S. Shklovsky in his article "Extraterrestrial Civilizations and Artificial Intelligence" talks about the fourth stage of the matter. He unfolds the following sequence of development: non-living matter—living matter—natural intelligence—artificial intelligence. It should be said that in dealing with such concepts one is bound to take a somewhat "speculative" approach from a rather "extreme" point of view. But this "speculative" approach and "extremism" come from an eminent scientist who, as a professional astronomer, has a real notion of the extent of the Universe in terms of space and time, who puts forth tenable hypotheses, and who, in contrast to a layman, can fully assess the incredible idea that we are alone in the whole universe and our civilization is unique not only in space but also in time.

Understandably, assertions about the feasibility of creating an artificial intelligent life like our own or strikingly

---

* see Россоховатский И. и Стогний А., *КД — Кибернетический двойник* (Киев, 1975).

different from our own (artificial "intelligence", "thinking" machines, the cybernetic double, and so forth) produce numerous objections. Even people who comprehend the concept of producing highly organized artificial life are in their heart of hearts repelled.

Academician Kolmogorov says in his article that the all-out invasion of the mysteries of human existence, up to the possibility of encoding a persons' self and dispatching it elsewhere, seems frightening and repulsive to many people. He claims that this fear is preposterous and groundless and that it must be replaced with a feeling of great satisfaction that such elaborate and miraculous feats can be accomplished by man.*

Of course, the "cybernetic double", "artificial brain", "artificial intelligence" and other cybernetics concepts at the bounds of the possible are now only predictions. But while the value of a prediction depends on the degree to which the basic data used are objective and reliable, one must not forget that prediction as such is systematic research into the prospects of the development of phenomena or processes by means of science.

Our vision of the future can only be shaped consistently through elaborate scientific methods. None the less, the fact remains that knowledge alone is not enough for prediction. No less important is inspiration and imagination, which are sometimes capable of ignoring logic itself. Without them it is difficult to cross the line which divides the possible and the probable, that is, something that can be accomplished and something that can only be imagined.

Optimists and pessimists can also be found among those who make predictions. Their approach to the same problem is made from different angles, coloured by different indivi-

---

* see pp. 40-41.

dual attitudes, temperaments, and so on. Although facts often speak for themselves, "facts" of the future are a special matter and allow diametrically opposite conclusions.

Thus, pessimists, who look even into the nearest future, are concerned with what they believe to be a certain intellectual barrier in the further improvement and application of digital computers. Some assert that there is a psychological barrier, as it were, in the path of the development of cybernetics, and with time it will grow stronger, not weaker.

It cannot be denied, of course, that advances in computer technology create various difficulties, primarily intellectual in nature. Paradoxically, these difficulties contribute to progress in applying computers.

N. Wiener, one of the fathers of cybernetics and its greatest optimist, once said that cybernetics as a science had just begun its life, and that it would find diverse and unpredictable uses.

That, of course, was a general forecast that cybernetics would evolve, and it would be interesting to know more specific prognostications. Unfortunately, there have been hardly any special publications on the future of cybernetics; as a rule the speculations on the theme are scattered through works that endeavour to predict the shape of things to come on a global scale. Take such books as *The Forseeable Future* by G. Thompson (1955), *Industrial Dynamics* by J. Forrester (1961), *Profiles of the Future* by A. Clarke (1962), *Наука в 2000 году* by Kuznetsov (1969), *Окно в будущее* by Bestuzhev-Lada (1970), *The Things to Come* by H. Kahn and B. Bruce-Briggs (1972), *Fahrplan in die Zukunft. Digest internationaler Prognozen*, by H. Beinhauer and E. Schmacke (1970), *The Next 200 Years* by H. Kahn, W. Brown and L. Martel (1977), the collections of papers *Future of Science. International Yearbook* (1966-1983); and some other books, and you can see that all those authors in some way or other touch upon cybernetics and computer technology.

Now, which view of the future of cybernetics should be chosen?

As one cybernetics expert wittily put it, the simplest and most common way is to prefer that which confirms our current beliefs and former misjudgements. And with computer technology and automation, he says, it is easy to find such a confirmation.

Perhaps nobody can avoid making a choice like this, but in trying to answer the question: "Cybernetics—what next?" one should bear in mind the following.

A new science often goes through three stages in its evolution: first, it inspires enthusiasm and catches the imagination, then comes a period of a more sober approach and practical use, and finally enthusiastic interest flares up again, this time based on a real knowledge of its capabilities and ways in which it can be developed. This also holds true with cybernetics.

At which stage is cybernetics today?

I think, it is the stage of a sober approach and practical use, although a new interest—in artificial intelligence—is coming. And what the future has in store for us can to some extent be found in the articles of this book.

When discussing the future, the authors specify or imply different points in time when their forecasts are likely to materialize. The forecasts can be divided into three groups: short-term, up to the end of the 20th century; medium-term, for the next century; and long-term, for the distant future.

This division is more or less in agreement with some important objective criteria.

One of these relates to the life span of a human being and mankind as a whole: short-term forecasts cover the active life span of one generation, medium-term forecasts corres-

2—01169

pond to life expectancy, and long-term forecasts deal with the 21st century and farther ahead.

The second criterion relates to the development of science, technology, and production. Thus, the time between a scientific discovery and its commercial realization is 20 years on average. Several decades must elapse before the new technology has taken over from the old one in many fields of human activity. The distant future will see global revolutionary changes in science, technology, and civilization as a whole.

Naturally, long-term forecasting brings science closer to science fiction. But fiction, if it is really scientific, is known to set imaginative tasks before science. Even the most practical experts believe that problems "at the edge of the imaginable" might serve as tomorrow's stock of material for science.

Medium-term forecasts, which cover the next century, also have to do with a distant future. Although they only offer hypotheses and give a general outline of what may come, this makes it possible to look into the future and see the horizons.

No doubt, short-term forecasts are the most valuable and critical, because they urge scientists to "invent" the immediate future all the time, and to substantiate development in technical and socio-economic terms. These forecasts can be corrected as technical progress reveals obvious flaws.

In this country, the programme that determines the development of national life for 5-10 years, pays great attention to technological progress and, specifically, to fundamental research into the scientific problems which are discussed by the authors of this book. For example, development of mathematical theory and its greater efficiency in practical applications have been projected to help write the software to solve scientific and technical problems. This provision will lay a solid groundwork for theoretical and practical research and development in cybernetics and computers. The task is to improve computer technology in terms of hardware, software, and data collection, transfer, and processing systems with a view to promoting wider use of computer-aided research and design, improving the efficiency of automated control systems, and expanding networks of computers and multi-user computer centres. All this will in turn spur the development, production and extensive use of industrial robots, integrated automatic control systems based on microprocessor and microcomputer technology, and automated production shops and entire plants.

The prospects for Soviet science are impressive. They can be seen today not only in outline but also in more definite terms, and fairly far ahead—up to the year 2000. This date may seem to have been chosen only for the sake of convenience, but it is not arbitrary. It defines a period of time in which a series of interconnected scientific and industrial programmes is to be implemented, something that is very important for economic planning.

Although concrete plans call for concrete actions, bold forecasts should not be avoided. The outstanding Soviet scientist Academician Keldysh once said that the breathtaking developments in science and technology pushed closer to realization projects that not long ago had seemed fantastic, and so it was unwise to confine ourselves to dealing with apparently feasible short-term problems and plans.

The year 2000 is significant for this book, too. By that time cybernetics will be half-a-century old. What will it have brought to the date? Will the hopes and predictions discussed by the present authors come true? Or have they, in the heat of debate, failed to see the course that cybernetics will really take?

V. Pekelis

From Discussions of Different Years

Considering debates on the various problems of cybernetics, we come to the following conclusion, which is now unanimous: as we go deeper into cybernetic problems, it is becoming apparent that, despite certain achievements, our knowledge in this new field is still inadequate. Our achievements can be regarded as only "tactical and local". Some experts believe the enthusiasm that the advent of cybernetics was met with has now flagged. Perhaps too much was expected of it; the hopes that cybernetics will solve all problems, that it will promptly explain all psychological and biological phenomena, and so on, have turned out to be largely utopian.

This situation is reflected in the articles of this chapter, which, in addition to critical analysis, outlines practical prospects for cybernetics in new conditions of the current revolution in science and technology.

Automata and Life

A. N. KOLMOGOROV

My paper, "Automata and Life", which I wrote for a seminar at the faculty of Mechanics and Mathematics at Moscow State University, aroused wide public interest. A popular version of the paper was prepared by N.G. Rychkova, my colleague at the University's Laboratory of Probability and Statistics Methods. This version is essentially true to the original, although the wording and hence the shades of meaning of some statements belong to Rychkova. Let me highlight the main points in the paper which seemed to be of general interest.

I. The definition of life as a special form of existence of protein bodies which was given by Engels is correct and fruitful so far as it relates to the forms of life which have evolved on Earth. In the space age, we are faced with the real possibility of encountering "forms of the movement of matter", which may be living and even thinking organisms while being structurally quite different. For this reason, the need for a more general definition of life becomes apparent.

II. Modern electronics opens wide possibilities of modelling life and intelligence. The discrete (arithmetic) nature of digital electronic computers and automata is not overly limiting in this respect. Systems composed of a very large number of elements, each acting purely "arithmetically", can acquire qualitatively new properties.

III. If the property of a material system to be "living" or to have the ability "to think" is defined purely functionally (for example, a material system capable of having a meaningful discussion of modern science or literature is regarded as intelligent), then the artificial creation of living and intelligent beings should, in principle, be recognized as quite feasible.

IV. It should be borne in mind, however, that the progress cybernetics and automation have actually made towards this goal is much more moderate than is described in most books and articles on science. For example, authors describing "self-learning" automata or those capable of composing music or writing poetry tend to oversimplify the real character of man's higher nervous activity and creative work in particular.

V. Real progress in understanding higher nervous activity, including the highest endeavours of man's creative power, obviously cannot detract from the value and beauty of human achievements. I think that such an understanding could legitimately be considered as one of these achievements, and the motto "Materialism is the thing!", which is used as a section heading later in my paper, testifies to this.

I side with those extremely bold cyberneticists who see no fundamental restrictions in the cybernetic attitude towards the problem of life, and who believe that life as a whole, human consciousness included, may be analyzed by cybernetic methods.

The following questions are posed very frequently.

Can machines reproduce themselves and can there be in the course of this duplication a progressive evolution that would result in more advanced machines than the original ones?

Can machines have emotions: happiness, sadness, discontent or desire?

Finally, can machines set aims for themselves, aims which have not been given them by their developers?

One way to get rid of these questions or justify negative answers is to define a machine as something artificially created by man. If such a definition is adopted, some of the questions, say, the first one, are meaningless. But a stubborn refusal to consider the really interesting and complicated problems hiding behind the shield of arbitrarily limited terminology is not reasonable.

Whether a cybernetic approach can create a real form of life which will continue and develop is a topical problem of our time. It must be answered and ought to be seriously discussed because the study of the similarities between man-made automata and really living systems has become a method of investigating life phenomena on the one hand, and a method for developing new automata, on the other.

There is another way to answer all these questions at once, which is to face it from the point of view of the mathematical theory of algorithms. Mathematicians are well aware that within any formally defined system, which is rich enough mathematically, one can formulate apparently meaningful questions that presuppose the existence of an answer, although within the limits of the system, the answer cannot be found. It is declared, therefore, that the development of the formal system itself is the task for the machine, whereas seeking the correct answers is the prerogative of man, the predominant characteristic of human intelligence.

Such an argument, however, is based on an idealized interpretation of intelligence, and can be used to prove that man himself, and not just the machine, is unable to think. This is because man is supposed to be capable of correctly answering any question, including that raised in an informal manner, and the human brain is supposed to be able to make calculations of any complexity.

In fact, there are no grounds whatsoever for this idealized concept of man as an infinitely complex organism holding an infinite number of truths. In order to achieve this, mankind would presumably have to be scattered across the universe so as to perform propositional-calculus operations in infinite space and even hand them down to descendants as a legacy. Only then could we consider mankind to be able infinitely to develop any mathematical algorithm.

This reasoning is not relevant to a real problem. Anyway, it cannot be regarded as an objection to posing the question of whether artificial beings can be created capable of replicating and progressively evolving and in their most developed form, capable of emotion, free-will, and intelligence.

The same question was put ingeniously but formally by the mathematician Turing in his *Computing Machinery and Intelligence*. Can a machine indistinguishable from man be built? This formulation seems to be in no way worse than ours, and besides it is simpler and shorter. Actually it does not really get to the heart of the matter. What is essentially of interest is not whether automata possessing specific human traits can be made. What we want to know is whether a new sort of life can be created, as highly organized as ours, although perhaps in an unusual and dissimilar form from us. Papers that touch upon this topic are beginning to emerge in modern science fiction. However, these writers have not shown sufficient ingenuity. I.A. Efremov, for example, suggested that "all perfect beings are similar to each other." Hence any highly organized being must have a pair of eyes and a nose, although, perhaps, they would be somewhat different in shape. In our space age, it may be presumed that we might encounter other beings, extremely organized, but at the same time utterly dissimilar to us. Shall we be able to get to know what the inner world of those beings is like, are they capable of thinking, do they feel aesthetic emotion, and so on? Why for instance, should a highly organized being not exist in the form of a thin film, a mould spread over stones?

What Is Life? Is Artificial Intelligence Feasible?

This question is closely related to others such as what is life, what is intelligence, what is emotion and aesthetic experience? How does the latter differ from simple pleasures, such as eating a pie? Tackling the problem philosophically, we can say that no accurate definitions of such concepts as free-will, the ability to think, or emotion, have yet been formulated. But definitions with the degree of exactness required by natural science can be made. If we refuse to recognize such a possibility, we shall leave ourselves disarmed before the arguments of solipsism.

We would like, for instance, to learn how to diagnose the inner state of a highly-organized creature by its behaviour.

How can a cybernetic approach be pursued in the study of higher nervous activity? Firstly, one could study the behaviour of animals or man; secondly, one could investigate the structure of their brains; and finally, one could use empathic understanding, which may be sufficient in some cases. If, for instance, we carefully observe a cat or dog, then even without knowing about ethology or conditioned reflexes, we can figure out what they want or what they intend. Understanding birds or fish this way is more difficult, but not impossible. The problem is not new and while some of its aspects are easy to solve, some are more difficult; it has been partially solved already. The inductive evolution of science testifies that every problem which has stubbornly resisted solution is eventually worked out, and there is no reason to believe in the existence of any limits beyond which science cannot go.

If we assume that cybernetics naturally includes the analysis of any highly-organized system, then the wide-spread opinion that cybernetics deals exclusively with systems which are oriented towards specific goals must be abandoned. Cybernetics is often defined as the science of control systems. All such systems are considered to have common characteristics, the main one being the existence of an aim. This view is only correct as long as what we choose for an organized system controlling its own activities is similar to ourselves. However, if we want to study cybernetically the origin and evolution of these systems, this definition is incomplete. It is hardly to be expected that cybernetics should relegate to other sciences the task of clarifying how a common cause-

and-effect relationship in a complex system naturally develops the system to the point where it can be regarded as intelligent.

The concept of "intelligence" usually includes the ability to protect itself against destructive environmental forces or includes, say, the ability to reproduce itself. It may be asked whether crystals act intelligently and whether the "embryo" of a crystal would develop if placed in a non-crystalline medium. Since no separate members can be differentiated in it, a crystal must be regarded as an intermediate form. And the existence of such forms is indispensable.

The solution of problems like this is apparently the prerogative of related sciences and experience gained in them should not be neglected. But general notions about the cause-and-effect relationships in intelligent systems that set aims for themselves cannot be excluded from the scope of cybernetics just as it is impossible when imitating life by automata, not to consider, say, that these aims and accordingly attitudes towards them change in the course of evolution.

When it is stated that the genetic mechanism, which helps a living being transfer its rational structure to its descendants, has as its purpose the reproduction of the organism, the passing on of its specific properties and the realization of a capacity to mutate and progressively evolve, then where does this purpose come from? Or, if the system is taken as a whole, who if not the system itself sets the aim of evolving by discarding unfit variants and reproducing fit ones?

Thus, a general study of the origin of those systems that can be looked upon as intelligent is a major task of cybernetics. General study obviously implies knowledge abstracted from anatomy, energy problems, chemistry, technological feasibility, etc. Here, the only thing we are interested in is how the ability to store and accumulate information came into existence.

Such a comprehensive statement of the problem incurs many difficulties, but in the present state of science it cannot be dismissed.

If it is important for us to define in objective general terms the vital properties of the inner life (higher nervous activity) of a highly-organized system which is strange and dissimilar to us, then why cannot the same approach be applied to our system, that is, human society? It would seem desirable for us to use a general language that is common for all highly-organized systems for describing all the phenomena of human society. Let us suppose an alien is observing our life, and that it has neither sympathy for us nor the ability to understand what we think or feel. He simply watches a large body of highly-organized beings, just as we watch an ant-hill, and wants to find out how it is arranged. Over a period of time he will perhaps be able to understand the purpose of the information contained, for instance, in a railway timetable (a person losing his timetable can miss his train). True, the observer would face great difficulties. How, for example would he interpret the following event: a crowd of people gather in the evening in a large hall; a few people ascend a a platform and start making disorderly gestures while the others remain seated quietly; finally when the proceedings end they all leave without any discussion. One young mathematician wondered, perhaps jokingly, about another example of unaccountable behaviour; viz. men enter a room, get some bottles, and then start to gesticulate absurdly. An alien observer would find it difficult to ascertain what had happened, was there merely a fault in the system, or a break in its continuous intelligent operation, or something meaningful which could be described and analyzed in order to establish the difference between both cases.

Joking apart, let us seriously formulate the problem: it is essential to learn to describe objectively in behavioural terms the mechanism that generates a specific type of behaviour and to distinguish between particular activities of a highly-organized system. Pavlov was the first scientist to find that it was possible to study animal and human behaviour and the cerebral processes governing this behaviour objectively and without subjective hypotheses expressed in psychological terms. A thorough study of our problem is but the further development of the Pavlovian programme of analysis of higher nervous activity.

The creation of highly-organized living organisms is beyond the possibilities of present-day technology. But any restrictive tendencies, lack of belief or even negation of the feasibility of achieving a rational and objective description of human consciousness as a whole will hinder the development of science. This problem needs solution because even an interpretation of the various types of activity would boost the development of engineering and automation. On the other hand, the possibilities of objectively analysing the nervous system are nowadays so vast that it would be unreasonable to shy away from problems of whatever complexity.

Even if the technological difficulties were overcome, whether or not it would be practical to undertake a particular programme will remain at least debatable.

Nevertheless, a materialistic outlook holds no significant argument against a positive answer to our question. Moreover, this positive answer is a present-day expression of the belief in the natural origin of life and the material basis of consciousness.

Is Thought Discrete or Continuous?

To date, cybernetics and automata theory have elaborated the principles of discrete-action devices, which consist of a large number of separate elements and operate sequentially.

Each element can be in a small number of different states, and any change in state of an individual element depends on the preceding states of a relatively small number of elements. This is how digital electronic computers and presumably human brain are structured. A brain is believed to have 5×10^{10} or more separate elements (neurons). The genetic mechanism is somewhat simpler structurally but even larger in volume terms.

It is sometimes held that cybernetics should only deal with discrete automata. There are two arguments against this view. Firstly, really complex system—all living organisms as well as a host of machines—have in fact a variety of continuous actions. A car steering wheel is an example of machines of a continuous mechanism. If we turn to human activity we find it is conscious but follows no laws of formal logic, i.e. it is voluntary or semi-voluntary (our locomotive reactions are semi-voluntary, for example). We also find that the high performance and accuracy of a continuous motion mechanism is determined by its very continuity and the geometric character of the motion. If an athlete completes a triple jump, or a pole vault, or, for instance, is preparing for a slalom, his motion should be traced beforehand as a continuous path (for a mathematician, a slalom path happens to be an analytical curve). This is not, however, a crucial argument against discrete mechanisms. The intuitive sense of a continuous path is most probably produced in the brain by a discrete mechanism.

The second contention against the discrete approach is that human brains and even, unfortunately, electronic computers act in many instances far from predictably. Their action at a given instant of time (and in a given cell) is often a matter of chance. To forestall these arguments, we can say that "randomness" can be introduced into automata, too. Needing to imitate random events (that is, substituting some pattern unconnected with the situation) is unlikely to seriously tamper with the process of life modelling. Certainly, the approach often adopted for introducing randomness is somewhat simplistic, viz. a long series of random numbers recorded on tape is used to imitate random events in various tasks, and, in the long run, too frequent a use takes these prefabricated occurrences out of the realm of chance. For this reason, the imitation of randomness in automata should be tackled very cautiously, but it is nevertheless practicable in principle.

Our discussion leads us to the vital conclusion that information and control processes in living organisms are undoubtedly based on a complex interaction between discrete (digital) and continuous mechanisms which perform both deterministically and probabilistically. The discrete mechanisms, however, play a leading part in the information and control processes in living organisms. We see no substantial argument to support the view that discrete mechanisms are basically more restricted than continuous mechanisms.

What Is Very Many?

The doubt whether modelling human consciousness on automata is feasible often proceeds from the assumption that the number of functions in the higher cortical activity of man is infinitely large and no machine can fully model his conscious activity. The number of nerve cells in the brain cortex alone amounts to 5×10^{10}. How many elements are thus needed in a machine to imitate all the kinds of complicated higher nervous activities of man?

The activity, however, is associated with large aggregates of nerve cells rather than with single cells. It is difficult to believe that a mathematical theorem could “sit” in a dedicated nerve cell, or even in a number of cells. Obviously, the situation is quite different. Our mind consciously handles small quantities of information at a time. The number of units of information that man detects and processes in a second is rather small. And yet this is somewhat paradoxical, for a slalom skier grasps and processes much more information in ten seconds of skiing than the information dealt with during other seemingly more intellectual activities. At any rate, he processes more information than a mathematician does during 40 seconds of concentrated thinking. Human intelligence generally performs in a very peculiar and complicated manner, but when we learn how it acts, much fewer cells will be needed to model it than are needed to model the whole brain, strange as this may sound.

How much information then is required to create qualities peculiar to complex phenomena, such as life or intelligence?

All numbers may be divided into small, medium, large, and extra-large numbers. The classification is not rigorous for no precise boundary can be fixed beyond which, for instance, a medium number becomes large. Hence, the categories are known only to an order of magnitude, but we need no stricter accuracy than this. What then are these categories? We shall begin with mathematical definitions.

I. We call number A small if we can enumerate all combinations from A elements with two inputs and two outputs, or we can list all their Boolean algebra functions with A arguments.

II. Number B is called medium if we are unable in practice to identify every combination of B elements, but can enumerate the elements themselves or (which is more difficult) can elaborate a system of designations for any combination of B elements.

III. Number C is large if we cannot in practice enumerate every element, but can establish a system of designations for them.

IV. Finally, extra-large numbers are those for which a system of designations cannot practically be devised. As we see later, we shall not require this category.

Let us now clarify these definitions by way of examples.

Suppose we connect three switches, each of which can be in a left-hand (L) and a right-hand (R) position, to a single electric bulb. Then, we shall clearly have $2^3 = 8$ possible position combinations of the switches. Let us list them to make this clear:

(1) LLL	(3) LRR	(5) RLL	(7) RLR
(2) LRL	(4) LLR	(6) RRL	(8) RRR

Our switches can be wired so that the light is either on or off in any of their listed positions. We can calculate that there are $2^{(2^3)}$, that is, $2^8 = 256$ different switch positions in these two states. The reader may easily ascertain whether this is true by adding marks "on" or "off" to the above switch position designations.

The fact that such an exercise is within our power and does not take long just proves that the number 3 (the number of switches) is a small number. Should there be, say, five rather than three switches, we should have to identify $2^{(2^5)}$ different positions of the switches marked with the "on" and "off" designations. It can hardly be done within a reasonable length of time without error. Therefore, the number 5 may not be considered small.

In order to clarify the term "medium number", let us cite a different example. Suppose you are let into a hall where a thousand people are present and asked to shake hands with each one. Obviously, your hand will not feel well afterwards, but it can in practice (in reasonable time) be done. You would be able to walk up to each one of the thousand without getting confused and reach out your hand. But if the thousand people were to shake hands with each other, and in addition each group of three to shake hands among themselves, it would prove impracticable. The number 1 000 is thus a medium one. It can be said that we can "enumerate" a thousand elements, marking each one (with a handshake) individually.

The number of visible stars in the sky is a plain example of a large number. Everybody knows that the stars cannot be counted using a finger. Nevertheless, a catalogue of stars has been compiled (that is, a system of designations worked out) to which we can refer for information on any star.

Evidently, a computer can count without error for a much longer period of time and compose various combinations a good deal faster than man. For this reason, the respective numbers in each category for the machine are larger than those for man, viz.

Numbers	Man	Machine
Small	3	10
Medium	1 000	10^{10}
Large	10^{100}	$10^{(10^{10})}$

What does this table reveal? It shows that the respective numbers for the machine while being much larger than those for man, remain close to them in the order of magnitude. At the same time, there is an insuperable boundary between the numbers of different categories: the numbers that are medium for man are not small for a machine, just as the numbers large for man are not medium for a machine. The cube of ten is incomparably larger than ten, and 10^{100} is even larger than 10^{10}. It is noteworthy that the memory capacity of a living being and even of a computer is characterized by medium numbers, whereas many of the problems that must be solved by what are called exhaustive enumeration techniques are characterized by large numbers.

Thus we immediately leave the realms of possibility with respect to exhaustive search. Problems that can only be solved with this search method will remain out of reach for computers whatever the stage of development of technology and culture.

We have come to this conclusion without resorting to the concept of infinity. We have had no need for it, and scarcely ever will when solving real problems that may arise in the way of the cybernetic analysis of life.

Instead, it becomes vital to know whether problems exist that can be posed and solved without the need for exhaustive search. These problems must be of the greatest interest to cyberneticists since they lend themselves to practical solution.

The feasibility of creating sound living organisms built wholly from discrete (digital) control and information-processing mechanisms does not fundamentally contradict the principles of the materialistic dialectic. A belief to the contrary can only arise because some people are not used to seeing dialectics where infinity is not involved. In order to analyze life, however, the dialectics of large numbers is essential rather than the dialectics of infinity.

Caution, We Are Going too Far!

At present, cybernetics is more susceptible to what is being written about it than any other science. I am not very enthusiastic about all cybernetic literature, which is so abundant nowadays. I see a good deal of exaggerations on the one hand, and oversimplifications, on the other.

Not that this literature suggests anything totally impracticable, but one often comes across articles full of euphoria, with the very titles proclaiming success achieved in modelling various complex kinds of human activities which have so far been modelled quite unsatisfactorily. For example, both American and Soviet cybernetic literature, and even serious scientific magazines, publish from time to time rather simplistic works on the so-called machine composition of music (this does not apply to works by R.Kh. Zaripov). The procedure usually used is to enter a large number (70, say) of country songs or hymns into the computer's memory, and then the computer uses the first four notes in one of the songs, finds all the songs where these four notes occur in the same order, and choosing one of these songs at random, takes the next, the fifth, note out of it. The machine again has four notes (2nd, 3rd, 4th and 5th), and again it carries out a search and selection in the same sequence. Thus, the computer feels its way through the "composition" of a new melody. Something cowboyish is claimed to be heard in a melody if it was taken from country songs, and something religious if it was hymns that were entered into the computer memory. But what will happen if the computer makes its search by seven successive notes rather than by four? As two compositions containing seven identical notes in a row are very rarely encountered in reality, then the machine will have to "sing" them through its entire "composition". If, on the other hand, the machine used only two notes for "creation" (and there is a host of compositions with two identical notes), it would face such a wide choice that it would produce a cacophony in place of a melody.

This rather primitive scheme is declared to be the composition of music by a machine, and the computer can compose more serious, classically sounding music with a larger starting batch of notes, and lighter music with a smaller number of notes.

Today, we are still a long way off the description and analysis of the higher forms of human activity, nor have we even learnt how to define its categories and concepts in objective terms, let alone how to simulate such complex tasks as the composition of music. If we are not able to understand how living beings that need music differ from those who do not, then any early attempt to tackle the machine composition of music will be just the modelling of purely external factors.

"The machine composition of music" is but one example of the simplistic approach to cybernetics. Another widespread fallacy of people carried away with the desire to apply the cybernetic approach to any problem, however difficult, is the tendency to neglect the experience other sciences have amassed over the centuries. They often pass over the fact that the analysis of the higher forms of human activity was started very long ago and has made good progress. Although it is described in non-cybernetic terms, this analysis is essentially objective and should be studied and used. By contrast, what cyberneticists have achieved without taking too much trouble and what they have praised so loudly is often restricted to very primitive phenomena. At a meeting at the Moscow Centre for Writers, a speaker asserted that we were to see and indeed have seen the creation of a new medicine. This new medicine must be the responsibility and the subject of study of experts in automatic control theory rather than doctors! "The most essential thing about medicine", said the speaker, "involves the cyclic processes occurring in the human organism. But these processes are described by the differential equations studied in the theory of automatic control. So the study of medicine in medical colleges has outlived itself and should be transferred to technical colleges and the mathematical departments of universities". Conceivably, experts in automatic control may have a say in solving some medical problems, but to take part in this work, they would require an extensive medical education.

The wealth of knowledge accumulated by medicine, one of the oldest sciences, is immense, and it has to be mastered if anything significant is to be achieved.

Why the Extremes Only?

Cybernetic analysis of higher nervous activity has so far been concentrated at two extremes. On the one hand, cyberneticists are engaged in an active study of conditioned reflexes, that is, the simplest kind of higher nervous activity. Most people will know what a conditioned reflex is. If two stimuli occur together repeatedly (for example, a ring is made to sound simultaneously with the presentation of food), then one of the stimuli (ring) elicits the response reaction (saliva) to the other stimulus (the food offer). This connection is temporary and gradually disappears if not constantly supported. A considerable number of cybernetic problems, which are today known as the mathematical theory of learning, also cover very simple schemes, and these are far from exhausting even a small part of the whole complex of higher nervous activity. In fact, they are the very first steps in the analysis of conditioned-reflex activities.

At the other extreme is the theory of propositional calculus. This area of higher nervous activity in man lends itself to investigation by mathematical methods, and with the development of computer technology and computational mathematics, these studies have made a rapid progress. Here cyberneticists have been doing fairly well.

But the immense range between these two poles—the most basic and the most complex manifestations of the human psyche—is investigated very little, if at all.

Cybernetics and Language

At present mathematical linguistics holds a special place. This science is still at the initial stage of development; it evolves with accumulation of language-related cybernetic problems. The sphere of mathematical linguistics is the analysis of those higher forms on human activity that are based on intuition rather than on formal logic, and which defy description in rigorous terms. Everyone knows what a grammatically correct phrase or the correct coordination of words is, but no one has been able so far to communicate this knowledge to a computer. An accurate, and logically and grammatically irreproachable machine translation might now be possible from Latin and into Latin, because its grammar is sufficiently well elaborated and defined. However, the grammars of the younger languages are inadequate for use in machine translation. This problem has been studied for a fairly long time now, and today machine translation has become a well-established and important field of activity. It is in translation that the bulk of attention from mathematical linguists seems to be centred.

Theoretical papers on mathematical linguistics, however, tend to ignore the fact that language originated much earlier than did logical thought, in the formal sense. The study of word formation process as a second signal system, which can harmoniously combine the concepts of cybernetics, new mathematical methods and modern logic, may prove promising from a theoretical point of view. Initially, when notions are not yet entirely formed, words appear as signals that elicit a particular reaction. The origin of logic is usually traced to relatively recent times. That words are not only symbols for certain concrete ideas and images, but represent also abstract notions which can be separated from them, was apparently only understood and formulated as late as ancient Greece.

Prior to development of really logical thought, ideas, rather than being formal conceptual categories, arose as word combinations followed by other words, and were attempts to pin the flow of images running in the person's mind, and so on. To trace this mechanism of the crystallization of words as signals carrying a series of images, as well as the development of early logic on this base, is a very promising task for a mathematician, a fact which has been repeatedly noted in cybernetic literature.

It is also interesting to see how logical thought forms in a human mind. In order to follow the stages of this process, let us take, by way of example, the ideas of a mathematician as he works on a problem. The first thing to emerge is the desire to investigate the problem, then a rough and spontaneous idea of what he hopes to achieve and how it could be done, and at the next stage, the mechanism of formal logical judgement is started. Apparently this is how logical thought forms and is the scheme of a creative process. It may prove interesting not only to investigate the first, intuitive stage of this process but also to try develop a machine capable of helping man by registering the results of his mental work (for instance, to assist the mathematician when he puts his calculations in order). Such a machine could be assigned to the task of interpreting and setting down in full the dim outlines of drawings, incomplete sketches or formulas which every mathematician writes down in the course of his search, constructing his multi-dimensional figures from their sketches, etc. In short, it would be interesting to think about the development of machines that could even today assist man, rather than replace him, in his complicated creative activities. It has been very difficult so far even to figure out how this task could be approached. But although the problem is still a long way from solution, it has already been raised in cybernetic literature, something to be approved.

As can be seen from the examples above, an objective understanding of the most complex and subtle manifestations of the higher nervous activity in man engenders many problems. They all deserve attention from cyberneticists.

Materialism Is the Thing

In conclusion we should touch upon what may be called the ethical aspects of cybernetics. Rejection or disapproval of many cybernetic concepts frequently arises from the unwillingness to admit that man, though a really complex material system, is nevertheless system of finite complexity and for this reason amenable to imitation. Many people consider this point of view to be humiliating and dreadful. But even when this idea is accepted in principle, some people cannot resign themselves to it. Such a complete penetration into the mystery of human nature, including the possibility, as it were, of "coding" a human being and "sending it by telex" to another place seems repulsive and horrifying to some.

There is also scepticism about our ability to arrive at a comprehensive and objective description of a human being's internal structure. For example, we have wondered whether we can learn to distinguish objectively beings that require harmonious music from those that do not. But—who knows?—an analysis may show that there is no reason to give preference to this kind of music over other combinations of sounds.

It seems to me to be very important to understand that the urge towards complete self-knowledge is not in any way fearful or humiliating. These fears can only arise from half-knowledge: a real understanding of our immense capacities, the existence of age-old human culture, which is our greatest asset and help, should give us joy! While we are aware of the limitations of our physical structure, we also know that it has enormous, virtually boundless capacities.

In fact, we should try to replace this silly and meaningless fear of human-imitating automata by the great satisfaction that man can create such complex and magnificent things, whereas not so long ago he looked upon simple arithmetic as something incomprehensible and awesome.

Cybernetics Today

B. N. PETROV

Our task is to review the history of cybernetics to the present and forecast its movement forward. Without doubt cybernetics has rapidly and fruitfully developed in this country over the past years. Powerful theoretical advances have been made and the technology of cybernetics has taken shape, its mathematical and computing base has been formed, its methods, primarily the simulation of complex systems and processes, have been worked out, tested, and have shown to be effective. So exactly where are we? Which problems (and how) have we been solving, have already solved, and have yet to solve?

The answers to these questions may profoundly influence the progress of cybernetics, for they will determine the important areas of research into which our activity must be channeled and intensified. The answers can, however, only be obtained through collaboration of theorists and practical workers, experts in different branches of science and technology. The task is largely methodological in character, and

I think that not only mathematicians, or applied-cybernetics engineers, but also philosophers and logicians should participate.

We should first agree on what ought to be understood as cybernetics for there are too many definitions in the literature both theoretical and applied. The definitions differ from those given when the discipline was first studied. There is now a trend abroad to replace the term "cybernetics" by other terms. In France, for example, the word "informatique" is used, but it is clear that cybernetics and "informatique" (the science of data processing) are not the same thing. In the USA and Great Britain, the term "computer science" and "systems theory" have begun to be used instead of cybernetics. It is obvious that cybernetics is not the same thing as computer technology and mathematics, that the study of systems at an extremely high level of abstraction (the general theory of systems) is much narrower than the wide scope of cybernetics as we see it.

Hence it is necessary to work out a clear-cut definition of cybernetics, one that corresponds to the present situation in this field. To do so, we should proceed not only from the fact that those definitions are not equivalent but also, and mainly, from the historical viewpoint. This view helps us, I believe, understand that cybernetics is today increasingly an area which deals with unconventional problems of control (in formulation, complexity, and method), including processes related but not identical to control, such as design. It also deals with the development of the various theoretical and engineering means for solving these problems.

Of course, the concept "unconventional" requires clarification. The following discussion should help explain what is meant.

The main tasks now in cybernetics are: to determine priorities in the research areas; to focus on complex problems where cybernetics interacts with other scientific and engineering disciplines; and hence to coordinate work in the various fields which are faced with a cybernetic problem. Here, we should also bear in mind the general methodology of our approach to cybernetics, ensuring that our philosophers cooperate with mathematicians and engineers to contribute to finding new ways and successful solutions. This calls for effective criticism of the shortcomings that took place in the past and for working out new and positive ideas rather than remaining preoccupied with questions which have been discussed for many years, sometimes fruitfully and sometimes not.

We should concentrate on generating new promising ideas and approaches, on developing new principles of building and modelling complex systems, and not only control systems in the conventional sense originating from automatic control theory. What we mean is that we should concentrate on principles and concepts that go beyond the range of traditional approach. This is essential if we are to increase the efficiency of control and data processing in those areas where the methods suitable for building simple systems are inadequate and where purely cybernetic methods are required to solve the problems that arise.

We should, of course, use our experience and the results that have already been obtained, and so move forward steadily but with discretion. As we enrich the traditions of the Soviet school of cybernetics, we should remember that developing science and technology always poses new problems. Therefore when we demand a generation of new ideas we should not pursue innovation at the cost of leaving the "old" results and methods behind without having explored their full potential. Our experience of cybernetics teaches us that a new task should only be posed when there is a real need for it and when it becomes practicable. In the 1960's, when it was decided to apply cybernetics to teaching—an important and needed task—neither cybernetics nor education were ready, and that was discovered in the 1970's. Such situations should be avoided.

To accomplsih what we have set out above, we have to decide which goals in cybernetics have really been achieved out of all those set in confidence that they would soon be attained. Take, for instance, computerized translation. It once seemed so close and yet as the work proceeded the problem turned out to be much tougher than it had appeared at the outset. But the effort has not been wasted, and although feasible automatic translation from one natural language into another is not possible, we can boast some interesting solutions in the automatic preparation of texts for man-computer conversational systems, which are important in many applications. This example demonstrates that it is important to clear up what must be done and how it should be done.

As we mentioned above, the principal problem in cybernetics is to develop unconventional approaches to control and data processing, to computer technology and software, to automation in the different branches of science, industry, economy, and culture. What seems to be essential in this respect? In our view, it is the search for new ways of developing and using computers, ways that will radically extend the capabilities of data processing and computer technology.

I should like to dwell on this point. Cybernetics, and this has already been said above, is not directly identified with computer technology and mathematics, but these, in their modern sophisticated form, make up its base. Moreover, present-day data processing systems provide a foundation for developing cybernetic methods. It should be noted that the traditional (three decades old) approach to research and development, engineering, programming, and the application of digital computers does not really require cybernetic concepts. The principles actually used in computer technology were formed over twenty years ago and are intrinsically remote from such concepts of cybernetics as self-organization, adaptability, and active search. At present, the theory and available technology make possible time-sharing computer operation, flexible arrangement of the system's hardware, and flexible memory structure; in fact, these are important steps in developing adaptive computer systems.

A computer based on the sequential data processing principle and the rigid structure of the data stored in its memory is not of interest any more. Today's requirements call for flexible time-sharing computer systems with a memory that allows the input of randomly structured information and that provides for connections between units of information and its associative search.

One trend in computers is the development of brain-like systems that are approaching the human ability to handle data in a flexible way and to find heuristic (approximate) solutions, which often prove to be rational. But in our view there is no need to run to extremes. Imitating the human brain is not necessarily the only way of refining computers. Although all the principles of brain-like systems that can be adapted to engineering should be used, none the less the benefits given by electronics, lasers, holography, optoelectronics and other technologies, all of which differ from the principles underlying living organisms must be exploited for computers, data processors, and control systems.

Another way of improving the operation of computers to help them solve complex problems that are hard to formalize is to use man-machine systems. The human side of the system has more limitations from the technical standpoint than the machine side. At the same time man is infinitely more flexible than machine. So there is a problem of putting the two together and this is still far from being satisfactorily solved.

Time-sharing operation is not merely a computer hardware or software problem, it is a theoretical or rather mathematical problem. According to Soviet scientists, efficient parallel processing requires new areas of discrete mathematics to be developed.

New scientific problems call for new logical methods. These new methods have recently been useful for helping to construct failure-free programs and for automated programming in block-structured computer procedures. Recursive function theory is used extensively and the development of recursive computers is now uppermost. This, however, is only some of the potential of logic, that is, logic oriented to the expression of laws governing data processing by intellect rather than mathematical demonstrative logic. Some experts believe that such logic theories as intuitionistic and combinatorial logic, modal or temporal logic systems, and some others may prove helpful, but whether this is so must be carefully studied. We must be circumspect about some of the ideas that come into vogue in cybernetics every now and then. Although promising concepts should not be rejected, for example the theory of "fuzzy" sets and algorithms, which are now very popular, we caution against converting familiar things into something else by using "fuzzy" terminology and against rediscovering results already known in other branches of mathematics.

The principal method of cybernetics is modelling and it has been widely discussed, particularly by philosophers. However, it was sometimes overlooked that modelling in cybernetics is primarily computer simulation. In some studies the concept of modelling is blurred and devoid of that specific cybernetic meaning which results from both orientation towards computer output and the character of simulation in cybernetics associated with having to overcome considerable complications.

Modelling in cybernetics means the simulation of the process being studied via a computerized experiment, which radically differs from a conventional experiment conducted in a natural science, such as physics. It should be borne in mind that the model put into a computer's memory (and then processed and modified) is not a theoretical description of the process. The nature of the computer requires, for example, that continuous relations and time be presented discretely, and that special synchronizing procedures should be provided for simulation of parallel processes, and so on.

Modelling in cybernetics is inseparable from the associated technology, and informational computer networks are being used increasingly for solving control problems (specifically, on a real-time basis) in multi-user systems. It is these systems that require parallel data processing and large data bases that can cope with many thousand parameters in models.

Computer networks are not only the technology underlying cybernetics but also its object of study. Their development helps understand the phenomenon of complexity, a problem peculiar to "large systems". The difficulties of solving multi-parameter problems are familiar to all those who deal with computers. Methods suitable for tackling problems with small numbers of parameters are often inoperable when this number becomes an order of magnitude greater. So informational computer networks, which combine the computing capacities of many computers, require new programming concepts to overcome these difficulties and to achieve different "thresholds of complexity" in computer simulation. It must be pointed out that this opens the possibility of simulating processes characterized not only by accurately measured quantitative parameters but also by the substantially qualitative attributes characteristic of most biological, economic, and social systems.

When we talk about unconventional problems in cybernetics, or about devising new non-standard methods and concepts, we must bear in mind primarily adaptative phenomena. Cybernetics must provide the tools for building adaptive technology of control and data processing that take account of the external situation and the internal condition of the system. What is especially important, these systems must respond to changes in the qualitative criteria of control and produce new criteria according to the problem being solved. Special algorithms need to be developed for problems in which the criteria can be changed in the course of solution, and in which several criteria can be reduced to a single criterion.

Some experience has already been gained in this area, but we seem to neglect somewhat the application (in cybernetic form) of the human methods of solving complex problems. Whether it is possible to program a computer to solve a problem in a human way so that its operation is formally similar to human thought (and if so to what extent) will require extensive research to answer. A first step in this direction has been made in this country in recent years and this is an investigation into the use of logic and semiotic models to formalize human experience in complex systems control. Another application of this kind is computer-aided design. Although very important in itself because it substantially upgrades the quality of design and releases many skilled workers for other tasks, CAD is a good testing ground for refining unconventional cybernetic methods. Computer simulation of the design process models the design system that has been entered into the computer. This is a typically cybernetic approach to solving a complex problem.

The investigations into interactive systems, that is, how to arrange for efficient interaction between the computer and its user, or between a set of computers and a team of its users, are an important sphere of cybernetics. Many problems have yet to be solved. One is the question of the qualitative distribution of functions between the human intelligence and the cybernetic "tools" that man is using to control a process. Such questions can be solved by planning the human activity in complex engineering systems, by substantially improving the reliability of the interactive systems, and by developing and studying control systems intended for applications which can only be accomplished interactively.

We already have some positive experience of interactive systems in such important areas as industrial planning or distribution control. It should be pointed out that the formulation of problems and the use of methods typical of cybernetics apply not just to man-computer interaction but also to "conventional" man-machine systems engineering.

The man-machine systems aspect of cybernetics is an essential part of that area of research for which the term "artificial intelligence" was coined. The term may seem controversial, for it gives rise to irrelevant associations. However, the field has nothing to do with the far-fetched idea of "thinking machines", a favourite topic with some thinkers. Whatever the term may be, this aspect of cybernetics must not be underestimated.

"Artificial intelligence" deserves a separate discussion. We will only touch upon some crucial points here. Artificial intelligence is closely associated with the non-traditional problems of control and information handling. One important question is the development of interactive dialogue systems, including dialogue-oriented languages that approximate natural human languages. It seems that the intricacies of human psychology which are important for efficient interactive communication will have to be taken into account.

4—01169

Dialogue systems in this country have been developed with success. Definite progress has been achieved in engineering systems that can discern fluent speech and in application-oriented dialogue languages. Soviet dialogue systems such as DISPUT (from the Institute of Control Problems), DILOS (from the Computer Center of the USSR Academy of Sciences), and some others show that this line of research is quite promising.

Another field where artificial intelligence is being applied and which should be mentioned is the automated demonstration of theorems in formal mathematical theories.

One of the first research projects in this field that was started in the USSR was the automation of proofs and logical deductions. It has gradually turned out that solutions of this kind are applicable not only to relatively simple formal systems but also to more complex areas of mathematics. A team led by Academician Glushkov at the Cybernetics Institute under the Ukranian Academy of Sciences applied these techniques to attain more general and important results, namely to increase the productivity of mathematicians. They formulated an approach which they called the algorithm of the evident, which revolved around organizing the mathematicians—the users of the system—in such a way that the computer system takes over increasingly more of the complex functions of the mathematical deductions and verifications of the proofs of theorems offered to the system, and seeks for new non-trivial solutions.

The formalization of proving is closely related to the problem of compiling modular computer programs from standard blocks giving word-formulated initial instructions. In the USSR, the research has resulted in the PRIZ system (developed by the Cybernetics Institute under Estonian Academy of Sciences). It is the first system of its kind to accomplish this task. Such systems seem to hold great promise.

The automation of games is also promising in the context of man-computer interaction. In the case of chess, for instance, such a system can help the player find the best moves, and Soviet cybernetists have had some tangible success in this area. The Soviet chess program "Kaissa" has scored highly in computer tournaments because, among other things, it used effective search procedures worked out at the Institute of Control Problems.

It is impossible to overestimate the significance of robotics. In addition to the robots and manipulators built on engineering principles, those using biomechanical concepts, or independent, particularly adaptive, robots, or robots monitored by the human voice will require new ideas. Engineering designs based on cybernetic technology must be supported by studies of living organisms, in particular, the systems for perceiving the environment and storing the perceptions. The mechanism of orientation, navigation, and communication in nature may be promising for building robots or teams of robots capable of functioning in an unfamiliar environment.

These questions usually converge on the problem of the robot's "intelligence". Its solution will probably require the study and simulation of neurons and neuron-like structures on an increasing scale. An artificial intelligence based on these structures, but using the capabilities of electronics and other technologies, may open a new chapter in the development of adaptive computer systems.

The theoretical and practical aspects of cybernetics make up an organic whole. The solutions offered by cybernetics must serve practical purposes. In this respect, we could give numerous examples of real achievements. Thus, positive results have been obtained in the automated testing of complex apparatus and in experimental studies of complex engineering systems (including flight control equipment).

We could also mention successes in designing on-board computers which made airborn systems more automated. An automatic flight control unit puts in a program for the systems, checks the operation of their components, and takes a decision on what must be actuated and what must be shut down. It also provides information for the crew, who can supervise its operation via a display unit.

However, many more problems have yet to be solved.

In the USSR, cybernetic research has also been applied to socio-economic problems, biology, medicine, and the humanities. But here, we must admit that our achievements are much more modest.

Automation in the sphere of managerial, business, and office activities is universally acknowledged as being of great importance. An efficient way towards this goal is to rationalize cybernetically the process of management on the basis of paperless procedures. Ultimately, automatic systems could obviate the need for conventional documentation. This problem is specifically cybernetic in nature because it can only be fully solved by using adaptive models that encompass fairly high levels of control. Research in this field should be continued and intensified.

Bionics, biological and medical cybernetics all require profound discussion, but this is beyond the scope of this paper. We shall only mention a few of the points in bionics, which are important for engineering cybernetics.

Today, the traditional content of bionics has been enriched. New kinds of closed systems are being developed where man (and his individual organs) are acted upon by technological systems or receive information from sensors incorporated in engineering systems. This is the principle behind the bioengineering systems being constructed for medical purposes. They hold out promise as efficient artificial organs. Compensatory "automation", the combination of living organisms, primarily human, and engineering systems, the development of artificial organs such as hearts and limbs, all these human-oriented applications of bionics are of great importance.

The humanities are a special sphere for the application of cybernetics. Although we have made certain achievements in linguistics, informational psychology, economics, and law (specifically, the use of computer technology in criminology), it must be remembered that no steady progress has been made. There have been alternating periods of enthusiasm and flagging interest but now clear and realistic problems have been put forward in these areas. However, cyberneticists cannot come to grip with these problems on their own. They need the cooperation of those working in the appropriate disciplines (which, of course, is true for work in biological and medical cybernetics).

This is evident, for example, from the application of cybernetics to linguistics. These studies are very significant for automatic control, data handling, and computer software generation. Without progress in this area we will not have any adequate languages for doing information search or implementing interactive communication and no way of ensuring that the computer understands texts given in natural languages. It must be remembered that these tasks cannot be accomplished without further development of linguistics, psycho-linguistics, psychology, and also without development of logical and semantic formalization.

The same can be said about the simulation of the creative processes. We have been posing more questions than getting concrete results, so it is time to determine in which direction we must move. Answers to all these questions should be expected in the first place from psychologists and logicians collaborating with mathematicians and cyberneticists.

In conclusion a few words must be said about the philosophical and methodological aspects of cybernetics. Those who neglect these topics may fail to see prospects and difficulties in their way. The main thing is to turn to the methodological side of the work at the planning stage, and not in the process itself, as the more practically minded people do.

The importance of the philosophical and methodological approach is especially manifest with respect to artificial intelligence. The scope of the problem is such that cyberneticists, mathematicians, engineers, physiologists, or psychologists working by themselves will not be able to break through its baffling complexity. This is an interdisciplinary problem of great significance to science as a whole, and therefore it cannot be solved without a serious philosophical and methodological substantiation.

Cooperation between research workers of different specialities is not easy because of their widely dissimilar scientific backgrounds. To overcome this, they should familiarize themselves with the various aspects that pertain to the other disciplines. Good quality literature that is comprehensible to a non-professional in a particular area but at the same time scientifically accurate and free from oversimplification and primitiveness is what is needed here.

Where Is Cybernetics Heading?

M. G. GAAZE-RAPOPORT

This article is a brief survey of the evolution of cybernetics and an attempt to outline some of the more important ways in which it is likely to develop. Even though this paper will be somewhat subjective and despite the conceptual difficulties of prediction, an effort to make predictions is undisputably worthwhile.

Cybernetics. There are many definitions of cybernetics that start from the basic idea that it deals with the control of different kinds of systems (technological, biological, economic, social, and so on). With the passage of time, the range of systems to which the cybernetic approach was thought to be applicable (at first it only embraced technological and biological systems) has expanded considerably and is continuing to expand. Accordingly, we have witnessed the emergence of neurocybernetics, economic cybernetics, law cybernetics, agricultural cybernetics and the like.

The various definitions of cybernetics tend to reflect the concerns of their authors such as the systems approach, complexity, dependability, and the use of models and computers. It has been noted that various sources indicate that cybernetics is made up of dozens of sciences and scientific disciplines often distantly related. May such an agglomeration be considered a science or a scientific discipline? Can all these disciplines and branches of other sciences be incorporated into the single concept of cybernetics? The answer seems to be unambiguously negative. Should this then lead us to conclude that cybernetics is non-existent? Perhaps, cybernetics is a fashionable term for the modern field of automatic control, a field which has existed and been developing for more than half a century. We feel these questions should also be answered in the negative.

The actual state of affairs appears to be this. Cybernetics is first and foremost a scientific and methodological discipline which considers the whole objective world from a single, namely informational, point of view. Cybernetics is an intentional abstraction from the material side of the world and its energy aspects (though, of course, they are borne in mind); rather it regards and studies only the informational side of the world, that is the receiving, coding, and processing, in the broad sense of the word, of information, including its transmission and use. Here, information is not understood in the narrow, Shannonian sense, but more broadly, as all the data, knowledge, and facts, required for making control decisions. It is this methodological approach, the "cybernetic outlook", as it were, that determines the objective significance of cybernetic concepts, the penetration of the cybernetic approach into every field of modern science and technology, and into every sphere of human activity. This is where the main value of cybernetics has been found to lie in recent years.

We believe that this is sufficient to reject as incorrect and unfounded the view sometimes encountered that cybernetics has been discredited and has not lived up to expectations.

The value and importance of cybernetics is measured not by obtaining some purely, "cybernetic" results or mathematically formulated cybernetic laws, but by the extent to which cybernetic concepts and the cybernetic outlook have found their way into particular sciences, have stimulated their development, and have led to new results in these specialized disciplines.

One striking example that confirms the fruitfulness and methodological viability of the cybernetic approach is the problem of deciphering the genetic code and the study of the transmission of information from nucleic acids to proteins. The very statement of the problem by Gamov, Rich, and Yčas[1-3,5] would not have been possible without the cybernetic ideas about information, its coding, and the necessity of a channel and transmission media. At the same time, finding a solution to this problem is a complicated biochemical rather than cybernetic task, and it was accomplished by biochemists Watson, Crick, Ochoa and others[4] using sophisticated specialized techniques.

Another typical example concerns the studies now underway of the neuron-level control processes in animal behaviour, particularly in the flight of insects[6]. This exciting biological work is also, to a large extent, based on the cybernetic concepts of the control system as a feedback system that receives, processes, and uses information. These studies could not be carried out without this concept.

I think these two examples are sufficient, although many more could be culled from different branches of science.

Cybernetics and the computer. One frequently encountered fallacy is the identification of problems connected with the development and use of electronic computers with cybernetics. Many people believe that the application of computers in some branch of knowledge means the application of cybernetics, that is, the cybernetic approach and techniques. Actually, this is not so. If the use of information and its processing are not themselves the subject of study, they may not be considered cybernetics.

Computers, their inception and development are in fact closely associated with cybernetics. To begin with, computers are employed for processing information and are not simply machines. It is even thought that they should be called "maperins" (an acronym for a machine-like device used for data processing)[7]. What is meant here is not just the hardware, the computer, which cannot do anything by itself, but the computer together with the software, the programs entered into it. From this point of view, the extention of the computer to new areas in order to perform both computing and logic-informational tasks and to model and research information processes, obviously has much in common with cybernetics and the propagation of its concepts and makes the computer a tool for cybernetic research.

Second, computers themselves, which are data processing equipment, their logic, architecture, and programming (excluding the purely technological problems of their design and manufacture) are objects of study from the mathematical and cybernetic (informational) point of view.

Thus, the computer appears in three entities: first, as a tool which drastically speeds up computations and data processing in the various branches of science and the economy; second, it is a means for extending the application of cybernetic principles and ideas to different scientific and practical fields; and third, it is itself an object for the application and development of cybernetic concepts and methods.

Being a powerful information-processing tool, the computer has played and continues to play a very important part in the generation, development, and dissemination of cybernetic ideas and methods. It is this that breeds the erroneous tendency to relate all that is connected with the computer to cybernetics.

The multiple status of the computer also gives rise to the notion that cybernetics has not proved itself, that although it promised the solution of the problem of machine translation, the creation of a thinking machine and so on, these problems are now as far from being solved as they have ever been, and the difficulties in their way are even believed to have grown rather than diminished.

In fact, the resistance of many cybernetic problems to solution is not due to the shortcomings of the cybernetic approach. True, this approach, which regards only the informational aspect of systems, is not universal and cannot be a magic way of overcoming any scientific and practical difficulty. But in reality these problems have remained intractable because they are intrinsically difficult and the capabilities of the computer, large as they are, have certain limits. Thus, as regards the problem of translation, it should be noted that its linguistic and psychological foundations are not yet sufficiently understood. Now, purely linguistic difficulties and unsolved problems that hinder the progress of machine translation have been discovered and continue to emerge. Cybernetics and computers are a great help in the attempts to solve this problem, but they cannot be blamed for the failure so far to create a viable system of machine translation.

The situation is similar for another problem, namely the problem of artificial intelligence. Our notions of consciousness, reason, and intelligence are still far from complete; they have not yet gone beyond largely superficial assumptions and do not yield results adequate enough to build machine interpretations. Moreover, it is thought by some that intelligence cannot in principle be abstracted from the body and, accordingly, created without it because they are greatly interdependent. If this is true, we can suppose that the informational approach alone, which leaves aside bodily aspects, is insufficient for creating "intelligent" machines and that other approaches need to be followed in addition to the cybernetic one. This does not mean, however, that the application of the cybernetic approach and the computer cannot assist psychologists in their pursuit of an understanding of consciousness and intelligence.

To date, the overwhelming majority of experts in various fields have become aware that science and technology cannot evolve much further without the extensive use of cybernetic concepts and the application of computers.

Simulation, or modelling, has been known as an efficient method of scientific research long before the cybernetics came into existence.

There are various classes of models. We shall consider only one of them, which is widely used in scientific research. The models in this class, referred to as computer models, provide descriptions of the properties and characteristics of the object being modelled in some sort of synthetic or natural language rather than reproduce its properties and characteristics themselves. The success and accuracy of computer simulation is determined here exclusively by the exactness of description of the object, its characteristics, and the relationships between them.

The possibility of varying and refining the basic description, which helps the investigator single out the essential properties of the object is a notable advantage of computer models. The application of the computer to model generation not only makes it possible to increase dramatically the efficiency of research work; it also allows the description of the object to be refined and developed as new knowledge of its properties is gained. Such models can be successfully used for verifying hypotheses. If the computer model reproduces the conditions under which a real object works and the data on its structure, then by comparing the function of the object and its model in identical conditions we can ascertain how correct our knowledge about the object is. Similarly, if the investigator knows the operating conditions of the object and reproduces its known reactions to these conditions on the model, he may formulate hypotheses about the possible structure of the object by analyzing the structure of the model. Using models in this way has been called "black-box" simulation.

The informational approach to modelling, the feasibility of realizing complex models on the computer, and the availability of hardware capable of converting the information signals coming from the computer into informational and physical actions directed to real objects under control, have lead to the penetration of computer-aided modelling into various branches of science and technology. The identification of modelling with cybernetics, however, has resulted in the importance of simulation being overestimated; it was thought that modelling was itself omnipotent and could easily handle any task. A period of what may be called "modelling euphoria" came. It was believed that because the processes of thinking, decision making, creativity, brain functioning, translation, and many others were information-processing phenomena and could be described, they could be reproduced (that is, simulated) on the computer. Whereas the premise was correct in principle, what was overlooked was the need for specific data on the properties and peculiarities of objects, which would be accurate enough to be entered into a computer.

The exaggerated notions about the abilities of simulation were also based on the fact that it offered a route towards obtaining new knowledge about the simuland. It was held to be self-evident that the approach could provide all the data required for the model to be refined and made more sophisticated.

Also passed over was the fact that the very process of translating data into a machine language is a difficult task which is made more complicated as the complexity of the problem to be solved grows. Moreover, the auxiliary tasks that arose require specialized software and specialized input hardware for entering large volumes of information into a computer.

As far as artificial intelligence is concerned, the research conducted in recent years has yielded considerable progress; however, it has also revealed serious difficulties caused by our inadequate knowledge of the objects to be modelled rather than by the cybernetic approach. These difficulties can only be overcome by well-oriented research in the appropriate branches of science with a wide application of cybernetic techniques. Such investigations should be conducted in consecutive stages in which the aim is approached step by step. First, experts describe the known characteristics of the object and formulate hypotheses. Then the simulation follows, its results are evaluated, and the hypotheses and the starting data on the simuland are refined. Then the procedure is repeated. In such a way, work has been conducted for a long time now on the computer simulation of the musical composition process.

The application of cybernetic approaches to the study of the information processes in complex systems of various kinds is found in practically every field of knowledge. If at the outset this approach was only considered to be applicable to technology and some branches of biology, today no one is surprised by successful use of cybernetics in economics, law, agriculture, neurophysiology, medicine, and some other fields.

The penetration of cybernetic concepts and methods into the humanities: literature, arts, history, sociology and others, has been somewhat slower. Cybernetic ideas are used there only for solving auxiliary problems. This is explained both by the complexity of the objects of study and a different style of thought that sets people in the humanities apart from those in the natural sciences and technology. For this reason, a long time is likely to be needed for establishing a closer contact between the liberal-arts people and experts in systems-cybernetic methodology and computer applications.

We should like to emphasize that what is in question here is not the creation of a new "cybernetics of the humanities" but the penetration of cybernetic ways of thinking and cybernetic techniques into the humanities, thereby promoting their development.

One example that confirms this attitude towards the "non-cybernetic" disciplines as the correct one is the latest developments in morphology. Some 10-15 years ago, morphology, one of the traditional branches of biology, did not seem to be very promising any more and was thought to be scarcely able to yield results of value to modern biology. It was even proposed that research on morphology should be scaled down. However, the bionic concepts, the need for developing precision transducers for engineering applications, the task of building walking vehicles, industrial robots, and the research on the flapping type of flight have greatly boosted new research in morphology. At present vigorous studies are being conducted into the receptor and locomotion members of many animals, in particular, crustacea and insects.

Owing to cybernetic ideas, these investigations came into contact with neurophysiological studies and new interesting facts on the neuron-level structure and operation of the systems that control motion, flight, and other functions were brought to light.

Structuring and formalizing knowledge. The complexity and specific nature of objects studied by the social sciences (man, social groupings, creativity, social processes and so on) determined the largely descriptive character of their investigations. Many of the concepts and laws in these disciplines are formulated in qualitative terms. Meanwhile, the importance of quantitative methods is appreciated today in every branch of science.

The application of the cybernetic approach, the need for exact descriptions to be used when modelling tasks, and the character of the problems encountered in present-day science and economics, have contributed to the penetration of exact methods, the systems-cybernetic way of thinking, and the formalized statement of problems into all branches of learning. Thus, the development of computer programming systems and languages, has brought about a considerable formalization and structuring of linguistics. The discipline of structural linguistics has emerged, and as it evolves it increases the share of quantitative results in the body of knowledge about linguistics as a whole.

The structuring and formalizing of other humanities, primarily psychology, are the main problems confronting us today. Human communication, the factors influencing human consciousness, and the management of social groups are essentially informational problems, and our knowledge in this field cannot be efficiently used without structuring and formalizing it.

The complexity and variety of objects such as man, thought and human activity naturally force the investigator to concentrate on individual features and special cases and make it difficult for him to find any of these objects' essential properties and characteristics. Computer simulation appears to open up the possibility of evaluating how essential each of the factors or group of factors is and finding basic and fairly formalized laws that underlie the phenomena being studied.

It can be stated with a measure of certainty that the structuring and formalizing of the humanities will bring about their partial mathematicization and make it possible to estimate more objectively the level of learning at any given instant.

Integrated research of man-machine systems. The development of science and technology leads to continuous growth in complexity of systems man has to deal with. They include large industrial complexes, branches of the economy, the economy itself, and finally the entire biosphere, of which man is a constituent part. It is becoming more and more important to ensure that man interacts rationally with the systems and to provide for their effective functioning.

Direct human interaction with the environment is steadily giving place to interaction via artificial devices and systems. Besides the material and energy factors and the large-scale use of machinery, the informational factor (that is, obtaining and processing information about the environment, the machines acting upon it, and the activities of other people taking part in this purposeful co-operation) plays an ever increasing role. The intensive development of automatic information-processing equipment has had the effect of bringing into man's communication channels machines that handle flows of information coming to and from the user.

Thus, man, his environment and all the interactions between them are transformed into a complex man-machine system in which information processes are gaining in importance. At the same time, this makes crucial the collective action of people and their joint efforts to solve common problems and attain common goals.

It is apparent therefore that the quality of the information flow between people and machines in large man-machine systems becomes an essential and often the decisive factor for the effective function of all the systems. Accordingly, informational interaction (conversation) in complex man-machine systems is a vital object of scientific research, whose results have a great practical importance.

The foregoing discussion shows that these interwoven problems, which require the joint attention of many branches of science, provide an extensive field for the application of cybernetic ideas.

Of the various aspects of cybernetic and systems approaches, the problem of communication (dialogue) arouses the greatest interest. It has many constituents: the problem of understanding, the choice of language, the problem of decision-making with regard to the aims and motivations that affect the process, the correlation of aims, the use of different kinds of information, the problem of psychological comfort, the problem of information requirements, and many others. The problem of communication breaks down into two parts: the dialogue between people and the dialogue between man and machine. Obviously, a complete solution to the man-machine problem is impossible without re-evaluating and rational using the data on human communication that has been accumulated by psychology and sociology. Nevertheless, the informational character of both components of this problem is bound to give the central role in the problem's solution to experts in cybernetics.

Further, although the man-machine dialogue must also draw upon the experience of human communication, both human and machine factors are interrelated to such an extent that they must be dealt with together. For this reason, the experimental data on man-machine dialogue are, in turn, very important for understanding purely human communication.

Linguistic aspects are also important in this problem. Without tackling them, no significant progress can be expected in machine translation and in developing methods for representing and storing knowledge in computer systems. Research in this field is now being conducted within the framework of artificial intelligence studies.

References

1. Gamov, G., *Nature* **173**: 318 (1954).
2. Gamov, G., *Kgl. Dansk. Videnskab Selskab Biol. Med.*: **22**: 1-13 (1954).
3. Gamov, G., A. Rich, and M. Y̌cas, In: *Advances in Biological and Medical Physics*. Ed. by J. Lawrence and C. Tobias (New York, 1956).

4. Watson J. D. and F. H. C. Crick, *Nature* **171**: 737 (1953).
5. Y̌cas, M., *The Biological Code* (Amsterdam, 1969).
6. Свидерский В. П., *Полет насекомого* (Москва: Наука, 1980).
7. Будько Н. С., *Вопросы философии* 11, 75-80 (1966).

The State of the Art

The title of this chapter could serve as a heading for a great variety of papers on current achievements of cybernetics and computer technology. But only some of the more important topics have been selected, which show the practical application of cybernetics in computer networks, automation, robots, and robot systems.

Cybernetics and Practice

O. M. BELOTSERKOVSKY

A notable feature of modern science is the growth of its economic efficiency. Science today belongs to great productive forces in a developed socialist society. Putting the results of scientific research to use in the shortest possible time is, therefore, one of the chief tasks placed before scientists and production engineers.

The interrelation between theory, science, practice, and production is well known. Cybernetics, as a branch of science, is no exception. Moreover, its ties with practice are more extensive because of its wide scope. One thing is certain—cybernetics as a science would not have won such a leading place as it holds in the general stream of scientific and technological progress had it not had to tackle continually vital practical problems.

Speeding up the pace of scientific and technological development is obviously a complex task. Its fulfillment calls for the integration of various branches of knowledge, requires experts versed in many fields of learning, and unites scientists into large teams. Fundamental and applied sciences have lately been enriched with new experimental discoveries and theoretical concepts, and many traditional concepts have been re-examined.

As we know, a scientific discovery can hardly be planned. No one can discover by decree a new phenomenon or formulate a law by a certain date. In contrast, the outcome of applied research and development is, to a considerable extent, amenable to forecasting. The development of complex, special-purpose programs is directed towards this objective. For instance, the USSR State Committee for Science and Technology, the USSR State Planning Committee, and the USSR Academy of Sciences worked out 170 scientific-technological programmes, among them 40 complex special-purpose programmes, which provide for large-scale application of the most outstanding scientific achievements in the economy. Implementation of such programmes opens new opportunities for strengthening the ties between science, technology, and industry.

In turn, the union of science and practice, and the comprehensive solution to problems favour the development of theory, giving rise to new branches of learning. Modern science in general is characterized by mutual penetration and enrichment of one branch of knowledge by another. The emergence and wide application of the methods of theoretical and applied cybernetics provide a striking example of such links.

The advent of electronic computers has given a great impetus to research into control processes in nature, technology, and society. It has paved the way for devising systems, which not only can perform functions traditionally thought to belong to the realm of human intelligence, but also allow a host of new control processes to be implemented. The vigorous penetration of the computer into human activities is likely to have an effect on the growth of production forces in human society similar to the one machine tools and other industrial equipment had in the epoch of industrial revolution.

It can generally be stated that mathematicization of physical knowledge and extensive use of mathematical-modelling methods have become typical of modern scientific research. Actual problems that practice places before science give rise to new features in the development of cybernetics. New lines of research are emerging, emphasis frequently shifts in the existing branches, and different problems appear. But, of course, cybernetics retains its significance as a science of control and information handling (mathematical and technical cybernetics), as well as the theory of data transmitting and processing.

Cybernetics is now tackling technological and production problems on an ever increasing scale. Even such purely theoretical disciplines as mathematical logic and algorithms theory, which deal with investigation into propositional calculus and methods of theorem proving, direct their efforts towards evolving software for high-speed electronic computers and methods of automating their design. The development of new aspects of mathematical logic and probability theory is also directly related to creating more powerful electronic computing systems and automata.

Discrete ("machine") mathematics, likewise, is turning to the study of the general principles that underlie the creation of algorithms for control systems and investigation into functional systems determining the operation of automata, their synthesis, complexity, dependability, and conversion,

Mathematical techniques are being developed for solving practical control problems as well as for research into control processes. The theory of adaptive teaching and self-learning systems helps towards organization of control processes in systems which follow complex cause-and-effect relationships or are behaviourally unpredictable. The theory of optimum control has a direct bearing on systems design.

Practice poses such problems of cybernetics development as the automation of experimental research and engineering design, and elaboration of methodology for structuring robot systems. Applied mechanics and physics combined with cybernetics yield direct results in the study of aerospace problems or controlled thermonuclear fusion.

The development of modern wide-capability computers and advances in computer simulation have opened new ways for theoretical research. Today, practice poses problems before the applied-science worker that can in most cases be investigated only by calculation or by carefully conducted physical experiment. That is why general calculation techniques (algorithms) are so important for studying problems in mathematical physics.

So what is computer simulation? This is essentially the finding of properties and characteristics of the phenomenon, process, or condition under investigation by solving, with the aid of a computer, a system of equations which represent a mathematical model. The model should be so devised as to reflect the characteristic properties of the simuland and, at the same time, be amenable to investigation. Obviously, the task is difficult. Up-to-date electronic computers alone can cope with the simulation of complex natural and engineering systems.

Mathematical modelling considers jointly the statement of the problem, the method of its solution, and the realization of the algorithm by the computer. As compared with physical modelling, mathematical modelling, performed by means of computers, is substantially more economical, and in some instances, where physical modelling is virtually not feasible, it is the only research tool. The initial statement of the problem is refined in the course of mathematical modelling. The processing of different variants in the computer enables the investigator to accummulate facts which allow the choice of the most real and probable situations.

Wide use of mathematical models was a leading factor to ensure savings of time needed to implement scientific and engineering programmes. This was demonstrated, for instance, by research into aerospace problems, as was mentioned before. The metal content of structures can also be reduced through improvements in strength calculation methods. Automated systems oriented on high-efficiency computers and using for strength calculations present-day mathematical methods, optimization techniques, information systems, and data bases are being put to use on an ever increasing scale. Research into destruction mechanisms and strength criteria, as well as the clarification of the character and magnitude of loads acting on structures, have made it possible to improve strength specifications, which are fundamental to the design of structures.

Owing to the computer, mathematical methods have found use in non-traditional areas, where compact mathematical models like differential equations have not so far been arrived at, but where models that lend themselves to investigation with the computer are nevertheless feasible. In this case, modelling is reduced to digital coding of the simuland (for example, language) and relationships between its elements (words or phrases).

A comprehensive approach, which takes advantage of both mathematical and physical types of simulation, holds the greatest promise. Functions are re-distributed between the analytical approach and mathematical and physical modelling. Such a new methodology of scientific research ties together more strongly the physical essence of the simuland, the mathematical statement of the problem, and its numerical solution on a computer. It also gives rise to a new style of investigation in the various scientific disciplines enabling the researcher to develop a broader outlook on the problems studied and to tackle them more efficiently. As a result, better ways to solve problems are found and the time needed for putting the obtained results to use is shortened. The extensive practical application of the computer and the development of techniques of mathematical simulation should go hand in hand with progress in understanding the role and place of the latter. The new methodology does not emerge instantly; it evolves in the process of work, grows and is refined as new knowledge is gained. A key to success in this important matter is the preparation of research workers versed in the new methodology and willing to develop it.

Let us touch upon another vital problem. Industrial methods of developing automatic control systems required the automation of their design, the working-out of mathematical models for typical manufacturing processes and the creation of standard software packages. Computer-aided design has found use, and control theory has been applied to specific types of manufacturing processes, industrial enterprises, transportation, and communications.

Manipulators and robots of the first and second generations are being developed along with more complex, third generation, and sophisticated "intelligent" robots. To help towards their progress, scientific research should be directed to development of multi-link mechanisms and structures with reliably controlled characteristics. These mechanisms must be functionally adapted to production conditions and provided with engineering analogues of human sensory organs (sight, hearing, tactile perception and others). Science should give assistance to robot developers in building speedy and efficient data processing systems for planning and programming the operation of robots. It should also provide help in setting up batch production of these automatic devices with the view to their performance reliability, standardization, and unification of their parts and convenience of handling, and ensure comprehensive and economical use of this equipment in industry. These conditions are imperative if robotization is to exercise positive influence on society.

Cybernetics is of much help in securing and maintaining high dependability of engineering products and systems in their manufacture and service.

Regardless of the progress made by our national economy, the performance of the control and planning mechanism as a whole does not still satisfy the present-day requirements. It is for just this reason that it is necessary to improve administrative structure and management methods on a scientific basis, with the orientation towards final objectives and optimum solutions to standing problems.

One route to this end is the application of the latest scientific advances, including the extensive use of modern computing technology to analysis, planning, and control of economic activities.

Such novel methods as systems analysis and artificial intelligence open up great possibilities for accomplishing control and planning tasks. For this reason, there has been a growing interaction of cybernetics with systems analysis, one line of which, operations research, played at one time a vital part in the formation of the basic concepts of cybernetics. Such problems as control of the development of complex systems, automation in the administrative sphere, informational aspects of scientific and technological progress are coming into prominence.

Among new developments in the field are methods of formalized description and identification of situations and scenarios of processes in large economy systems and practical methods of predicting on the basis of the models that represent the objects of prediction.

In such "traditional" complex problems as "Cybernetics and Semiotics" and "Cybernetics and Psychology", a shift can be observed towards elaboration of linguistic and psychologic models of information processing, which are significant both theoretically and practically.

On the side of artificial intelligence, in addition to research oriented towards practice, an active search is being made for the use of cybernetically related non-classical logics.

In biological and medical cybernetics, problems yielding direct results in public health, the economy, and technology are coming to forefront. Effective automatic means for monitoring the condition of patients are under development, the principles of computer application in medicine are being worked out, as are cybernetic systems for continuously monitoring a person's physical state under extreme conditions and methods for synthesizing bio-engineering control systems for dynamic objects.

It is noteworthy that, contrary to what popular magazines may churn out, the present-day progress of cybernetics is determined not so much by the achievements in the field of artificial intelligence as by working out engineering analogues of biologically regulated systems used in various engineering applications—from control of moving objects to automation of processes in industry, engineering design, and scientific research. Successful developments in this area include the principles of self-adjustment, adaptation, invariance, optimization, compromise choice, and homeostasis,

At the same time, the logico-mathematical and informational methodology of cybernetics is closely connected with widening penetration of the computer in all spheres of control and management. It is two features of cybernetics that determine the practical line of its development, namely, the engineering imitation of natural, biological control, and the creation of an informational and mathematical basis for the further advance of computer technology.

The main direction of progress in cybernetics in the near future is likely to be the continued development of high-capacity general- and special-purpose computers (both hardware and software) and applied mathematics. Achievements in this field will certainly have an immense influence on the very style of mathematical and applied research.

These lines of research are gaining in significance as the chief methodology for applying mathematics to technology and economics. Development of multi-processor and multi-computer complexes is under way. New structural principles and designs of computers radically different from the existing ones are being sought. The aim is to raise the efficiency of computers, that is, their speed of operation per unit cost.

Many efforts are now being expended in order to ease man-machine interaction and extend computer applications. To this end, data-processing means are being given some radically new features which will allow them to receive visual or verbal information or to use it directly for controlling manufacturing processes in real time.

Particularly worth mentioning is the search for new data-processing means, for instance, optical and opto-electronic means that make use of logic arrays, which can have a substantial effect on the structure of computers and on the data-processing methods. Related to this field of research is work on high-capacity holographic memory devices, on using laser rays for transmitting information, and on improving the speed of operation of fibre optics, photodiodes, phototransistors, and the like. Such research and development programmes are under way in a number of countries.

Great efforts are being made towards producing microcomputers oriented on interaction either with man, or directly with the controlled object. Microcomputers find increasing application in control systems for manufacturing processes and scientific experiments, in computer-control systems for metal-working equipment, in the lower levels of automated management and control systems, in computer-aided design systems, in communication systems, and in robots. Here both microprocessors and microcomputers are coming into extensive use.

Analysis of the prospective development of computer-oriented mathematics and computing equipment shows that a fifth generation of computers is about to enter the scene. As follows from projects carried out in a number of countries, the hardware, machine complexes, and communication lines in fifth-generation computers are bound to differ drastically from their predecessors. They will be a family of multiprocessor computers built on super-large integrated circuits, with an architecture, components and software providing for extra-high efficiency (up to billions of operations per second). The new machines will be highly dependable owing to novel components and the use of noise-protected coding of information. The application of changeable structures and other promising technologies will effectively provide for the control of information flows. These computers will be produced in different types and sizes and for different purposes: from supercomputers to high-performance mini- and microcomputers. Even today they are invading not only the world of mathematics, but also the practical activities of people and even their everyday lives.

These will be computers organically tied up with input

and output equipment that will permit information to be represented in various forms (alpha-numeric, graphic, audio, and so on). And, last, but not least, these computers will work on the time-sharing principle for handling flows of information in parallel at different levels—from breaking down the tasks themselves into relatively independent blocks that can be run in parallel to the level at which many processors and their components simultaneously perform a host of operations.

Obviously, the development of such computers, computer systems and complexes is an extremely difficult task. The elaboration of their architecture, their inner structure, algorithms and programs, and making them reliable calls for the solution of a great many complicated problems. The physico-chemical, "extremum", properties of the materials to be used for elements and blocks of such computers and the physics of the respective processes will have to be carefully studied. Systems aimed at optimizing hardware, devising and proving out the manufacturing processes for making the components, and carrying out the simulation and test procedures will have to be designed. And, finally, we shall need new mathematical methods, programmes of dividing information flows for parallel handling and retrieval of data from memory devices, systems software, and programming automation means.

The new generation of computers will undoubtedly bring new elements into mathematical thought. But, conversely, difficult mathematical problems, especially "bulky" ones which require devising powerful non-heuristic and heuristic algorithms, will inevitably place serious demands on computer technology, and hence, on structuring informational-computing man-machine systems.

Besides the already mentioned directions that computer technology, mathematical techniques, and programming may take, we can indicate the potential of the so-called vector-type information processing method, which requires an extended range of languages for man-machine dialogue, and the application of effective computer programs for implementing this method. The prospects of developing territorial information networks based on the use of the computer, and the growing importance of large data bases, whose handling becomes a serious problem, should be looked upon in the same light. These networks and data bases will in future become an everyday auxiliary tool for mathematical, though not exclusively mathematical, work.

We are convinced that in the next decades cybernetics will necessarily change the style of thinking of mathematicians and many other specialists in different branches of science, technology, and industry. Mathematicians and research workers will have at their disposal powerful, new means for enabling them to develop new mathematical theories in the man-machine conversation mode. And who knows what mathematical disciplines, what theoretical concepts, what new practical applications will be brought about by the development of computer technology itself, in which hardware and software will intertwine to an ever increasing degree?

Ways of Developing Automation

I. A. APOKIN

The history of technical progress testifies that any type of technological object has a spectrum of practical features and applications. "The technological object" concept can refer to a material (for example, wood or iron tools), to the principle of operation (mechanical or electronic devices), and to different kinds of energy used to drive machines (water, wind, nuclear energy, and so on).

Depending on the technology used, the spectrum of features may be relatively wide, but there are definite limits as to how far any type of technological object can be improved. For example, if we were to design a digital computing device, we would have to consider the fact that a relatively low-level computing capability can be obtained with mechanical components; another, higher level, with electromechanical components; and, finally, a substantially higher level, with electronic components. Even the most perfect systems of all known to us—biological systems—have their obvious limitations. Thus, man is able to solve fairly complex problems in seconds. But even the simplest problem is absolutely impossible to solve in a microsecond or nanosecond. None the less modern electronic computers can easily do it, although they are infinitely more primitive than the human brain. This is only because the speed at which signals are transmitted and handled in electronic systems is five to six orders of magnitude higher than in biological systems, and so electronic computers provide incomparably higher productivity when performing some intellectual tasks.

Fixed Programming

Let us consider the principles underlying modern automation from the "maximum possibilities" standpoint. The concept of "fixed programming" is treated in this article in a broader sense than that commonly used. What we mean by "fixed programming" is a method for controlling a system that requires relatively simple algorithms. In effect, this pertains to automatic equipment and systems that can be controlled without large modern general-purpose digital computers.

There are numerous examples of such relatively simple (in terms of control algorithms) systems; they include automatic transfer lines and machines in factories, various types of automatic vending machines, automatic telephone exchanges, various types of automatic weapons, and so on.

How far can systems with "fixed programming" be developed and used? Theoretically, such systems could be used to automate the bulk of modern production operations provided that they are static, that is, they produce identical items with no change in the product. This is unrealistic. Even so complete automation would be enormously expensive, and many processes, including production management, would remain beyond the scope of such automation and would require many more office workers. In many cases automation would not be cost effective because it would not increase the productivity of labour.

"Fixed programming" automation came into extensive use in industrially developed countries in the 1920-30s and continued making strides in the following years. In the USSR, the milestones of automation were the first automated power plant (1932), the first automatic transfer line (1940) and some other facilities. The initial achievements in complete automation of production plants have also been associated with the "fixed programming" concept. An automated plant for making motor car chassis was commissioned in Milwaukee, USA, in 1921 and cut the labour requirements by 95%. An automated tyre factory and several automated oil refineries came on stream in the USSR during World War II. The first postwar decade witnessed the start-up of an automatic truck-engine piston factory (1950), automated mobile concrete plants and a number of other automated production facilities. In later years, "fixed-programmed" automated machinery was designed and put into operation on a large scale. In 1965 Soviet industry had some six thousand automatic transfer lines in service and in 1979 more than twenty-four thousand were operational. We should say in passing that standardization, an important feature of technological development, encourages "fixed-programmed" automation. A relatively limited variety of highly standardized products can be turned out in large quantities making it possible to employ widely automatic transfer lines. Nevertheless, complete automation of the main sectors of the manufacturing industry using "fixed-programmed" automatic machinery and equipment is impracticable because of the continual product changes.

Computerized Systems

The current revolution in science and technology has drastically increased the rate at which not merely improved products but also radically new products are introduced. In this situation "fixed programming" cannot be the principal method of automation, although it is valid method for mechanizing some production processes. Automatic machine tools and transfer lines, automatic control systems for production processes, railways, power plants, and so on, will be used in ever growing numbers. However, in the second half of the 20th century there has been a shift from "fixed programming" control towards the use of computer control of automated systems, and this has opened up unmatched possibilities.

Soon after the first digital electronic computers had come into being, they were viewed as the key to automation. Thus, Wiener in his book *The Human Use of Human Beings; Cybernetics and Society* (Boston, 1950) gave an amazingly accurate prediction of the changes that would occur in industrial production, although he was too optimistic in terms of time. According to Wiener, the industrial cycle would be controlled by computers, which would be used both to monitor machinery and to handle business information. At a time when computers were used mainly for scientific research purposes, Wiener predicted that similar machines would be at the hub of an industrial revolution, and that they would become dominant 10 to 20 years later.

Although time amended the terms given by Wiener, his predictions have come true. After the 1950s, when computers were used primarily for scientific and engineering calculations, came the period of their predominant use for processing large amounts of data, mainly economic in character. Typically, computers were now incorporated into information or information/control systems rather than used singly as before.

Information and information/control systems belong to the class of automated man-machine systems, with the role of the machine in each specific area growing more and more important in terms of decision making and implementation. The extreme case where the computer is fully responsible for making decisions and implementing them is usually considered to be a separate sphere of computer application, namely real-time automatic control. Here, the computer provides a feedback function for the control system, that is, the control process runs without a human operator.

The essential difference between computer-controlled automated systems and fixed-programmed control systems is that the change of parameters of the process under control is either provided for by the program or can be introduced by modifying the program, which is much simpler than changing (resetting) a fixed-programmed system. As each new generation of computers acquires an increasingly higher operating speed and larger memory, they can handle more and more complex programs. As a result, the computer as a tool for data processing and automation of complex engineering systems is steadily gaining in importance.

Computer-controlled systems have an extensive field of application: automated management information systems (MIS), continuous production processes, military and aerospace installations, information search systems, programmed instruction systems, medical diagnostic systems, experiment procedures, and so on. Industry has a lead in the application of computer control, and it is followed by other sectors of the economy.

In the USSR, the first computer-controlled systems came into existence back in 1950s. One of the world's first control systems with direct control of the production process by a digital computer (the Autooperator system for chemical production developed in the Lisichansk Division of the Automation Institute) was put into operation in 1962. A number of successful MIS's were developed and put into service in the 1960s (at the Optical and Mechanical Engineering Association in Leningrad, the Freser Tool-Making Plant in Moscow, the Television Equipment Factory in Lvov, the Radio Equipment Factory in Barnaul) and brought considerable cost benefits. The use of computer control systems in the economy on a relatively large scale began in the second half of the 1960s, when more than 400 such systems came on stream, including 170 systems for manufacturing process control. In the 1970s the scale of this activity tangibly increased. Thus, for instance, in 1972 some 40 thousand experts were engaged in the design and engineering of MIS, which were installed at every fifth industrial enterprise. In all, about four thousand computer control systems were put into use between 1971 and 1979, among them 1 475 systems for production process control.

During the 1960-1970s, computers gradually increased

their share of automation expenses. Thus, in the USSR computers accounted for 8 percent of the total output of instrumentation in 1960. This figure doubled over eight years, reaching 16.4 percent in 1968. The rate of computer production then increased again, so that the fraction of computers in the total output of the instrument-making industry reached 40.1 percent in 1972, 69 percent in 1975, and around 80 percent in 1980.

In recent years the role of the computer as a means of automated control has increased still more owing to introduction of multi-user computer systems, namely time-sharing systems and information-handling networks. The development of multi-user computer systems has promoted the use of computers to such an extent that in this respect it ranks in importance with the development of the digital computer as such.

The concept of time-sharing is based on the use of the fundamental difference between the speeds of transmitting and handling signals in living organisms and in electronic systems. As a result, a computer can be accessed by several users so that it interacts (solves problems and answers enquiries) with each user in sequence. As the time of response in a human being is thousands of times longer than in a computer, the impression is that one user has an uninterrupted dialogue with the computer. In practice, the time-sharing principle enables a large computer to be wired to a number of terminals placed perhaps at place of work or at home. As the computer is supposed to operate round the clock, it can be accessed from any terminal at any time, or from all terminals at once, as the case may be. In the USSR the development of such systems began at the computer centre of the Siberian Division of the USSR Academy of Sciences (the AIST project—an automatic information centre). The AIST-0 system was commissioned along with a general-purpose time-sharing system based on the BESM-6 series digital computer.

The most significant outcome of the development of time-sharing systems is the information and computer networks incorporating dozens and even hundreds of computers, all exchanging information. The aim of these networks is to provide a whole spectrum of services for users on a time-sharing basis, that is, calculation, computer-aided design, reference data retrieval, business information processing, computer simulation, and other tasks according to the programs available. Information and computer networks ensure better utilization of computers through pooling hardware, data banks, software, and experts. The idea of an all-embracing information and computing service envisages that the networks' terminals located at factories, offices, and homes will become no less widely used than our present-day telephones and television sets. In general, information and computing networks provide a powerful tool for increasing the overall level of automation, primarily in the areas of production control and information servicing.

In the mid-1970s over 250 information and computing networks of different capacities and purposes operated throughout the world. In the USSR the concept of the State network of computer centres proposed by V. M. Glushkov provides for several stages in its formation. The network will include the country's main computing capacities and provide a base for an All-Union automated system for collection and processing of information for planning, accounting, and controlling the economy. Specialized networks (such as the Sirena system, an airline-ticket booking system), industrial MIS networks (MORFLOT, PRIBOR, and some others), and some regional computer networks were put into operation in the 1970s.

At present, the main prospects for automation are seen

in the use of computer control. The principal problems of automation are to be solved so that automatic machinery and equipment will take over from man nearly all his heavy, monotonous, and primitive tasks. Are these hopes justified? Are there any limitations to modern computer-controlled systems, and if there are, what are they?

To answer these questions, we need to consider the distribution of workforce in the two main sectors of the economy: production and non-production. The latter part of the 20th century has witnessed a gradual decrease of employment in the production sector, while the non-production sector absorbs more and more people. In the United States, where this process is especially manifest, people employed in the non-production sector now outnumber those in the production sector, reaching, according to different estimates, from 54 to 60 percent.*

This process has two causes. First, a well-developed industrial structure depends on efficient non-production activities such as scientific research, education, and health service. A high industrial level is associated with high living standards, which include housing, services, home appliances, private cars, good infrastructure, mass communication, and so on.

The second reason for the rapid rise of people employed in the non-production sector is that non-industrial occupations are neither easily automated nor easily mechanized. Far be it from us to regard the automation of the entire non-production sector as the goal of technical progress, but

* The difference depends on which occupations are classed as non-production and on the method of adapting US statistical data to the classification accepted in the USSR. USSR statistics include the public health service, education, science, culture, the arts, government, services, housing and social construction, passenger transport, and finance, in the non-production sector.

it is obvious that we must aim at developing some way of eliminating, as much as possible, unskilled manual labour, such as cleaning and servicing public buildings, tourist facilities, hospitals, and the like. Industrial development will involve a further expansion of housing (probably at a higher rate than the growth of the population), public buildings, hotels, transport, roads, and so on. Each of these facilities will require more people for servicing, maintenance, and similar jobs. Automating these areas often requires solutions that radically differ from computer-controlled systems.

What is important is that in the production sector, too, there are many areas that require low-skilled labour and that are not easily automated. Take, for instance, engineering, one of the key areas of the production sector. The level of automation in mechanical engineering industries is substantially lower than in power generation, chemical, or food processing which use continuous production processes. Fully automated chemical production in the USA is known to account for 50 to 60 percent of all chemical processes. The figure is 10 to 15 percent for the US automobile industry, which is the most heavily automated of all engineering, whereas in the heavy engineering and metalworking industries as a whole it is much lower. This is the situation despite the high level of expenditure on automation (25 to 26 percent of the total investment in new equipment in 1973-1974). In the Soviet Union the share of fully mechanized and automated production systems in the mechanical engineering and metalworking industries was only 1.9 percent in 1977, whereas in the electrical power industry it was 30 percent, and in the textile industry it was 46 percent.

The low level of automation in mechanical engineering can be put down to the discrete nature of the manufacturing process and the predominance of small-lot production enterprises. None the less, state-of-the art automation looks promising for most metalworking operations. Thus, machining operations in small-lot production can be automated using numerically controlled multi-operation machine tools known as machining centres. Such machining centres can make up a computer-controlled production cell complete with automatic workpiece transfer and loading/unloading systems.

On the other hand, a labour-consuming process such as assembly is very difficult to mechanize. About 90 percent of the assembly operations in US industries are performed manually, employing some 700 000 people in the mechanical engineering industries. Although automatic assembly equipment has been introduced on a large scale (about 17 000 units were operational in 1973), it has only replaced manual labour in 20 percent of the operations. In the automobile industry, for instance, experts believe that about 70 percent of all assembly operations still cannot be automated.

Intelligent Automata

It follows from the foregoing that not only the service sector, but also part of the modern production sector cannot be automated using either fixed-programmed systems or present-day computer control systems. What properties should be provided for devices that are capable of performing tasks which cannot be tackled by today's automated systems? Some, though very rough, ideas can be formed by considering the main directions in the research and development of third generation robots.

It is opportune to note here that first generation robots, which are being used extensively in industry (by the end of 1980 nearly 20 000 robots were being used in capitalist countries, and about 6 000 robots in the USSR) belong somewhere between fixed-programmed and computer-controlled systems. They can be likened to fixed-programmed systems because they are designed to perform specific operations and require relatively simple algorithms for their function. Characteristically they have no "feedback" from the environment. In common with computer-controlled systems, these robots are multi-program devices, that is, they can be changed from one job to another by putting in a new program, and not by mechanical resetting, as is the case with fixed-programmed systems. Together with first generation robots, this intermediate class includes numerically controlled machine tools, most programmable teaching systems, and some others. Second generation robots (which respond to the environment through special sensors) can be placed into the class of computerized systems. Volume production of such robots is forecast for the mid-1980s.

Various concepts for robots of the third generation are now under development in a number of laboratories (such as the ones at the Institute of Cybernetics, at the Institute of Applied Mathematics, at the Bauman Higher Technological School, at the Engineering-Cybernetics Design Office at the Leningrad Polytechnical Institute). The aim is to upgrade the intelligence of the robots (first generation robots cannot simulate any intelligent action at all and second generation robots are extremely primitive in this respect). Remotely controlled "intelligent" robots, that is, those operating under human supervision are a variety of "intelligent" robots which are close to robots of the third generation. The highest level of remote control—dialogue-type control—implies contact between the robot and the human operator when carrying out a task (formulating the task, discussing emergencies and unforeseen circumstances, and so on).

A spectacular example of the initial steps towards "intelligent" robots is a robot built by Stanford University (USA). It can solve problems of the "monkey-and-banana" type in which a monkey trying to get a banana has either to find a chair in the room, carry it to the right spot and climb it, or to find a stick and throw it at the banana to bring it down, or to use both the chair and the stick. The Stanford robot has to deliver an object placed on a platform to a specified location. As the robot, which moves on wheels, cannot climb the platform, it finds a skid, brings it to the platform, rides up the skid onto the platform, pushes the object down and takes it to the right spot.

The general problem being solved by different research teams is to form an adequate model of the working environment in the robot's memory (possession of such a model is acknowledged to be the distinguishing feature of third generation robots). An important area of research within the scope of the general problem is improving "hand-eye" systems, with the eye being a computer-controlled television camera. Such systems, capable of performing numerous assembly tasks, will signify an important advance in the development of third generation industrial robots. Other and no less important research programmes involve the spatial motion of robots, reception of oral commands, and so on. According to some estimates, the first practicable third generation robots, though very expensive, will be commercially available in the late 1980s. Some domestic-robot projects have also been proposed.

At present, a concept of a radically new automatic device has been outlined which could be termed an "intelligent automaton" (specifically—"intelligent robot"). "Intelligent" automata differ in principle from today's computers and computerized control systems. The efficiency with which computers can carry out some tasks by imitating mental activity is determined solely by the programs put in these machines. "Intelligent" automata will be given the "principles for compiling programs", "the general principles underlying particular tasks" and some specific problems rather than individual programs, as is the case with computers now. "Intelligent" automata will be instructed how to generate programs for accomplishing specific tasks or will do it on their own. The programs will not have their final form, they will be modified as the task is carried out. In other words "intelligent" automata, having received a basic intelligence through instruction, will themselves create the algorithms for the problems of the class for which they have been designed. This is a striking difference between them and modern computers. In addition, more sophisticated servomechanisms (mechanical hands, for example) will be used in combination with these new automata when required.

The classes of automatic systems discussed above (fixed-programmed, computer controlled, and "intelligent" automata) reflect the evolution of automation; each class will be refined and used in future, that is, no single type of automatic device will push out all the others. Thus, modern computers will gradually evolve into powerful "intelligent" automata of the universal type with large information and computing capacities. At the same time, robots will also be provided with "intelligence"; some of them will be operated by "intelligent" computers, and the others will operate independently, that is, run by their own built-in "intelligent" minicomputers. Fixed-programmed automation will also be employed. The engineering industry will use automatic transfer lines (for volume production), computer-controlled systems (manufacturing cells with machining centres for small-lot production, MIS for manufacturing plants as a whole, and so on), and "intelligent" robots (for assembly and auxiliary operations).

Each class has a definite range of capabilities, but, put together, all these capabilities will encompass most kinds of human activity, almost completely including the spheres of unskilled and low-skilled labour.

Production-Methods Approach to Automation

It must be noted that the use of automatic devices as such is not the only way to automating production, as it might at first seem. There are some other ways, which, on the whole, could be termed the "production-methods approach" to automation.

The approach is best explained by way of example. Suppose, an automobile component that has until now been machined on a conventional lathe is now to be produced using an automated technique. We could switch over from the standard lathe to an NC turning machine linked to a pick-and-place robot. The problem could also be solved by producing the same part another way, for example, by moulding it from a plastic. The result will be the same: the part will have been produced without manual labour. To sum up, the production-methods approach is to introduce new manufacturing techniques for the production of items that are functionally identical to those obtained using the automated equivalent of the existing method.

Considering the relationship between automation and manufacturing technology, two aspects affecting automation are apparent. First, advances in manufacturing technology make it possible for automation to advance (a spectacular example is the evolution of semiconductor and integration-circuit techniques, which have drastically changed many of the characteristics of computers and other electronic devices). Second, in some situations automation can be attained either by using automated equipment or by resorting to a new manufacturing process.

As with automation, the evolution of production techniques, where one manufacturing method replaces another, is governed by definite laws of development peculiar to every field of technology and perhaps general for technology as a whole. Thus, in the 20th century, the role of chemical engineering has increased considerably, and biotechnology is gradually being applied more and more extensively. We can thus say that there is a trend towards the use of more highly organized structural levels of matter for production processes. Another trend is towards the industrial use of results obtained in physical studies of microcosm, atomic, and subatomic levels of matter's structure. In power engineering, for instance, the role of nuclear energy is growing rapidly despite the currently predominant use of chemical processes based on coal, oil, gas, and so on. In engineering production, the prevalence of machining is accompanied by the growing importance of non-traditional methods, such as laser and electron beam machining, electrical discharge machining, and the like.

Automation is developing under conditions of a rapidly changing world of production technology, where sometimes the manufacturing methods themselves perform the role of automation in addition to the ever extending use of automatic devices.

References

1. *Народное хозяйство в СССР в 1979 г. Статистический ежегодник* (Москва: Статистика, 1980).
2. *Мировая экономика и международные отношения*, 2, 146-157 (1975).
3. Супян В. Б. *США. Экономика, политика, идеология*, 2, 66-67 (1976).

The Emergence of Computer Networks

E. A. YAKUBAITIS

In recent years we have witnessed a rapid change in the approach to computers and their capabilities. Electronic computers were initially designed for complex scientific and engineering calculations. It soon turned out that the computer had become an indispensable tool for information handling and production control tasks.

These capabilities are particularly important at the present stage of the development of the economy. The links between industrial enterprises and organizations are becoming ever more complex, and the dynamic development of the economy requires competent management and prompt decisions. Traditional methods of administration and control are no longer efficient, while planning at enterprise and industry levels is becoming more and more critical.

These needs brought about the emergence and development of a new discipline known as information science, or informatics. It embraces the methods and means that provide for high-speed collection, transmission, processing, and release of data in formats convenient for management and production.

What is the technological basis of informatics? Consider these data. In recent years the cost of electronic computers has gone down by about 28 percent annually. Communication channel costs have dropped by 11 percent. Mini- and microcomputers have come into being. Information teleprocessing systems have been developed which allow communication with computers located at long distances from their users. Dialogue methods for operating computers in different parts of the world have been put to practical use.

Taken together this has laid the groundwork for a breakthrough in computer engineering whose significance ranks with the computer's advent about 40 years ago. I think we could talk about a revolution in information handling without any exaggeration. A key role here was played by the emerging computer networks. Each network consists of a number of large and small computers interlinked by communication channels. By connecting terminals and peripheral equipment (electric typewriters, CRT displays, drafting machines, and so on) to a computer network, distant users can gain access to information stored in the memory of any of the computers in the network.

Computer networks have resulted from joint research and development programmes carried out by experts in cybernetics, computer technology, and communication engineering. They proposed the general principles and methods for collecting, storing, processing, transmitting, and outputting the information. These methods made it possible to bring together the processes of computing, economic modelling, and management in various sectors of the economy, production, and scientific research.

A modern computer network consists of a number of user systems which come in contact with each other through the communications system. Each user system includes one or more computers, terminals, printers, copying and graphics devices and other more specialized input-output devices.

There are a number of different sorts of communication networks which provide for the transmission of information between the user systems. This is used for networks spread out over large territories (a region, country or group of countries). The heart of the network is the data transmission system, which consists of communication centres and channels connecting them. A communication centre has several micromachines which distribute information.

Small local networks generally take two forms. The first is very simple in structure. Here an electrical coaxial cable or an optical light conductor interconnects the computers in a single network. The second kind of system connects all the user systems via a ring of information carrying channels.

Large multi-purpose computer networks have been created in central planning and control departments, industrial associations, and scientific centres, where large flows of information have to be dealt with. Such networks are already in operation in Moscow, Leningrad, Kiev, Novosibirsk, and Riga. They will largely determine the progress in the information handling industry, serving the economy and the general public.

In view of their importance, computer networks have been earmarked for rapid development. Ultimately, they must make up the integral national computer network in this country.

The essential part of a computer network is its data banks. These provide the basis for comprehensive information services. Relevant economic data, such as statistical data and information on the activities of an industrial enterprise, trade association or region, are entered into the computer memory. These data banks can be set up at different locations throughout the country. A user can reach every data bank via the communication links and promptly, in the conversational mode, obtain the necessary data at any time round the clock.

Complex data processing systems are formed around data banks. As an example, Soviet and Bulgarian scientists have proposed a standardized set of programs for the automated control of an engineering or instrument-making factory (or association). The programs are used to plan for production, to monitor the industrial cycle, to supervise the utilization of materials, and so on.

7—01169

An important feature of computer networks is their ability in a matter of minutes to transmit documents in any form: texts, tables, diagrams, and drawings. "Electronic mail" looks promising for arranging teleconferences, symposia, discussions, and the like. The participants will be provided with means for data input and output, including small electronic terminals, which can be used to write a text or to draw a diagram or a sketch. The information will be reproduced on the displays used by other participants. The diagrams and drawings can be accompanied by oral commentaries.

Office information systems having one or more minicomputers and several dozens of terminals will be used extensively. Such systems will release office workers from the tedious routine tasks, taking over the compiling, editing, searching, and selecting of documents, and warning about the coming deadlines. They can help prepare financial reports, accounts, requisitions, legal documents, and so on.

A mass media systems, tentatively named VIDEOTEST, will appear in the coming years. Every user will have a home television set, a telephone, and a plain cassette recorder, which are supplemented with a small box (the size of a transistor radio set) housing a microprocessor and a typewriter keyboard. In this way, millions of users will be able to have quick access to a wide range of information: to go through the pages of electronic "newspapers", to reply to inquiries about weather forecasts, to obtain information about various services and entertainments, to carry out transactions in savings banks, and to book tickets for shows and journeys. Computer-aided teleinstruction and training on individual programs will become a reality.

It is clear therefore that the development of data banks and information systems is very important though perhaps complex. Several serious obstacles will have to be overcome. The first is to devise and put into use a large number of standards establishing the rules and procedures of processing and transmitting information.

This is necessary to prevent the breeding of a great variety of data banks that operate in different computer languages and employ different methods of interaction with users. Diversity would inevitably make the banks incompatible with one another and with other networks.

Another problem is to change the habits and attitudes of office workers who have got used to documents coming by mail or telegraph. It must be realized that new up-to-date information systems require new forms of handling documentation.

I should like to conclude that standardized data banks with ramified telecommunication systems for information handling are a promising development.

Extensive application of computer networks with dynamic data banks and information handling systems will help to provide management and production personnel with information for efficient control of the industrial cycle.

The Robots in Present-Day Industry

I. M. MAKAROV

Why is there such a great need for robotic devices in the economy?

The reason is that robots have concentrated in them all the latest advances in automation that have been brought about by the scientific and technological revolution. They incorporate the theoretical progress in engineering cybernetics and its practical achievements; the essential results of information and control theory; the new electronic components developed for automatic machinery and computers; the extra-sensitive micro-transducers; and miniature drives. Robotics is rightly at the forefront of modern industry.

According to plans made by the USSR State Committee for Science and Technology, the technological basis for robotizing Soviet industry is being established in the current five-year period. Science and industry have developed ingenious industrial robots, and there is now a considerable population of them in this country.

Robots can be classified by their applications.

Remotely-controlled robots are used extensively for handling a variety of tasks from industrial operations that do not lend themselves to the traditional methods of automation to work in difficult environments that are hostile to man, such as extremely low or high temperatures, the presence of radioactivity, chemically toxic environments, outer space, and beneath the ocean. Industrial robots are used to stamp, grind, weld, classify, and transfer components and finished parts. They are also used in various branches of industry, combining high accuracy and efficiency.

Industrial robots are chiefly manipulators handling "manual" jobs, but some of them perform informational tasks using sensors to collect information and output it immediately.

The "intelligent" robots have different applications. They automatically accomplish tasks associated with mental activity, which had always been regarded as belonging exclusively to man. We can rightly classify as such robots like automatic drafting system, "automatic librarians", and of course automatic "composers" and "poetry writers".

Three Generations of Robots

Over their relatively short history, industrial robots have been assigned to several generations depending on the type of their control systems.

The first generation is the numerically controlled robots capable of performing only programmed movements.

The second generation contains robots with sensors and adaptive controls. These are more flexible and compliant. They are taught to "sense" and act upon the guidance of their sensors, thus adapting themselves to conditions in order to fulfill their tasks better.

The third generation of robots is used for various control functions and for imitating intelligence.

Although this classification is arbitrary, one cannot but feel the sharp division between the generations, a division that strikingly manifests the advance towards the creation of an "intelligent" robot and shows up the results that have already been achieved.

True, the term "generation" as applied to robots is peculiar. It does not imply change, the substitution of one type of system for another, it rather means their refinement, improvement, and optimization. Since the needs of industry are very diverse, each generation requires an assessment of where and when it will be suitable and efficient. Hence robots from all the three generations may work side by side. And each generation must be continuously developed and improved. But how?

Concerning robotics, no definite answer can be expected. Several methods and several approaches are always available. Hence, we have the somewhat contradictory concept of the poly-alternative solution to the problems of robot systems.

Take for instance first generation robots. Their main disadvantage is the difficulty of adjusting the control program whilst they are in operation. Where should improvement in this type of robots be sought?

One way is to orient the program towards specific requirements dictated by the job that must be done. Suppose we are faced with a situation where the optimum control of a process is only possible if the control procedure itself changes. Then, we have to complicate the program so that it can both select and optimize the type of control.

Another way is to assign the programming tasks to different levels in a control hierarchy, that is, to create programs oriented to particular types of equipment or manufacturing processes. Specific, clear, and unambiguous solutions and the elimination of "yaws" in the process of seeking the right way are in itself an optimization.

What about the second generation of robots? Here, also, we have a host of problems.

The very question of making robot systems sensitive was generated by the problem of complexity. It was necessary to attain a high operating accuracy of pick-and-place robots without resorting to engineering imitations of biological sensory organs, that is, to make robots feel robot-like rather than human-like.

A variety of available sensor devices enabled designers to produce adaptive-control systems that can receive data from external sources, analyze them and adapt themselves to changing conditions. The problem seems very clear: a single approach is required to pull together all the different sensing devices so that the outside world can be perceived.

Of course, this approach should be pattern recognition. The clear picture becomes blurred when one considers a specific robot application.

It took scientists a lot of difficult work and argument before they could come to the present-day division of pattern recognition techniques into syntactic, opto-spectral, and resolution methods.

The first category of methods is best if the pattern can be described in a special language. The optical and spectral method has shown its advantages in systems where the objects being classified by the robot are slowly and fully scanned. By contrast, the resolution method has been successful when time is short and the robot must use less data since the time available to survey the object is short. Without any doubt, most difficulties are encountered when dealing with what may be referred to as "control and intelligence". This is fundamental to research on rationally-acting robot systems.

This problem too can be approached in more than one way. Two relatively independent methods—neurocybernetic and semiotic—yield dissimilar but interesting results.

The neurocybernetic approach is based on a simulation of the nervous system, which works by processing information hierarchically. Neuron-like structures are now used to control material-handling and excavator robots.

In contrast, the complicated problems of independent intelligent action in robot systems require something like a symbiose of the processes of perception, formation of concepts, generalization, action planning, and behaviour.

What progress the semiotic approach has made and what is its contribution to the creation of an intelligent robot? Basically, this approach is quite attractive and promising—it seeks to provide a robot with the ability of analyzing sensory information, comparing it with its inner knowledge, and acting upon the results of the comparison.

This superior ability is implemented through semiotic networks which form the inner notions by describing for the system the relationships between notions. The system is taught the skill of generalization by forming higher-level notions from simple notions. In order to do this, the system is given a certain knowledge with different levels of sophistication.

The semiotic approach to artificial intelligence has made possible the appearance of robots with a measure of speech such as can be understood as a human language. These systems can converse with man within the limits of a topic. Systems that can prove mathematically stated assertions, and some solving and planning systems also act on semiotic principles.

Although each of the methods is independent, this does not mean they are isolated from each other. Quite the reverse is true: the neurocybernetic methods for directly processing sensory information and the semiotic methods for analysing and transforming data can and should be combined to solve practical problems.

The Mechanics, Kinematics, and Dynamics of Robots

We have so far dealt with the problems associated with the "brain" of robots, that is, the control of their actions. But robots also have operative members and these too have their own problems.

Scientists attach great importance to the mechanics, kinematics, and dynamics of robots because they are vital when developing robot drives and limbs.

Here too, every problem can be answered in various ways.

For instance, what type of drive will prevail in future robots: hydraulic, electric, or pneumatic?

Using criteria such as maximum drive torque, response to command signals, number of working positions, and positional accuracy shows that hydraulic drives are well ahead of the other types. A robot using a hydraulic drive can attain a load-carrying capacity over 100 kg, a maximum weight handling speed of 2 m/sec, and a positioning accuracy of 1 mm.

Precision engineering, however, in which light weight and compactness are essential, will obviously require robots that carry a minimum of additional equipment, and electric drives are best here. Fluidic devices are the most suitable for robots operating in hostile or blast-hazard environments where thermal or electric energy may accumulate or be released.

Therefore, all three types of drive are not exclusive and should be developed together to suit specific robot applications.

There has been a notorious controversy over whether to make the working members of robots imitate human limbs. The disagreement is not dictated by emotional or aesthetic considerations; anthropomorphism, which has been the subject of discussion for many years now, is often looked upon as the measure of robots' performance and efficiency.

Undoubtedly, the flexibility and adaptability of manipulation attained by natural limbs are in many respects out of the reach of robots. The angular, brusque, and awkward grip of mechanical manipulators cannot be compared with elastic, smooth, and sparing movements of the human hand. But do we need manipulations that are so perfect always and everywhere? No, as it happens, not always and not everywhere. Anthropomorphism need not therefore be the ultimate goal to strive for. More than that, we often wish to endow robots with abilities man himself does not possess and teach it to do what man is not able to.

Therefore, a co-operative approach is likely to prevail in future. Robots will combine working members similar to human arms with more complex sensor-information systems. Robots already exist that, for instance, not only see the light, hear sounds, sense heat, detect obstacles, and pass them deftly, but also react to radioactivity, slight pressure changes, and so on.

Robots and Information

Information processing is also a challenging problem for robots.

The large scale use of robot systems first of all requires large concentrations of sophisticated equipment. Groups of robots and manipulators including telecommunication devices, interfaces, and control apparatus are often spread out over production areas. The first requirement for robots to function, therefore, is to process all of the input and output information. The bulk of this data-processing work has often to be shifted from the robot itself to a computer. This is a way out, and there was no other way before the advent of microprocessors.

"Microprocessor" is a term which is extensively used today. It sometimes appears that there is a single approach to the architecture and work of this miniature computing device. Actually, microprocessors tend to develop along two fairly independent lines: microcomputers and functional microprocessor units for specific applications.

The second sort of microprocessors have attracted the most attention from robot designers. They have many advantages: first, they are made in the form of functional integrated circuits; second, they are suited to solving the logical problems which prevail in robots; third, they are easily incorporated and adjusted; and, finally, programming them is fairly easy.

It follows that the functional units can provide add-on intelligence to a robot in order to deal with the routine tasks that need frequently repeated control programs. Where a task involves large volumes of unconventional computations, the microprocessors in the other subclass, that is microcomputers, are best suited.

Microprocessors have had a notable effect on information-processing techniques. In the past, there was only one way of data processing—the centralized method. The tasks were handled using a single data base and a single programming language. Under such conditions, solving even a rather simple task required a high speed computer with an efficient central processing unit, a large-capacity memory, and a high-level programming language. Such a centralized system is very sophisticated, and programming and executing instructions and subroutines overweight the operations needed to process the work program itself. Hence, the centralized method is rather inflexible and therefore inadequate for use with robot systems.

Microprocessors have made it feasible to adopt a radically new approach to information processing. It has been called control by distributed intelligence: information here is processed independently by individual units of the system.

This method has a host of advantages, and some of them are really outstanding. For example, the arrangement of information handling agrees with the group structure of robot systems; the data processing tasks can be performed in parallel on a real-time or faster-than-real-time basis; the control process itself and the respective software can easily be adapted to different robot applications; and the whole system remains in operation even if some of its parts fail.

There is also a drawback to the new method, namely, coordination between the individual units of the system is difficult.

Understandably, scientists have wanted to combine the benefits of the centralized and distributed methods of data processing. Hence, a new control method has emerged based on a hierarchical principle.

Thus, we have three methods of information processing instead of one and can choose whichever is best for a particular application.

The centralized method, which makes use of a large computer, is expedient where the stages of the controlled process are difficult to separate as happens in chemical processing, or the interdependent process stages are performed in sequence as in building by industrial methods.

Distributed data processing is best where the process under control breaks down easily into separate operations, and their sequence is not crucial for the process as a whole, as happens, for instance, when manufacturing semi-finished products and spare components for the electronics industry.

Where the process comprises a number of separate, but closely interconnected stages, which is typical of most robot applications, hierarchical control should be used.

Robots and Human Labour

In conclusion, let us take up another aspect of robotics which cannot be ignored today, namely its social and economic significance and its effect on life in human society.

The use of robots releases people from arduous and hazardous work. At the same time, it extends the sphere of labour to environments inaccessible to man.

But there is more to it than this. The socio-economic effect of robotization, even in the areas of production involving hard and monotonous jobs, goes beyond the number of people released. Robots offer a way to relieve the general labour shortage, to make work more attractive and to bring a creative element into it. And this will certainly improve the general quality of work.

Of course, it is very important to create a good, reliable and "intelligent" robot. But still more important is a consideration of how it will affect people's work, how it will change their lives, and what contribution it will make to the improvement of production.

Artificial Intelligence: Pros and Cons

Artificial intelligence and its implications have been in the limelight in recent years. Engineers, cyberneticists, philosophers, linguists, logicians, psychologists, sociologists, and economists have all been attracted to the topic.

Research in artificial intelligence covers automated decisionmaking processes, the development of interactive systems for communication between human beings and computers in natural languages, computerized translation, automated theorem demonstration, design, and simulation of complex systems, and automated computer programming and program verification. Other important areas of research are situational control of complex objects, intellectual data banks, systems of self-instruction and information searching, perception of images in real time, and "intelligent" robots.

These research efforts are aimed not at the replacement of man with machines but at the imitation of man's mental activity to allow the transfer of routine and repetitive tasks to computers and to ensure more efficient decisionmaking. Human mental processes, therefore, must be studied with a view to formalizing them and expressing them in algorithmic form.

The time has passed when experts in cybernetics considered it possible and even necessary to formalize and automate human activities completely. Practice has shown that often these goals are not only impracticable (regardless of the state of the art in technology) but also unnecessary or economically unjustified. Nevertheless, the idea of total automation still surfaces from time to time when certain engineering, scientific, and even philosophical problems are being considered.

An algorithmic (formalized) approach to human mental activity can be useful in description of most routine tasks such as accounting, simple engineering calculations, and so on, and attempts at automation of such operations have had positive results. Automation of creative activities, such as decisionmaking, the modification of decisions, or the analysis of complex situations, has so far been unsuccessful. The development of partly automated, man-machine systems necessarily involves the appraisal of factors for or against automation. Each system must be evaluated individually to decide whether automation or optimization by some other method will be more efficient. Automation, apart from its purely mechanizing aspect, has many other implications—economic, organizational, psychological, and so on—which are no less and, often, even more weighty. The implementation of automated man-machine systems, therefore, should not be regarded as a means for replacing man with machines but as a reorganization of certain areas of human activity in all the aspects mentioned above, with the aid of machines and other devices (not only computers but also various supplementary equipment, displays, control panels, and so on). If viewed otherwise, automation will simply preserve existing routines in human activity. In other words, automation must be used as a means of rationalizing human activity rather than as a substitution for man.

The problem of automation is closely related to the equally important problem of the feasibility of cybernetic concepts for analysis of social, psychological, economic, and other aspects of human activity. Cybernetic models and concepts are fairly general in character. Their successful application in other areas depends on successes reached in studies of mechanical, electronic, biological, social, and other processes. Since cybernetic concepts and principles tend to be universal in character, there is a danger of considering them to be absolute. In its extreme forms this absolutism may appear as "cybernetic reductionism", which ultimately repeats the errors of physicalism (only instead of the language of physics, the language of cybernetics is proclaimed to be the universal language of science). It is particularly important to emphasize this potential hazard now, since not long ago excessive early scepticism towards cybernetics changed to an uncritical approach of total "cybernetization" on the wave of undisputed successes in the practical application of cybernetics. Fortunately, most philosophers and practical engineers have now adopted more sober and realistic views, and today all those dealing with the problem of artificial intelligence realize that purely cybernetic methods are not enough for its solution.

New Approach to Computer Application

G. S. POSPELOV

The exceptionally important role played by the computer in the current scientific and technological revolution can be measured by the enormous progress of computer technology in the past few decades. Capable of serving as a means of automation and as a tool for considerably increasing the efficiency of mental activity, the computer ranks in importance with the steam engine of the first industrial revolution.

At the outset, digital computers processed numerical data (and they got their name from this basic function). The first computer languages were oriented towards mathematical models in physics, mechanics, economics, management, and so on. All these models are universal in character. That means that the same models—systems of algebraic and differential equations or various models of optimization (linear or non-linear programming, optimum control, game theory and the like)—can describe in mathematical language phenomena and processes in diverse problem domains.

Computers operate and handle numerical data on the syntactic (formal) level and the meaning of the input and output data is hidden from the computer. This meaning must be interpreted by the user, an expert in a specific target area. Extensive application of the computer and its success in handling numerical data on the basis of universal mathematical models and syntactic functioning caused the computer to be used like a large, speedy, automatic calculator.

With time, however, the situation changed. Gradually at first and then more rapidly, the computer extended its field of application to processing symbolic data in addition to numerical data (or, as it is sometimes inaccurately termed, alphanumeric information). The ability to handle symbols, transform their sequences and aggregates, and subject them to various operations and procedures lies at the heart of all kinds of communication in human society. Audible or visual symbols or signs arranged according to syntactic rules reflect the meaning (semantics) and pragmatics of human relations and form natural languages and the numerous languages of natural sciences. The language of mathematics, for instance, is an excellent illustration of the significance of symbols and their transformations. The history of mathematical symbols and their transformations is virtually the history of mathematics itself. Often, as the following two examples make clear, the most important factor in creative thinking is the concise symbolic designation of the given concepts and their relationships.

In the Middle Ages one had to study at a university to learn arithmetical operations. Not just any university would do; only Italian universities could teach the art. Roman numerals were used then, and the problem of division of large numbers could take a lifetime to master. The situation changed dramatically with the introduction of Arabic numerals and the concept of zero and its designation. At present the algorithm of division is easily learnt at primary school.

Ten years after the appearance of work by Hamilton, Maxwell saw that two Hamilton's operators could reflect relations between the electric and the magnetic field. Two short lines in the Maxwell equations represented the entire theory of electricity, magnetism, and light as an electromagnetic field.

Beginning with the language of gestures used by our ape like ancestors, symbols and methods of symbolic transformation have developed simultaneously with the evolution of human intelligence and civilization. Calculating tasks apart, since computers and their programs became capable of processing data in symbolic form and thus of solving tasks traditionally thought to be intellectual, it became possible to speak about artificial intelligence. Computers of the MIR-2 and MIR-3 types, for instance, can among other operations find indefinite integrals, that is, produce the result of an operation in formulae. The increasing ability of computers to solve intellectual problems has led, naturally, to their inclusion as a kind of "intelligent" tool in human communications and interrelations.

That has created a number of difficult problems in artificial intelligence theory. Any communication between two people presupposes a certain commonality in their models of the outside world or roughly equal levels of knowledge of the topic of discussion. Given that, it is possible to omit whole sentences in a conversation without the risk of misunderstanding. Suppose Mr. A asks Mr. B: "Are we going to the country today?" If, for instance, the reply is: "No, my battery's run down", Mr. A will correctly perceive Mr. B's meaning since their common model of the world initiates the necessary chain of cause-and-effect relationships in his head. But if A is a computer, rather than a person, initiating such a chain of relationship is far from easy. Computers have now been taught a syntactic analysis of sentences. Human beings, owing to a common model of the world, can understand syntactically incorrect sentences like those uttered by Jingle, a character in Dickens's *Pickwick Papers.* If Jingle said in his typical manner "A highway-ice-skidding-crash-hospital", readers would most likely grasp the situation. But what about the computer?

If the computer is to be introduced into the sphere of human communication to increase the efficiency of mental activity, it must hold in its memory a semantic model of some segment of a target area. Specifically, if we consider communication through texts, the model must reflect "the text-the meaning-the reality". Using such semantic models, computers will be able to analyze and synthesize texts and speech. But semantic models can be formed if the computer memory contains knowledge and not simply data, as is currently the case. Today's computers are provided with software to manipulate data banks, which will be gradually changed to knowledge banks. The introduction of knowledge into the computer is one of the central problems of artificial intelligence, and from 25 to 35 percent of all papers read at international conferences on artificial intelligence are invariably dedicated to finding its solution.

We have touched on the first of the important computer properties to stem from the development of artificial-intelligence theory. This ability of the computer to analyze and synthesize texts and speech is realized in so-called question/

answer systems or in systems of communicative interaction with data bases in a modified natural language, limited by professional terminology*.

This ability of computers to analyze and synthesize texts and speech involves a qualitatively new application of computer technology when it is utilized directly without the programmer.

This new application of the computer also allows the use of computers to solve problems as initially formulated, using basic data without pre-programmed algorithms for the solution. The plan and the algorithm of the solution are developed automatically from a set of programmed modules by the master planning program. Since these modules are parts of the widely used, general-purpose mathematical models mentioned above, the importance of this feature of the computer cannot be overestimated. This new application of computer technology opens the way to the use of computers and their networks by numerous professionals in all branches of science and the economy.

Marx once wrote that "a spider conducts operations that resemble those of a weaver, and a bee puts to shame many an architect in the construction of her cells. But what distinguishes the worst architect from the best of bees is this that the architect raises his structure in imagination before he erects it in reality. At the end of every labour process, we get a result that already existed in the imagination of the labourer at its commencement."**

---

* One of the first Soviet question/answer systems, devised by E.V. Popov, was described in an article by V.N. Baklanov and E.V. Popov published in *Известия АН СССР. Техническая Кибернетика* (1978, 4).

** Marx, K. *Capital*, v. 1, 178. International Publishers, (New York, 1977).

If we consider the conventional functioning of computers and their current use from this point of view, the computer compares to the spider or bee rather than to the weaver or architect. The spider and the bee act on their genetical programs, whereas the computer operates according to programs written by the programmer in a certain language.

To perform its task like a human being, the computer must be provided with a semantic model or a model of some sphere of knowledge and a planning master program, which can generate an algorithm and an operative program from a set of program modules designed for solving problems of a specific class.

This second feature of the computer, which, like the first one, has unlocked the path to a new style of computer application, was facilitated by the evolution of computer software. Thus, computers of the Unified Range (UR) allow an unlimited number of programs to be stored on magnetic discs or in libraries in usable form. In addition, software for UR computers is modular, and all programs are arranged in standard modules which can be assembled into larger programs.

Software for UR computers makes use of three kinds of modules: source modules written in programming languages, object modules obtained by translating the source modules, and input modules obtained by combining and processing the object modules. Before modules can be put together into a final program, they must be called up by an operation code or macro instruction. So one more step has yet to be made: the automation of the assembly of a working program from a set of program modules relating to a specific problem area. The model of this area, the planner working out the plan, and the algorithm solving the problem are required to make that step*.

A few words should now be said about semantic models, which are used to encode the meaning of processes, phenomena, texts, sentences, and so on. There are several methods for composing semantic models. A fairly common semantic model is represented by the so-called semantic grid or graph that carries the meaning of a particular text or sentence. The peaks of the graph signify concepts, and the connecting curves signify relationships between the concepts. The creation of a semantic model of a specific target domain is feasible since such languages as Italian, Russian, and English have no more than 180 to 200 basic relationships to express action, motion, condition, and so on. With 500 concepts, a fairly large amount, from a definite sphere, we can create a graph quite suitable for processing in today's computers.

Obviously the computer is a tool to aid the mental activity of man, and the quest for artificial intelligence gives this tool a new dimension and provides new promising fields of application. Arguments for or against artificial intelligence, therefore, seem quite irrelevant.

As to the question of whether the machine thinks by itself like humans, the answer may be that the mental activity of a human being is initiated by his needs, wishes, interests, motivations, and so forth. Similar (if "similarity" is the right concept at all) "mental" activity of the computer is initiated entirely by the will of its human user. The computer, although already capable of defeating a human player at chess, does not enjoy the game, the player does.

---

* In the USSR this step was pioneered by E.Kh. Tiugu in the PRIZ software system, which is now in use. The DILOS system that combines the properties of dialogue systems with PRIZ-type systems has been developed by V.M. Bryabrin and D.A. Pospelov.

Why Artificial Intelligence?

M. M. BOTVINNIK

I cannot say I fully agree with G.S. Pospelov. In my view, we should get rid of our prejudices when talking about intelligence, both natural and artificial. Let us define the concept from the cybernetic point of view. What is it, then? I believe intelligence is the ability to make a decision—a sound decision — in a difficult situation by spending available resources in a most efficient way. From this point of view, there is no difference between natural and artificial intelligence.

How did the idea of artificial intelligence come into being in the first place? Since the amount of information we have to assimilate is growing at an unprecedented rate and the problems we must come to grip with are becoming increasingly difficult, we have trouble making decisions and, therefore, must be helped. This is why a device to handle information, an apparatus similar to the human brain, is needed. Artificial intelligence is based on the computer, a device whose essential features are high processing speed and memory capacity. And in these terms the computer has already outstripped the human brain.

But it is not enough to have a data-processing device. A program is needed to allow full use of the device. Certainly in this respect, man has great advantages over the computer. Computer software is still very crude, while man's "software" is very sophisticated. Thus, if we are going to create artificial intelligence as an aid to man in decisionmaking, we have to develop computer software that will equal and even surpass man's capabilities.

Such work has long been going on, and it is moving in two

directions. The first trend is based on the idea that computer software must be built by methods other than those used by man in his reasoning. Investigators moving in the second direction believe that computer software should be based on the principles that underlie human mental activity. Achievements of both schools of thought have turned out to be very modest. Apparently these theories are not proved by practice. We are now developing a program that, we hope, will enable the computer to play chess like a master. Some people wonder whether we have any grounds for cherishing such hopes. But the "Pioneer" program is already capable of solving chess problems similarly to human players, and every player knows that playing a game and solving a chess problem are comparable actions.

Occupation and Problem Oriented Intelligent Systems

D. A. POSPELOV

Considering the use of the computer for modelling intelligence, we must first ask what exactly we want to simulate. If, for instance, I wrote a good chess program, like the one mentioned by M.M. Botvinnik, and put it into a computer, would I be justified in saying that the computer playing chess according to the program represented artificial intelligence? I think not, for we would merely have an intelligent chess program. Let us now place in the computer a program of composing music, one devised, for instance, by the prominent Soviet scientist R.Kh. Zaripov. The computer now not only plays chess well but also composes fairly good waltzes and marches. Can that be called artificial intelligence? Apparently not. And if we provide the computer with a program enabling it to imitate discussions of the weather, what then?

It should be clear that such an approach to modelling individual aspects of mental activity will never be completed. In addition, all the programs we have placed into the computer are very narrow in scope, suitable only for simulating the procedures for which they have been designed. The main question remains: what should we simulate? The answer seems to be quite definite. Rather than simulate processes of playing chess, composing music, engaging in small talk, we need to simulate overall psychological mechanisms that help organize those processes. Unfortunately, psychology has yet to provide answers to all the questions concerning the structure and functioning of such mechanisms.

All this explains the importance given by artificial intelligence researchers to the task of developing a computer system that can understand and talk with man in a natural language. The natural language is the most powerful system modelling reality. Hence, the understandable desire to use this system in tomorrow's "intelligent" robots. All that can be expressed in words by human beings could, then, be introduced into an artificial system.

But the question arises as to whether is it right to stop at a verbal level in developing artificial intelligence? I think not. Enormous amounts of information are processed by man on a non-verbal level, and numerous processes important for mental activity also occur on a non-verbal level. How can that all be programmed in the computer? So far the task has simply been impossible. Computer programs require a textural description of processes, in the general terms of a natural language, if nothing more. But what cannot be expressed by words also cannot be transformed into a program. Recently, advances towards the realization of some models of non-verbal mental procedures have been reported. An example is the simulation of a general-perception mechanism by means of a device called Perceptron. Although this device has not lived up to expectations, it has nevertheless demonstrated that the computer is not the only method of creating artificial intelligence. Apparently, a symbiosis of computer systems and devices of a different nature, like the Perceptron, will make it possible to simulate many mental mechanisms inherent in natural intelligence.

Mental activity with no connection to the environment is impossible. Yet the computer has no sensations, no perception of the outside world. Modern robots fitted with sensors, however, are able to receive signals directly from the environment. These "organs of perception" are close in sensitivity to human organs and, in some instances, are more subtle and receptive than the latter. This necessitates the creation of a logic of perception and cognition of the outside world. And we are confronted with an interesting problem here. Neither classical systems of logic, created for the purposes of deduction and induction, nor derivative systems of classical mathematical logic or non-classical logic can be used directly in artificial intelligent systems. Different logical theories are needed, which can take into account the laws governing real processes in the outside world. Such systems include temporal, spatial, imperative, causal, and other logics. The creation of inductive and "fuzzy" methods of inference is the prime task in developing artificial intelligent systems.

From a practical standpoint, the problem of producing all-embracing artificial intelligence is hardly interesting. Such a problem cannot even be clearly defined. More promising are occupation and problem oriented systems designed to solve problems of specific types. The methodology of creating such intelligent systems forms that nucleus of artificial intelligence theory which deserves discussion and argument,

Why Artificial Intelligence Is Impossible

A. V. BRUSHLINSKY

The desire of modern cyberneticists to answer positively the question "Can the computer think?" has taken various forms. One approach has resulted in attempts to create artificial or machine intelligence. Such attempts have been criticized by scientists from an extreme cybernetic point of view based on the philosophico-psychological proof of the impossibility of machine intelligence. This criticism, first voiced in the USSR in the late 1950s and early 1960s by S.L. Rubinstein, E.V. Ilyenkov, M.M. Rosental, and other researchers, involves the critical comparison of natural and artificial intelligence. Such an approach, in my opinion, should be continued as follows.

Technology (for instance, artificial intelligence) and the mind (for instance, mental processes) are based on essentially different types of interconnection between their elements. Any machine built by man is a unified whole made up of clearly defined, separate component parts, assemblies, blocks, and so on. This intrinsic separateness between individual parts characterizes not only the structure of the whole, or its "morphology", but also its functioning, or "physiology". As M. Minsky aptly put it, machines and automated systems switch from one condition to another in clear-cut, "discrete" steps. The simplest example is provided by a motor as the driver starts up, changes speed, and shuts it off.

Similar relations between the elements within a unified whole are peculiar to the mathematical set, a concept which, according to many experts, is basic to mathematics. We will call such relations disjunctive. Mathematics, then, as well as engineering, is disjunctive: it idealizes the type of interrelation between elements that is realized in technology. This is true of both discrete and continuous mathematics. The term "disjunctive" is more appropriate in this context than the more specific term "discrete", which is inevitably associated with discrete mathematics, for instance, as opposed to continuous mathematics. Thus, a mathematical set, a machine, and an automaton all represent different varieties of basically similar, disjunctive systems composed of inherently individual elements separated inside a unified whole.

The functions of the mind represent a fundamentally different type of system. The actual process of mental activity in a human being, for instance, is never disjunctive in the sense mentioned above. The stages and elements of the natural thought process are so organically interconnected that they cannot be likened to disjunctive, individual machine components or set elements. The stages of such a mental process overlap, intertwine, arise genetically one from another, and so on. This non-disjunctive character of relations between the components of the mental process has been demonstrated experimentally in work showing that the thought process (for example, the solution of a problem) always results in the prediction of a solution to the given problem. Such a mental prediction makes a choice among alternative solutions unnecessary. The necessity of choosing reflects a formally logical relation between the results of the mental process, but not the process itself. Such a choice is a specific, although common, instance of disjunction, that is, of inherent separateness and mutual exclusion of alternatives.

Disjunctive relations are most adequately generalized in formal logic (in particular, mathematical logic), which, on a certain level of abstraction, can be very productive and promising, although it is detached from the development of the object being studied. Non-disjunctive relations are generalized in the terms of dialectical logic, which provides the methodological basis necessary for studying the development of an object. The psychology of thought based on dialectical logic also attempts to investigate systematically the micro- and macro-development of the mental process as well as the transformation of each of its stages, components, operations, and so on. Consequently, the highest level of such continuity (in the psychological sense described above rather than in the mathematical sense) in the shaping of the conscious and unconscious mental processes is non-disjunctive, that is, genetically continuous. It is clear from the foregoing that the psychological concept of continuance substantially differs from the mathematical (disjunctive).

This interpretation of the disjunctive and the non-disjunctive provides a clear answer to the question of machine "thinking", in general, and artificial intelligence, in particular. Artificial, machine intelligence is theoretically impossible to create since it is intrinsically disjunctive, whereas the natural mental process is always non-disjunctive. The machine and the living organism develop in essentially different ways. A living organism emerges from a single fertilized egg cell, which evolves by differentiation in a single, unbroken process. Machines are created by man in just the opposite manner, by the deliberate assembly of inherently separate, prefabricated parts. In this respect any modern or future machine (including the computer) can only be an artificial disjunctive formation, that is, secondary to and derivative of man and his activity. The machine is created by man and man alone, and therefore cannot be non-disjunctive. As a result, artificial intelligence is impossible.

The area of research erroneously referred to as "the design of artificial intelligence", however, remains important and fruitful because current and future machines are the necessary tools (and only tools!) of creative and non-creative human activity. Man has been and will be the only being truely capable of thinking.

Relative Capabilities of Natural and Artificial Intelligence

V. S. TYUKHTIN

Many of the theoretical miscalculations and inaccuracies characterizing research into artificial intelligence can be attributed to two methodological extremes. One extreme is a pessimistic attitude, in which the features of natural intelligence are overrated and the possibilities and prospects of artificial intelligence underrated. The other extreme is "superoptimism", which stems from initial successes in the application of cybernetics to the solution of relatively simple problems (those with a "good structure"). These advances lead to overestimation of the machine factor in solving complex and creative problems and to underestimation of the human factor, with the result of hypostatizing some formal methods regardless of difficulties in simulating natural intelligence.

Correct formulation and research of the problem of artificial intelligence depend on the interpretation of natural intelligence. A constructive approach to mental processes can be found in the works of I.M. Sechenov and I.P. Pavlov, who believed that thinking, in a broad sense, should be defined as the process of solving problems (from elementary behavioural problems to the most complex theoretical ones). Animals, human beings, and man-machine combinations, therefore, represent systems capable of solving problems. Problems can be of two types: *reproductive* problems in which conditions, means, and methods are adequate to achieve the aim; and *creative* or *productive* problems in which available conditions, means, and methods (algorithms) are incomplete and the missing links must be supplied by the system itself as it interacts with the environment and uses experience gained in the past.

The solution of any actual problem requires both reproductive and creative thinking. Whether a particular problem falls into the first or the second category depends on the predominance of reproductive or creative elements. Natural intelligence, therefore, can be defined as the ability of living systems (animals and man) to solve both types of problems. Accordingly, artificial intelligence can be defined as machine simulation of this process. This definition, however, avoids the questions of whether the machine can, in principle, solve creative problems, and whether natural and artificial intelligence have essentially equivalent substrate properties. A discussion of the sequestions would make for a more realistic understanding of artificial intelligence. From the outset, two principal approaches have been evident in computer simulation of natural intelligence. The first approach, which we will arbitrarily call descriptive (substrate structural), has been oriented towards modelling the structure and properties of the problem-solving system as well as the dynamic internal structures of the process of solution, externally represented by macroprograms for information processing. The second, normative functional approach has focused on the identity of results and their respective macroprograms for information processing. This approach, which in cybernetics is called functional modelling, has proved substantially limited in application to problems where the creative element is predominant.

The reasons for these limitations become obvious if we consider non-formal creative elements at all stages of solution as well as those elements that cannot yet be formalized. The first stage in problem solving is that of problem formulation. It involves the definition of the problem, the setting of new goals, and the establishment of new criteria for selecting responses, elements that have so far been the prerogative of man.

Analysis of the conditions of the problems, searches for the principles of solution, and planning for its realization make up the second stage. Non-formal elements of this stage include the stimulation of the search for the missing links in the solution process; the reinforcement, in the course of self-learning, of responses and associations required by the system; and the creative imagination (scientific, artistic, and engineering), which is expressed by the ability to generate possibilities, conjectures, and hypotheses for subsequent analysis, and the ability to synthesize to the highest level of integrity. A generator of random conditions provides the search with quantitative but not qualitative diversity. Combinatorial methods and non-linear methods of synthesis also fall short of the level of synthetic mental processes.

Elements of the third stage of problem solving—the interpretation of the formal solution and its symbolic expression, the transformation of the signal-exciter into an image (or model), and total comprehension—have not yet been simulated by computers.

Why do creative elements defy formalization? All non-formalized properties of the mental process are various manifestations of the phenomenon of activity, which depends on motivation. Motivation may be connected with basic needs (the result of hunger, thirst, and so forth) or with orientational needs and their modifications (cognition of the outside world, feelings, desires, and aspirations, for example). These needs are the primary source of creativity at all stages of problem solving, in other words, the source of the orientation of the problem-solving system towards the external world. Today's computers are not self-organizing systems. They have no needs and, therefore, cannot perform creative functions.

The functioning of creative thinking is impossible to simulate without the properties and structure of the bearer of natural intelligence—man and his brain. In the absence of needs which must be filled, for example, formal attempts to solve the problem of reinforcing responses have failed. Developing an internal model of the outer world with automated systems (for instance, the so-called Gyromat system) also proved impossible, since the conversion of a physical signal into the model or image of a real object requires "materialization" of the signal, that is, the projection of relations and structures back upon the object. This "departure" from the internal world requires that the vector of active orientation towards the outside world must be realized. In living systems such an orientation results from the desire to fulfill an actual need.

The complete and efficient simulation of creative thinking including mental traits and the capacity to respond to motivation must not be limited to the general level of logical and informational programs. Rather, it should be oriented towards deeper levels of natural intelligence organization. Different mental traits and functions can be understood through the levels of the problem-solving system specifically responsible for those traits and functions.

Basic research on human intellect is conducted on various levels: the information-logical level, which pertains to logical-syntactic structures of information processing; the gnoseological level, which discloses relations between the subject and logical forms of information processing; the psychological level aspect of human intelligence studies, which concerns special features of the individual condition and experience; the neuropsychic level, which describes physiological mechanisms of mental activity; the neurophysiological level, which deals with the physiology of the brain, receptors, and nerve communications; and the level of biochemical processes. Thus, the question of simulation of functions of native intelligence in informational machines or robots involves a number of branches of science that deal with life, psychology, and man.

The most promising and effective area of research is that of hybrid man-machine systems, where man does the creative thinking and the computer, which is algorithmically universal, carries out any program. Each creative problem has particular creative elements, which differ in number and distribution in the process of solving. The classification and study of creative problems to divide functions between man and the computer optimally is the task not only of cybernetics but of all sciences concerned with the creative activity of man. In the functional simulation of the thought process, that is, in the development of increasingly sophisticated programs, it is impossible to know before solving the problem which components are creative and which are routine. With the help of data gathered on the problem of intelligence, advances in the various sciences that study man, and, especially information on the psychology of creativity, it is possible to determine which aspects of a given problem in the man-computer dialogue happen to be creative and, therefore, best dealt with by man. In my opinion, it is this complex study of "man-machine" intelligence, that is, the study of natural intelligence aided by informational technology, that will dominate cybernetic research in the coming years.

On the Capabilities of Artificial Intelligence

B. V. BIRYUKOV

The question of whether artificial intelligence might be possible was first asked by the pioneers of cybernetics, particularly by A.M. Turing in his *Computing Machinery and Intelligence*[1]. This paper and the ensuing discussion showed how unclearly the problem had been stated. An exact statement of the problem is difficult to make because the brain and its through processes on the one hand, and modern data-processing systems, on the other, are described in terms of different scientific languages which have very little in common. For this reason the question "Can a machine think?", which at one time attracted so much attention, has now virtually ceased to be of any consequence. The question of how capable artificial intelligence may be is quite another matter. Artificial intelligence studies are usually divided between two areas: first, the simulation of the mental processes, and development of computer models and algorithms to describe, to some extent, a process of thinking close to man's; and second, work on automatic systems for solving difficult problems without seeing how a human mind would work in similar cases. These two lines of research make up what may be called "artificial intelligence".

In order to understand the capabilities and limitations of artificial intelligence it is essential to consider its logical sources. When it became necessary for the mental processes of intelligence to be automated, that is, when information processing using powerful "intelligence amplifiers" was necessary instead of just the human mind and primitive mechanical calculators, it was realized that the theoretical mathematical logic basis had already been laid, i.e. formal language theory had been developed, powerful methods of propositional calculus had been devised, algorithm theory had developed and theorems had been proved that stated that any information processing task presented in a clear language could be assigned to a certain idealized machine. The advent of the electronic computer has made it clear that it is an embodiment of the abstract devices for processing information digitally and that any process, including the workings of our mind, can in principle be simulated by an appropriate discrete automaton if we are aware of how this process evolves.

Back in the early 1970s my personal emphasis was on the feasibility of the cybernetic simulation of any adequately described process of information handling. My point of view has now changed. Now I do not attach much significance to this scientifically indisputable thesis. The fact is that the past decade has shown up limitations which are imposed by what is termed "complexity". It has become apparent that a number of abstractions made in the thesis that simulation is feasible such as the abstraction from limited human space, time, and material resources, the postulate of identity, which assumes that the objects under consideration can always be differentiated and identified, the postulate of correctness, which assumes that information can be processed without errors, and the idealization of the structural embodiment of the object, all these mathematical and logic idealizations fall to pieces when science is faced with the complex theoretical and practical problems.

It is worthwhile at this point remembering an idea stated at the outset of cybernetics by one of its pioneers, J. von Neumann, an idea that has not yet been sufficiently understood from a philosophical point of view. Von Neumann's approach is that the object and its description can be compared with respect to complexity. As is known, in order to understand a complex phenomenon we must simplify it, make it more comprehensible, and, in a sense, more manifest. Abstractions and idealizations are a route to simplification. If a process, object, or system is relatively simple, it can always be described so as to make it look simpler than it actually is. This property of understanding has been fundamental to the natural sciences, particularly those described in mathematical terms. Von Neumann's chief hypothesis is that there is a certain boundary of complexity beyond which a description simpler than the system to be described becomes impossible. Von Neumann exemplified this hypothesis using a visual analyzer and formulated it in the strict terms of automata theory. According to his postulate, one cannot probably build, beyond a certain threshold of complexity, an automaton simpler than the object it is to imitate.

The difficulties in developing the complex computer-programming and problem solving systems which have emerged over the past years seem to some degree to indicate that we are approaching von Neumann's complexity threshold. There seem to be some considerations pointing to the limited information-processing capabilities of computers as compared with the immense capabilities of the human brain.

In his treatise *What Computers Can't Do*[2] the American philosopher H. Dreyfus criticizes the research on artificial intelligence conducted in the USA between the late fifties and the late sixties. His criticism has not stood the test of time. Advances in the field in question refute Dreyfus's arguments. However, his critical opinion of "cybernetic atomism" is worthy of consideration. In particular, Dreyfus considered the following situation. In order to process information algorithmically, we must have appropriate rules. The more flexible the rules, the closer the information processing will be to similar human activity. How do we make them flexible? We could introduce rules, then amendments to the rules, then rules to amend the amendments to the rules, and so on. Clearly such a procedure must be interminable. As a result, either our information processing cannot occur at all or else we shall have to postulate some final rules. But then, there must inevitably be tasks that the algorithm cannot handle. Another form of this paradox relates to contexts required for understanding situations expressed in a natural language. In order to process information in a natural language (and this is a fact of which everyone studying automated translation and formal languages for describing new problems is aware) it is essential to take account of context. Understanding can only be gained within the given context but the context too needs to be understood. Hence, a broader context must be considered, and so on interminably, or up to some final context. The latter, however, will immediately restrict the capability of a cybernetic system to understand the texts it receives.

In the forms described, these paradoxes, which might be called the paradoxes of artificial intelligence, are reminiscent of Zeno's paradox, which postulates that no movement can ever start since before moving 100 paces, one must move first 50 paces, before which he must move 25 paces and so on. Man can resolve these paradoxes. He can successfully orient himself in dynamic situations, solve inadequately stated problems, and comprehend the meaning of texts given in a natural language with its subtle connotations. Obviously we would like to know whether something similar can be entered into a computer. The problem was discussed by Turing who suggested the idea of teaching a "child-machine" in a quasi-social environment. However, no real success in this direction has been made so far, and we do not know how far we can go.

In the book by Dreyfus that I have already talked about, the world and the personality of an individual human being are set starkly against the world of physical phenomena. The latter is an "atomized" world of events and can be entered into a large computer data base. The former, human, world is the one in which man, acting in accordance with his needs and objectives feels himself at home. Dreyfus criticizes the view that the computer only lacks an effective program in order to equal man in intelligence, a program that comprises all that surrounds man and describes his outer and inner world in scientific terms. But—and here we agree with Dreyfus—the human world cannot be interpreted in the same way as the machine world.

In his alternative approach to understanding the mechanism of rational behaviour, Dreyfus in *What Computers Can't Do* attaches a great importance to the human body, its biological needs, body functions, and so on.

Obviously, the body of a man is a real fact. His sensory perceptions are, indisputably, more "bodily" than the logic of his thought. It is, however, his logic, deductive logic, formal-logic processes that lend themselves relatively easily to formalization, whereas what relates to sensory perception, is much more difficult to formalize. Experts in automatic pattern recognition are well aware of this.

Of course, we should refrain in our discussion from placing too strong an emphasis on the biological nature of man since the human world itself, structured in terms of objectives and needs, is a social world. The capability to orient oneself in the ambient world and to feel at home in it, is indeed proper to man, but man is primarily a social being.

We should bear in mind that human needs are not solely the product of biological evolution; their difference from the animal needs lies in the history of society, in the socially determined development of the cognitive, creative, emotional, and volitional properties of a personality, in that these needs, motivations, and aims are formed in human social groups. Human aims are a combination of the objective and the subjective. This is impossible for the machine, which is a good deal more "purposeful" in its function, because any machine algorithm must satisfy the requirement that it should obtain definite results. Yet, man has variable and flexible objectives induced by the social components of his being.

Where then may we look for the source of progress in the field of the automatic handling of tests, automatic theorem proving, computerized solution to complex problems, and the design of independently acting robots? Here, seemingly, different strata of intelligence will be brought into play. We are still a long way off the intimate knowledge of our mental faculties. The human brain functions at various levels of consciousness. Some of them are well amenable to cybernetic simulation, others less so, and yet others, as I see it, will hardly lend themselves at all to a more or less complete formalization. I believe that there are spheres of human consciousness and self-awareness that will remain beyond the feasibility of cybernetic simulation and automation not only in the foreseeable future, but forever.

Certainly, nothing can keep us from discussing the "education" of machines in a "social environment", the development of a "machine" from biological components, and so on. But this is a different, and somewhat futuristic topic for the time being. But today, man-machine systems are at the forefront of artificial intelligence, and here I only can repeat the opinion of Academician Berg that the machine, as it is understood today, does not "think" (and can hardly be expected to "think" in future) in the same way as man does, that is, like an intelligent being living in a society, having a complex system of socially determined needs and objectives, and using a natural language for the exchange of thoughts with other intelligent beings. But, undoubtedly, a human possessing cybernetic amplifiers of his mental capacity will think better and deeper than one who has to be content with primitive aids to his mental work.

References

1. Turing, A.M. *Computing Machinery and Intelligence.* Mind., Vol. 59, October 1950. Reprinted in E. Feigenbaum and J. Feldman (eds). *Computers and Thought*, McGraw-Hill Book Company (New York, 1963).
2. Dreyfus, H. *What Computers Can't Do. A Critique of Artificial Intelligence*, Harper and Row (New York, 1972).

On Some Control Problems

This part of the book puts together articles dedicated to new ideas in cybernetic control methods.

Recent years have seen the advent of management information systems (MIS). These powerful systems do not just collect, process, and transfer information and automate the laborious record-keeping and document-handling processes; what is more important, they bring management to a radically new level, which allows decisions to be made correctly and on time.

But cybernetics does not rest on its laurels. Scientists continue to seek new, more efficient ways of processing control and management information, sometimes coming up with unusual ideas aimed at preparing and taking optimal decisions.

Semiotic Models in Control Systems

D. A. POSPELOV

For many years now, the theories of regulation and control have dealt with objects of a specific nature. These objects (machine tools, automobiles, rolling mills, and so on) were designed primarily for specific purposes. A machine tool was to process workpieces by a pre-determined method, an automobile was to move about and carry men and loads, and the purpose of rolling mills was to roll sheetmetal to a specified thickness. To put it in more generalized terms, the objects we were to control had a clear reason for existence. This reason enabled us to formulate a definite criterion of control which could take into account indispensable constraints dictated by the requirements for control reliability, ergonomics (convenience of handling), costs, and so on.

The dimensions of a machine-tool and the arrangement of controls in an automobile had to take into account a person's size, the required speed of reaction in controlling an airplane was not supposed to be beyond the pilot's capabilities. The rotational speed of rolls in a rolling mill had to depend on the quality of rolled stock, and speeds of the automobile and the airplane were a function of their aerodynamic characteristics, so that they would ride steadily.

Within the framework of such constraints, the developer could put before himself a task of optimization of a certain efficiency function. For example, in addition to the control of the rolling mill, the task could require a maximization of its production rates within given constraints, and an automobile control system could be designed with due regard for minimizing fuel consumption.

The whole of control theory rested on these three "whales" (the purpose for existing, the control criterion, and the constraints). They were the basis on which it posed its tasks and problems. The very notion of "control" was considered to be inseparable from the aim of the object under control, reflected in the efficiency function, control criterion, and constraints. Attainment of the objective by the best possible means was the motto of classical control theory.

Knowledge of the object's purpose for being and of the control criterion enabled one to answer the question about the quality of control, that is, whether the control system had been designed well or poorly. Obviously, the best control system was the one that ensured better efficiency function under the given constraints, with the object achieving the aim of its existence. For example, the best automobile control system provides for greater maneuverability, lower upkeep, easier repairs, and so on. The automobile which meets all the necessary requirements and constraints, determined by the reason for its existence (carrying people and loads), is the best.

We can note two more principles characteristic of the methods of traditional control theory. The controller always assumes that the object being controlled has no "freedom of will", is indifferent to the control system, and perceives command signals and instructions of the control system exactly as its developer has proposed. Indeed, presumably no one would risk driving a car without being certain that all his control actions will be processed as he expects. And the designer of an aircraft control system could hardly propose that a totally unprepared person be allowed to fly the plane.

The second principle of control theory is the "genericity" principle, well known in applied mathematics. It states that methods devised by a theory must find use in solving a set of problems of a definite type. For example, from school we know how to solve a quadratic equation $AX^2 + BX + C = 0$. This method is valid not just for a particular quadratic equation, $2x^2 + 7x - 4 = 0$ for instance, but for all equations of this type. The control system of the VAZ-2103 car is suitable for all cars put out by the factory in Togliatti.

Genericity makes theory "more solid" and abstract and allows one to consider not a particular car or lathe, but an idealized representative of a whole set of cars or lathes belonging to a certain type.

It is genericity that allows control theory to formalize controlled objects and control systems, substituting mathematical analogues for real physical and technological systems. The specialist in control theory has more and more acted as a mathematician rather than as an engineer; he has combined these two different ways of perceiving the world. That was very convenient. If a whole world of real controlled objects could be rendered in a category of formal models, then control theory could concentrate all its efforts on the study of these formal objects, setting for them the tasks of searching for control methods, for their optimization, and for the synthesis of the control system itself.

All this has brought syntax the victory over semantics, since any formalization means a transition from hazy semantics, which is used to describe the structure, functioning, reason for being, constraints, and control criteria of a real object, to an exact formal syntax of its theoretical analogue.

It seemed that control theory would soon be absorbed by mathematics to become one of its branches. But these hopes proved illusory. Why? In recent years controlled objects of a radically different nature have appeared (or rather, experts have included in the scope of control theory various objects that formerly lay beyond its province). Some of these new objects had no control criteria, for others, constraints could not be formulated, others refused to obey command signals passively, and still others were so unusual that they did not even have a purpose for existing, or at least, no purpose that could be formalized in any way. And these objects existed not in environments formerly inaccessible to man, in space or on the bottom of the ocean, but literally right next to us.

Let us consider one of these unusual objects. Suppose we are faced with developing a control system for a city or region. The first thing to find out is the reason for the city's existence. We want an answer to the question, "Why is the city needed?" Then other questions follow: "What city-control system will be adequate?" "What constraints on our control actions should be considered?" "Are we sure that our control actions will be responded to as we want?" There are a host of other questions which we should like to have exhaustively answered. The effectiveness of our expenditures on the city's control system will depend on how correct and complete these answers are.

Alas. We shall not succeed in getting answers to such questions as the expert accustomed to the rigorous syntacticality of classical control theory would like. A city is a fundamentally different kind of controlled objects as compared to a car, airplane, or machine tool. The reason for its being is not formally definable. Consequently, it is not possible to find a rigorous criterion of control. Neither can constraints be formulated exactly and completely. A city is populated by people whose behaviour strongly affects the control system. And we can never be absolutely certain that our control recommendations will be executed as we would like. Finally, any object out of this category (the city) is unique with respect to control and cannot be likened to other cities. A control system, if it can be found at all, should suit the unique features of this particular city.

Control decisions should be taken in any particular instance in strict accordance with the city's topography, the situation of industrial enterprises and housing, the distribution of working hours, the established pattern of traffic flows, and so on. As a result, to devise a control model for a city, we need a model of a given city with all its specific features rather than a model of a city in general—an abstract city—which was a favourite model in classical control theory.

A city is not a single representative of a host of controlled objects that do not measure up to the principles of conventional control theory. In tackling the problem of control of various sectors of the economy, territorial production complexes, power-generation systems, and territorial transportation systems, we are repeatedly faced with the necessity to review the principles and techniques of solution resulting from control theory.

This qualitatively new nature of controlled objects seems to be the source of the difficulties encountered over the last decade. It is just these difficulties that hinder the development of standardized methods and computer programs that would enable us to effect the automated control of manufacturing plants, branches of the economy, cities, and regions. All these objects belong to a category to which purely syntactic control models fail to apply.

So the need arose for models of controlled objects of the new type. They had to be based on a formalized (as far as possible) description of a specific object, taking into account all its distinctive characteristics vital for the control function. It was also essential to find a way to formalize our knowledge about what the purpose of control is, what specific, often contradictory, aims we intend to achieve, how the object reacts to control actions, and what constraints (also contradictory in many cases) should be taken into account.

Since in these new control models the semantics of the object in question and the pragmatics of the projected control system needed to be reflected in full detail, there was no hope of using old, formal syntactic models in the form of various equations, statistic distributions, and the like. Radically new means of description were required.

The new models were named semiotic models. This name reflects the fact that they are based on semiotic systems. Only a few people know about this concept, so we will try explaining it by way of some simple examples. Semiotic systems are studied in semiotics, which may be defined as the science of sign systems. The signs used in these systems are objects that exhibit three properties: syntax, semantics, and pragmatics. The syntax of a sign is a way of expressing it. If, for example, we take a playing card and call it "the ace of hearts", the syntax of this sign will be the card itself with a representation of the single heart suit symbol traditionally red in colour and placed at the edge of the card. The syntax of a street sign indicating a metro, or subway, entrance is the letter "M", in a shape and colour specific for a given city. The semantics of a sign reflects its meaning. As distinct from the syntax, the semantics of a sign can be understood only within the whole system of signs. For example, in a deck of playing cards, the ace of hearts has a quite definite semantics. It belongs to one of the suits and differs from the other cards of its suit by, say, priority. In the systems of signs connected with city transport, the sign standing for the metro indicates the specific type of transportation and differentiates it from a bus, tram, and trolley bus promising high speed and comfort, stable climatic conditions, and so on. Finally, the pragmatics of a sign can be found only in the presence of the sign's user. For a card player, the ace of hearts has an explicit pragmatic value determined by the rules of the game. The pedestrian intending to take the metro uses the sign of a station in its pragmatic aspect when he goes down into the station as the sign indicates.

The distinctive feature of signs is that these three aspects of theirs—syntax, semantics, and pragmatics—cannot be definitely formalized. One might simply substitute the words "The ace of hearts" for the traditional symbol on the card. The letter "M" at a metro entrance may be replaced by some other indication (for instance, an arrow accompanied by the words "Frunzenskaya station"). For a person strolling along the street, the pragmatic significance of a metro station indicator is quite different than for a person looking for the station entrance. The former may be thinking, for instance, that he can get change there or may remember a good cafe located next to the entrance. The semantics of a symbol is likewise uncertain. In one card game the king has priority over the ten, whereas in another, it may be vice versa.

This conventionality of a sign makes it an extremely flexible and convenient means of representing different models of both the surrounding world and man-made systems. It is no wonder that natural human language — the most powerful of the systems known to us for modelling reality—also belongs to the semiotic systems.

It would seem clear by now that the models of controlled objects and control systems themselves are bound to be semiotic if it is necessary to reflect with adequate completeness not only formal relationships and processes (that is, syntax), but also the semantics of the controlled object and the pragmatics of control.

Before proceeding to description of the principles that underlie such models, let us touch upon another important question. The appearance of the electronic computer gave rise to programming, whose purpose is to translate information into a language comprehensible to the computer. Without the programmer, the computer is dead. It is unable to communicate and cannot derive necessary information directly from the environment or from the information media used by man (books, conversation, cinema, etc.). Hence, a programmer is needed to act as an intermediary between the computer and the outside world. The programmer is the translator of our era. And although programming languages have been developing right in front of us, in practically no time, here, too, we encounter the problem of the Babylon tower. Different computers and the programmers who service them very often fail to understand each other. The avalanche of dissimilar languages is perilously gaining. At least several hundred languages are now used in practice. And no fewer than two thousand of them have been proposed and discussed in literature.

Such a large quantity of computer languages is not accidental. It testifies to a critical situation in the field. Each of the programming languages is in some respects better and in some respects worse than others. The developers of computer languages draw upon practice, ignoring, as a rule, psychological, linguistic, and psycholinguistic knowledge. Their pragmatic research, however, has borne fruit. One such fruit is the definite conclusion that the knowledge which must be entered into the computer in order to solve a problem breaks down into two radically different types. The descriptions of some procedures contain knowledge of the first type, appropriately called procedural knowledge. Culinary recipes are a good example of such knowledge. It can also be found in all kinds of instructions, rules of behaviour, military regulations and the like.

In data processing systems, procedural knowledge is embodied in programs, which the computer is expected to execute. The algorithms embodied in these programs are the top achievement of procedural knowledge. The programming languages that appeared in the initial period of the programming era, ALGOL, FORTRAN, COBOL, and many others, are languages for representing procedural knowledge.

Man, however, makes extensive use of another type of knowledge, too. He knows that a nut can be turned on a screw of the appropriate size, that two pieces of wood can be nailed together with a hammer, that the sun and the moon are not one and the same thing. In short, he is aware of a host of different facts that describe separate events, phenomena, and processes, and reflect relationships between them and the man's evaluation of them. All this knowledge is not procedural. It is referred to as declarative knowledge. And human memory stores an immense volume of knowledge of this type. Its total enables man to form and keep a mental model of the world, which conforms well to reality.

The languages for representing declarative knowledge and procedural knowledge are bound to be different because declarative knowledge reflects the structure and composition of the world, whereas procedural knowledge contains information on rational behaviour in it.

Our digression from the main topic was not irrelevant. Now we are able to indicate the basic difference between models in classical control theory and semiotic models. Models of the first type are largely procedural, whereas models of the second type must have, in principle, a great potential for representation of declarative knowledge. A model of the controlled object that discloses its inner structure and the character of its performance and response to control actions is a sum of declarative knowledge. The control procedures for the object, embodied in algorithms or computer programs, are the procedural part of our knowledge. These two types of knowledge should harmoniously combine in the framework of a semiotic model.

Semiotic models substantially extend the application of computers. If the model of the controlled object and a sufficient quantity of information on its control are present in the computer's memory, then we can instruct the computer to learn and generate procedural knowledge by processing the stored control data.

To illustrate the possibilities of semiotic models, let us consider an elementary example. Suppose we need to find the area of a triangle ABC. It is known from mathematics that the formula $S = ab \sin C$ can be used for this purpose (triangle ABC is shown in Fig. 1a). The calculation procedure will be as follows: Multiply a by b. Hold it in memory. Compute the sine of angle C. Keep it in memory. Multiply the two stored numbers. The calculating sequence represents the procedural knowledge that allows the area of a triangle to be found by two of the sides and the angle between them. If the procedure and the initial numerical data are entered into the computer, it will handle the task very well. Now, let us find the area of triangle ABC if it is known that $a = 5$, $b = 3$, and angles A and B are equal to 30° and 50°, respectively. Any person familiar with elementary mathematics will solve the problem easily, although the direct use of the foregoing formula for S proves impossible since angle C is unknown. From school we know that $A + B + C = 180°$, which permits C to be determined from the

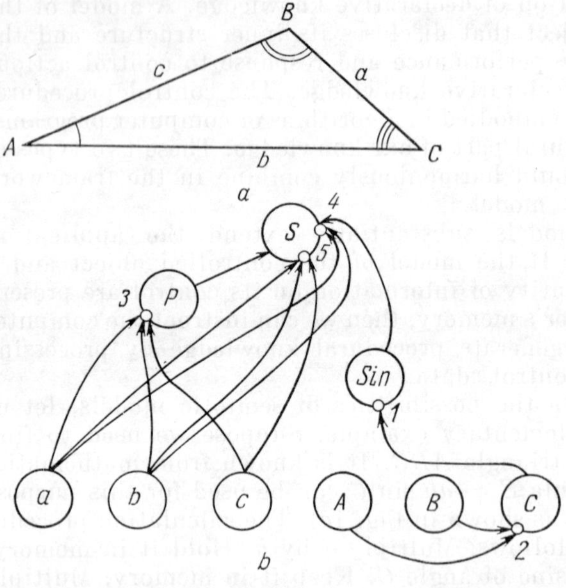

Fig. 1

known values of A and B. This relationship is declarative knowledge. It helps us use the procedure we have just described.

Assume we are now faced with the need to compute the area of triangle ABC if we know the three sides a, b, and c. In this case, as any school student knows, the Heron formula can be used:

$$S = \sqrt{p (p - a) (p - b) (p - c)},$$

where $p = 1/2 (a + b + c)$. But the computer does not know this and therefore refuses to determine the triangle's area. Of course, we could write up the procedure to get the computation, according to the Heron formula and feed it into the computer. But the need to choose a procedure adequate to the given basic data remains all the same, and the number of such separate procedures will constantly grow, making the problem of their selection increasingly complicated.

Consider the diagram shown in Fir. 1*b*. It illustrates a model of knowledge about a triangle (or, rather, a fragment of the model). The nodes stand for the basic concepts of the triangle's geometry. The points on the boundary of the nodes are called synapses. They can be in either of two states: excited or non-excited. If some of the synapses are excited, the respective node also becomes excited and this state is transmitted along all the outgoing pointers. These pointers come to other synapses. A synapse passes into the excited state only when all the incoming pointers are activated.

For the excited state to arise in this network (experts refer to it as a semantic network), some of the nodes will have to be activated from the outside. If this occurs, the excited state will begin propagating to activate other nodes of the network. Shortly the process will become stabilized to bring the network into a static excited state.

Let us initially activate the nodes designated by letters *a*, *b*, and *c*. All the pointers going out of them will then become activated. This will lead to initiation of synapse *1* at the node marked by Sin, and then, through the activation of the node itself and the outgoing pointer, to activation of synapse *4* at the boundary of node *S*. After the latter has become excited, the process of further activation will cease, and the network will come into a static excited state.

Now we shall use the process of activation in a semantic network for solving problems connected with the formation of procedural knowledge for the computer. Assume that every synapse stands for a certain procedure stored in the computer memory. The reference number of the synapse designates the name of the procedure, and the activation of the synapse is equivalent to the call of the respective procedure for execution. We shall associate the initiation of the network nodes with the presence of certain starting data required to solve the task. In this instance, these data are *a*, *b*, and *c*. The initiation of synapse *1* calls the procedure of the sine computation. The activation of the node marked by the sign "Sin" means that the sine has been computed. Synapse *4* calls the procedure of computation of the triangle's area by the first of the foregoing formulas. The activation of apex *S* signals that the area has been found. Transition of the network into the statically active state signals that the search for the required procedural information has been completed.

Let us turn to other variations of the problem with different starting data. If we are given sides *a* and *b*, and angles *A* and *B*, then their respective nodes in the semantic network and synapse *2* will be excited. Synapse *2* will then ask for angle *C* to be calculated by the formula $C = 180 - A - B$, and the process of activation will proceed as in the previous example. Given the sides *a*, *b*, and *c*, three left-side nodes of the semantic network will be initiated, which will bring about the activation of synapse *3* and the ensuing computation of half the perimeter. After that, synapse *5* will be excited, initiating the computation of the area by the Heron formula.

A semantic network of the type we have described also reveals situations where the starting data are not sufficient for solving the problem. If, for instance, only two sides of a triangle are given, then neither synapse *3* nor synapses *4* and *5* will ever become excited. In this case, the computer can generate a standard message: "No triangle's area can be found with the given starting data".

The foregoing example shows the difference in storing procedural and declarative knowledge. The first is stored in the computer memory as traditional programs and the second as a specially arranged model. A semantic network is but one of such models. At present, control systems based on semiotic models use three types of languages for knowledge representation: predicate, relational, and frame languages. To describe declarative knowledge, predicate languages employ a formula-type notation for computing predicates, whereas procedural knowledge rests, as a rule, on logical conclusions derived from basic descriptions. Relational languages are arranged like the semantic networks we have already discussed. They explicitly state the relationships between objects. In the semantic network we have just considered, these relationships are expressed by the pointers connecting the nodes.

The gist of these relationships may be expressed in words: "the node is used for computation by formula *i*", where *i* is the number of the formula corresponding to the reference number of the synapse that receives the given pointer. Such relationships can generally have various meanings.

For example, let us consider the following text: "a car with license plate 48-51 МОЮ pulls up to an intersection. The traffic light is red. The car must stop". Let us present this text in a relational language known as the language of syntagmatic chains. This language finds many applications in solving complex problems by the method of situational control, which we are going to discuss a bit later. The standard unit of the language of syntagmatic chains is the elementary syntagma. It has the form (a_1ra_2), where a_1 and a_2 are certain elements and r is the relationship between them. Let us try to present our text as a sequence of such syntagmas. Assume that a_1 corresponds to the notion of "car" and i_1, to the license plate number 48-51 МОЮ. Then, if the relation r_1 means "to have the name of", the first half of the starting sentence may be represented by an elementary syntagma $(a_1\ r_1i_1)$. The whole sentence will be described by syntagma $((a_1r_1i_1)\ r_2a_2)$, in which a_2 stands for the concept "intersection", and r_2, for the relationship "to pull up to". The second sentence will be rendered by the syntagma $((a_1r_1i_1)\ r_3\ (a_3r_1i_2))$, in which a_3 is the notion "traffic light", i_2, "red", and r_3, the relationship "to observe". Finally, the third sentence can be expressed by the syntagma $((a_1r_1i_1)\ p_1)$, in which p_1 designates the imperative "stop moving". The entire situation observed the moment before the intersection, important for the control of car 48-51 МОЮ, is described by a chain of three syntagmas we have built up.

It is very important to us that both declarative (the first two sentences) and procedural (the third sentence) components of knowledge be represented in a relational description. As in a natural language, these two categories of knowledge turned out to be described in an identical manner. It is just this circumstance that makes relational languages convenient for use in semiotic models. Predicate-type languages, which we briefly mentioned earlier, can also represent declarative and procedural knowledge concurrently; however, the greater formalism of these languages limits the capability.

It has already been noted that natural language is the most powerful of all known semiotic modelling systems. Data on the structure, functioning, and methods of controlling complex and non-formalized objects are, as a rule, supplied by control experts in the form of texts written in natural language. To use this information, the developer of a control system requires some means for turning informal-language texts into formalized concepts which can provide a basis for designing the control procedures and the structure of the control system. The language of syntagmatic chains offers one such means.

Earlier we mentioned one other class of languages for representing knowledge. These are frame languages. The word "frame" is interpreted in two ways by experts in control theory. There exist two types of frames which correspond to these interpretations: frames of basic description and octant frames. They could also be called frames of declarative knowledge and frames of procedural knowledge.

Let us clarify the notions by some examples. Suppose we need to come up with a control system for regulating the traffic light at a four-way intersection.

The aim of controlling the object is apparent. The control system should change the traffic light as the situation on the roads leading up to the light dictates. The system must take into account the number of vehicles approaching the light as well as those vehicles which have the right-of-way (ambulances, fire engines). Let us choose one of the directions in which traffic is going through the intersection. When speaking of the light signal, it is understood that we mean its change in this direction.

The light control system, then, must issue two different signals that will change the light from red to green and vice versa. This means that any current situation should be assigned to one of the two classes. All situations falling into the first class must initiate the switching of the light to green. The other class covers situations where the light should be changed to red.

This generates the problem which is central to the control system—the problem of classifying current situations. To solve this problem, one must specify a certain characteristic for relating the situation to a given class and then eliminate from the description of the situation irrelevant data, retaining only those which will permit classification. For example, there may be a great number of situations, where various combinations of the number, type, and speed of vehicles will arise in the reference direction, while from another direction, there are no vehicles at all. The absence of vehicles coming from another direction is the deciding factor for all these situations, because they are all similar as far as control is concerned. In any of them, the green light must be switched on. The fact that there are no vehicles from the other direction is a frame of basic description of situations about the intersection. Of course, this frame is not unique. There are other frames too, for instance, the presence of a special vehicle (an ambulance or other emergency vehicle) or the absence of vehicles in the reference traffic direction.

Generally, the basic-description frame, or the frame of declarative knowledge, is a body of knowledge that cannot be reduced without losing the meaning of the phenomenon, process, or event being described. This is the framework on which our ability to classify a given body of knowledge is based.

The octant frame performs the same task with regard to procedural knowledge. In semiotic models, it enables one to single out the minimal amount of information essential for the control process. In the example considered, one of the octant frames has the form "As a special vehicle approaches the intersection, turn the green light on in its direction".

Frame languages tend to summarize the languages of the relational type, to bring them onto a higher level. This occurs as a result of transition from single-level relational descriptions to multi-level hierarchical descriptions that use frames of various levels. In this way, the hierarchy of data on the surrounding world and methods of acting in it, which is characteristic of man, can be represented in the system of knowledge stored in the computer's memory.

Now we can formulate the main principles for using semiotic models in control systems.

1. The basic information for describing the controlled object, the processes occurring in it and the control methods, including the necessary constraints and requests for optimizing individual parameters, is given by texts written in ordinary, natural language.

2. The texts are translated into formal knowledge rendered in some special knowledge representation language, using a finite number of different elements (notions, relations, names, imperative forms, and so on) determined by a specific problem domain.

3. The system is provided with built-in means for summarizing the description and finding the frames required for classification of descriptions and procedures.

4. Control procedures are devised on the basis of the starting information entered into the system.

5. In experimental work, the information that has previously been placed into the system can be supplemented through an analysis of the results of control actions. This refines the control procedures.

To make the foregoing statements clearer, let us consider the structure of the systems of situational control. Situational control was historically the first attempt to apply semiotic models to the control of complex objects. In 1965, the first experimental program was developed on the basis of situational control for handling a system of sluice-gates. Ever since, situational control has been used effectively many times.

Examples of problems solved with its aid include dispatching the motion of special drilling equipment in oil fields, control of loading and unloading operations in a fishing harbour, and control of cement heating in a rotary kiln. Situational-control methods have found application in various dedicated management-information and production control systems (for example, in civil aviation and in assembly of engineering products).

The scheme of situational control is presented in Fig. 2. The information on the current situation at the controlled object or additional data concerning the object and its control is fed to the input of the system. A coder translates the diverse information into the language used in the system, for instance into the language of syntagmatic chains. The description obtained is fed to the input of an analyzer, whose purpose is to perform a preliminary classification of the information. When the information needs to be stored in the control system for future use, it is transferred to a knowledge model. If it describes a current situation whose category is unknown, a classifier is brought into play. In case the type of situation is clear from the basic description, the analyzer passes it to a correlator. The correlator serves to find the chain of control actions for a given situation; it uses data stored in the knowledge model. When necessary, the correlator may turn to the classifier for ascertaining the category of the current situation. Should there be a single control action, the correlator tells this to a solver. If there are alternative solutions, then, before reporting to the solver, the correlator

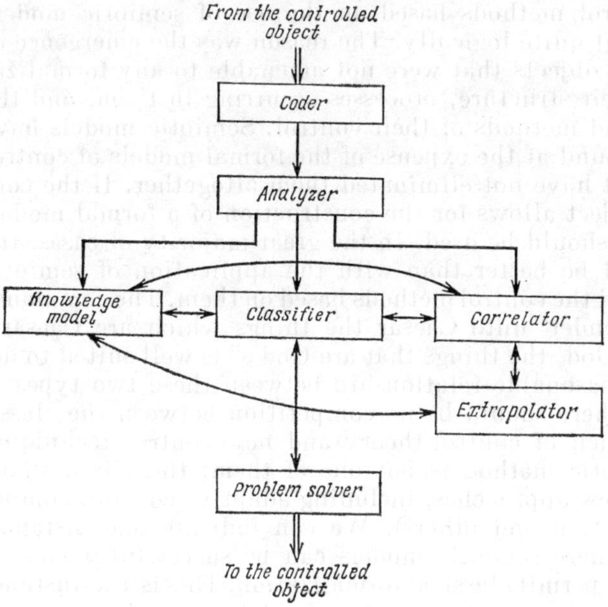

Fig. 2

checks their possible effect with the aid of an extrapolator. The extrapolator based on the knowledge of the controlled object predicts the likely consequences of various control actions. The responsibility for the final solution rests with the solver. After being coded, the solution is transferred to the controlled object or reported to the controller (when the system is used as an aid to a human controller).

In conclusion, let us make two notes, for which the reader should be prepared by the preceding discussion.

1. Control methods based on the use of semiotic models came about quite logically. The reason was the emergence of controlled objects that were not amenable to any formalization of their structure, processes occurring in them, and the criteria and methods of their control. Semiotic models have gained ground at the expense of the formal models of control theory but have not eliminated them altogether. If the controlled object allows for the construction of a formal model, the latter should be used. In the great majority of cases, the result will be better than with the application of semiotic models and the control methods based on them. The commandment "Render unto Caesar the things which are Caesar's and unto God, the things that are God's" is well suited to defining a reasonable relationship between these two types of models. There should be no competition between the classical approach of control theory and new control techniques (the semiotic method is but one of them; there is a whole range of new approaches, including adaptive control, computer simulation and others). We can indicate one instance, though, where semiotic models can be successful in control tasks that permit classical formalization. This is the instance when a control system is to operate on a real-time basis, that is, at the same speed as the controlled object itself, but the time allotted to the task does not permit its accomplishment with the required accuracy.

One American scientist has recently noted that although an absolutely accurate forecast of tomorrow's weather is within reach of today's science, it would take a month to prepare. It is just for this reason that the weather forecast is made on an approximate model which, as compared with the exact, formal model, yields somewhat inaccurate results, but in real time. Another example is the work of the operative system in modern electronic computers. The purpose of the system is the organization of the computing process. In particular, the structure of the computer allows simultaneous execution of tasks in several devices running in parallel. The operative system is to assign tasks to the devices. The problem of such a distribution, in which, for instance, the total requirements of time for the processing of a given package of tasks should be minimized, is well known in mathematics. The problem is easily formalized and methods exist for its accurate solution. Unfortunately, the time spent on such a solution consumes the whole gain yielded by the optimization of control. In instances like this, approximate (but, in a sense, quasi-optimal) solutions, which can be obtained in a short time, prove to be more beneficial. Such quasi-optimal solutions can be arrived at by techniques based on semiotic models.

2. Control systems that rest on semiotic models are basically open. They can always be improved by adding new information. Such information may be accumulated by the system itself during its service or supplied from outside by experts. The quality of control with semiotic models is wholly determined by the total experience put in by all experts who take part in shaping the system's model of knowledge and by the individual experience gained by the system during its field work. Practice has shown that the effect obtained from operating such systems is always higher than, or at least equal to, the effect of control actions performed by a most experienced specialist.

And, finally, we should like to note that semiotic models are indispensable in the control of artificial-intelligence systems called intelligent robots. Such robots will become an essential factor in new industrial and agricultural technology in the near future. But this topic is too broad and too specific to be treated within the bounds of this article.

Systems Analysis and Artificial Intelligence for Planning and Management

G. S. POSPELOV

Before starting to talk about the very complex and interesting problem indicated in the title of this article, I must make a clarifying digression. The term "artificial intelligence" is not really altogether apt. It hypnotizes a lot of people, particularly laymen, who see it as a token of unprecedented future achievements and possibilities.

For this reason, the bounds of the term should be outlined from the outset: artificial intelligence is not a synonym for artificial reasoning, but rather a line of scientific research concerned with problems and tasks of a non-computational nature that require largely the processing of semantic information. They obviously include management and planning tasks, the more so because these tasks have a substantial semantic component connected with the use of the computer.

From Data to Knowledge

The field of research on artificial intelligence is commonly divided into three parts.

The first includes the development of various models for solving problems that psychology regards as creative ones. The developers of such models do not propose to simulate the processes occurring in the mind of a person performing such a task. Comparison is made by other characteristics, namely, by the efficiency of obtaining the result and by its quality.

Research in the second area is, in contrast, directly oriented on simulation of the various psychological processes which man or animals go through. The purpose is to obtain, with the use of a model, the same results in problem solving as natural intelligence does.

The third part includes investigations which deal with the problem of interaction of man and artificial intelligence systems in the framework of a more comprehensive system. An example is work on the development of efficient man-machine systems for handling complex information processing and management tasks.

Any problem in each of these groups is not only difficult, but practically not amenable to general, abstract modelling; it requires a model for solving the given, specific problem with all its particulars.

For carrying out a creative task with the computer, a complicated model of the "outer machine world" needs to be built. To describe it, traditional methods and means prove to be inadequate. The connection between information units in the machine memory by means of addresses becomes "too small" for the new tasks; they simply cannot "squeeze" into it.

Just as data on the environment have a semantic value for man and animals, a description of the "machine environment", that is, certain data, facts, and rules essential for solving creative problems with the computer calls for semantic, meaningful relations. In other words, the computer cannot already manage with data, it needs knowledge. This makes a great difference.

The accumulation and use of knowledge, and the formation of models of the world, so common and natural for man, prove very complex and difficult to perform in the computer. All kinds and forms of communication activities within a human society are based on the ability of man to process symbols (signs), to transform them into sequences and sets and perform on them numerous and varied operations.

Sound or visual symbols and signs form natural languages and the various languages of exact sciences. Beginning with the language of gesticulation used by our ape-like ancestors, the evolution of human civilization and intelligence has gone hand in hand with the development of symbols and methods of their transformation. Therefore, artificial intelligence and new models for solving intellectual problems could come about only at the point where the computer acquired the capability of processing data in the symbolical rather than numerical form.

New models, as it was said in the preceding article, have been called semiotic models, after the name of that branch of linguistics which studies signs and sign systems. A symbol, or sign, is defined by three characteristics. The syntax of a sign is the method of its presentation. Its semantics is associated with its content or meaning and can be understood only within the framework of the whole sign system. The pragmatics of a sign expresses its utility and can manifest itself only in connection with its uses.

Conventionality is the peculiar feature of signs. It makes them an extremely flexible and suitable means of describing the surrounding world and artificial systems. Semiotic models are called upon to provide the computer with an understanding of the reality it is to deal with and, thereby, of the human partner who turns to it.

To enable the computer to work with semiotic models, it must be supplied with a special knowledge-representation languages which would act as the inner language of the artificial intelligence and describe situations in a standardized environment.

Text-Meaning-Reality

Knowledge is represented in computers most effectively with a model called "Text-Meaning-Reality". In fact, this title enumerates the main stages of the work. Models of this type are rather complex. For this reason, specific demands placed by various intelligent systems call for different approaches to developing knowledge representation languages. We shall discuss only some of the most promising approaches.

One of them includes models based on so-called frames, which are a systematic and structural description of the surrounding world. The term "frame" was proposed by the American cyberneticist M. Minsky. It means literally the framework, field, or sphere of a certain notion, event, or the like.

Essentially, a frame is a certain formal, symbolic pattern for an event, notion, phenomenon, or condition. It represents a set of questions which can be asked about a situation, object, state, and so on.

For example, the frame "day" implies the following questions: Of what year? In what month? What day in the month? What day of the week? Each of the questions corresponds to an empty position called a "slot". To obtain a frame, that is, a carrier of specific knowledge about reality, the slots must be filled with particular data.

The more slots in a frame, the more varied, many-sided and systematic the idea it describes.

The frame of the notion "operation" (undertaking, type of activity) may have the following slots: What to do? What for (reward, cause, motivation)? What will it bring in? What are the costs? What are the alternatives of the aim? Who does it, when, where, and so on?

Now, apply it to management and planning tasks. Is not the very first question, "What to do?", crucial for the activity? To answer it is to determine and formulate the objective of the activity as the desired result. In our time, it is a difficult matter to substantiate the objective of an activity so as not to commit an error of judgement.

The method of frames is related to the situational control method, whose concepts were developed by the Soviet scientists D.A. Pospelov and Yu. I. Klykov before the emergence of frames. Their reasoning, it would seem, was very simple.

For a number of traffic-control objects, such as a freight seaport, a town intersection, congested air-space around an airport, and the like, attempts to build management information systems on the traditional, formal, and mathematical basis have given no positive results because of difficulties in describing the task and the cumbersome solutions obtained. People, however, manage with the control of these complex objects using nothing more than phrases, or "texts", of their native language. Therefore, models should be designed in a similar fashion, by coding in the computer the semantic characteristics of a particular controlled object. The more so because despite there sometimes being an immense number of possible situations, the controller makes a limited number of decisions. For instance, only two decisions are taken in controlling the traffic at a simple crossroads: open traffic in one direction, close it in the cross direction and vice versa, although the number of particular situations is enormous.

This method attempts to consider yet another "human aspect" in approaching the problem: a fussiness of characteristics indicating in most cases the degree of reliability with which a particular object belongs to some class of objects. One can easily imagine a series of drawings on which, say, the image of a lion gradually changes into that of man. You cannot say exactly where in the intermediate drawings one should draw the line separating the notion of man (or, rather, the "picture" of man) from that of lion. A fuzzy area exists between them in which every object can be assigned subjectively to either notion with a certain degree of reliability.

To appreciate how difficult the work in this direction is, suffice it to say that no single program that forms fuzzy notions has so far been devised, and every step towards this goal is greeted with great interest.

Models known as semantic networks have also been used lately for representing knowledge.

A semantic network has nodes and pointers that connect them. Each node stands for a certain notion and the pointers indicate the relationships existing between the notions. The pointers can have different semantics.

We can illustrate this with some simple examples.

Take a genealogical tree. Here, the nodes represent particular persons and the pointers represent parentage. Each node receives two pointers designating the father and the mother of a person represented by this node.

Here is another example: systematization in zoology. The nodes designate the names of the classes, orders, suborders, genera, and species of animals. Each pointer describes the genus-to-species relation. Thus, for instance, the pointer denoting the Przevalsky horse comes from the node that stands for the genus "horse".

Semantic networks with functional relations have already found extensive use:

"Poet", "Priz", "Posokh" and others.

If we compare traditional computer tasks with those involving artificial intelligence, the difference will be apparent. In the first case, the user is bound to relate his semantic model of reality to formal mathematical models implemented in the machine. Artificial intelligence that brings into effect a semiotic model sharply raises the effectiveness of the use of computer technology in management and control and allows the computer to handle very important tasks. Some examples:

(1) The computer learns to "understand" a professionally-oriented natural language in the form of writing or speech and react accordingly to the input. (2) The computer acquires the capability of performing management tasks by their descriptions and initial data, automatically compiling the work program from a set of standard program modules. (3) Man-machine interaction systems, in which the user converses with the machine in a language of standard commands, become feasible.

Let us see how systems that "mastered" the new structuring and application style operate.

The "Poet" system designed to generate reports on the current status of production and economic indices works on the text-understanding principle. A requisition is made in a common business language. It is analyzed and translated into the internal knowledge-representation language. The internal representation is formed as a task-related semantic network and consists of an abstract and a concrete network. Essentially, the abstract network is a complex frame, and a concrete network is a specific example of this frame.

The notions are structured into a hierarchy whose generalization produces super-notions and whose elaboration produces sub-notions. The events are used for representing task-related actions. Analysis of the text separates a specific event, activating the appropriate frame in the semantic network.

Suppose you enter a requisition: "How much coal is shipped by rail from A to B in the course of a year?" The requisition starts the frame "to ship", which initiates the filling of slots: "What?", "By what means?", "Wherefrom?", "Where?", "In what period of time?". In this example, all the slots except the slot "how much?" are filled in the course of semantic analysis. To arrive at an answer to this question, the system addresses itself to the data base, finds the answer, and formulates it in the same business information language the user operates in.

One example of systems that solve problems by their description and basic data is the "Priz" system. The user can formulate his problem for the computer in a common natural language. The system singles the required objects out of the loaded text, enters them into the semantic network stored in the computer memory, and seeks the way leading from the initial to the end nodes just as is done in solving a quadratic equation. The result may prove to be a few variants of solution, only one of which should be selected. Such a variant is either chosen by the user or is determined automatically by a certain criterion.

While "Poet" is an "answer-question" type of system, and "Priz" allows various complex planning and design problems to be solved thanks to its ability to execute all the mathematical models relevant to the user's area of interest, there are also universal artificial-intelligence systems. They solve not only the first two problems, but also the problems of structuring conversational-mode man-machine systems.

The system "Dilos" was evidently one of the first conversational-mode information and logic systems; it proved itself as a tool for dialogue-type planning and was effectively used in interactive systems designed to control large complexes. The ability to output intermediate results of computations makes "Dilos" particularly attractive.

All operations are performed by a set of procedures grouped into four main program sections. A linguistic section transforms the business-language text and command instructions into an internal language used to operate information-retrieving, computing, and logical sections. The logical section is the principal part of the system and the leading one with respect to the information-retrieving and computing sections: it is the logical system that controls analysis of modifications of models of the outside world, the design of problem solutions, and the handling of user requisitions for which conventional information retrieval is inadequate.

Conversation in man-machine systems may be led either by the user or by the machine. In the first and most common case, the problem-solving procedure and the refinement of the basic data are controlled by man. In the second case, where the computer takes over, use is made essentially of the ideas of programmed learning, according to which the machine automatically acquires the skill of using the conversational and programming languages, designing the algorithm for solving a problem by the starting data, and some other operations. Both conversational modes can be used to advantage when the user is still at the stage of acquainting himself with the system.

One of the most important problems of artificial intelligence is the development of software in order to implement semantic systems.

An example is the multi-purpose, question-answer "Mivos" system and its further development in "Posokh".

Thus, certain progress has now been made in theoretical research and some experience gained in bringing artificial intelligence systems into existence.

Artificial Intelligence and Systems Analysis

Undoubtedly, two present-day branches of scientific research dealing with problems of semantic character and using a rational method of investigation could not help but combine their efforts and potentials. The importance of the interpenetration of the ideas of systems analysis (which has been called, "enlightened common sense with mathematical models at its service") and artificial intelligence (figuratively called "the science of making a machine do what an intelligent man can) for solving problems of this class is now clear to everyone.

What is the primary goal of artificial intelligence when it turns to a specific problem? It is to break it down, separate, and reduce it to a number of subproblems, in other words. to structure it. The problem-reduction approach allows the use of mathematical, technical, programming, and other means for obtaining an acceptable solution.

In systems analysis, such problems are divided into subproblems until direct particular solutions are arrived at, that is, problems are analyzed.

The process of "putting together", or synthesizing the solution to the whole problem out of solutions to constituent problems, is then carried out. In case the problem of synthesis also proves non-structured, it is then "taken apart" into subproblems as well.

Thus, in applying systems analysis to solving the problems of management and planning at some organization, the problem may be considered structured when it answers a detailed list of questions. It is essential that planning should be started from the end goals, from the desired end results; that rules and procedures of decision-making should be unambiguously stated; that the decisions should be presented in a clear, not a "fuzzy", form, that is, as a choice of several alternative methods of achieving the goal or alternative plans of operations or events; that one could ascertain, when and where a decision was made and whether it was correct, who is responsible for the decision; and whether to reward him for efficient performance and high-quality results or penalize him for bad or erroneous decisions.

We already know that the problems of pattern recognition as well as identification, inference, and the representation of the incoming information are central for artificial intelligence. Since any information makes sense only in connection with a certain activity, "understanding" consists in structuring the incoming information in accordance with its proposed use.

Thus, we are faced with an insufficiently structured problem which is solved on the same principles as those which underlie systems analysis.

If we turn to programming for the electronic computer, we shall have to recognize that the customer's assignment for developing and implementing a software complex is typically an inadequately structured problem. By applying the systems analysis approach, scientists have developed special programming techniques, for instance, a "downwards" process for software complexes.

Cooperation of artificial intelligence and systems analysis goes in another direction as well.

Systems analysis arose from the need to solve large-scale problems and consequently to justify large-scale goals first of all. The problem of justifying objectives was not so pressing before the advent of the scientific and technical revolution: no large and complex problems had been tackled then simply because there were no means for doing so. Experience and intuition of management were sufficient.

With the advent of the scientific and technical revolution, intuition and experience have started to fail; misjudgements in the end results and expenditures, as well as the oversight of the consequences and side-effects, especially distant ones, have become rather frequent.

Systems analysis offers a general approach to complex situations, namely, problem reduction. It should be clear that this approach requires work at various levels, with problems differing both semantically and mathematically. The same methodology applies to selecting aims and forming assessment criteria.

The problem of choosing objectives can be solved by the development of predictions and scenarios of future events based on the thorough study of precedents. It is evident that such complex problems can hardly be solved by a single person and even by a large group of experts in acceptable deadlines and with acceptable quality if they apply methods of representation, processing, and information retrieval traditionally used in systems analysis.

Here the use of artificial-intelligence systems may prove invaluable not only to store, systematize, and search for information, but also to organize the joint work of different experts.

Artificial intelligence provides systems analysis with a method of creating data banks for collective use based on frames. This opens up great possibilities for justifying objectives. Messages can be checked for completeness, input information can be selected and restructured, standards of performance can be maintained, and the computer can be protected from human errors. Last, but not least, forecasts and scenarios can be constructed in a man-machine conversation mode, and experts, when necessary, can address the machine in a language they understand.

The prospects of mutual penetration and enrichment of systems analysis and artificial intelligence are very attractive. Work in this direction was begun quite recently and is awaiting further development. But it is clear that new approaches will generate new interesting problems in both systems analysis and artificial intelligence and in their application to management and planning.

A New Branch of Economy: Information Handling Industry

V. M. GLUSHKOV and Yu. M. KANYGIN

How Did Information Science Come into Being?

First, the very first steps have now been taken, when the period of pilot computers and not their commercially produced counterparts were being used and questions like "What is all this going to come to?" and not "How do we use them best?" were prevalent. Today, the economy has reached a certain level of saturation with computers and increasingly sophisticated data processing equipment is now mass produced.

From being exotic instruments used solely for complex scientific and engineering calculations in some top-priority science and industrial areas, computers have become the work horses for numerous users.

Second, individual computer centres have begun to be integrated into large multi-user networks. We can see here a definite "chain-reaction" pattern in computer application, the development of computer networks and advances in computer technology producing a sharp rise in the number of users. This together with heavy capital investment has made the study of the cost effectiveness of computer centres differing in grade and purpose very relevant.

Third, a distinct new industry, the information-handling sector, has come into being and grown stupendously since its inception. The output of computer products in the Soviet Union has multiplied tenfold over the last decade, outstripping every other sector of industry in growth. The USSR's computing capacity doubles every three to four years. Predictions for growth in this area are stunning: the growth curves sky-rocket, approaching a vertical line.

But there is more to the phenomenon than the mere increase in the number of computers. What matters is the impact of computer technology on the structure of the economy. The spreading information and computer network is gradually encompassing the entire economy and requires a complex organization, more complex than that adopted in the more traditional sectors of the economy. On the other hand, tackling the problems of data processing for production control and management purposes not only improves the effectiveness of existing or projected MIS's (management information systems) and computer centres but also largely shapes national scientific and industrial progress.

This is the background for our discussion of computerized information science. It should thus be apparent that computer data processing has currently become a special field of application with a high labour content. In terms of employment and investment, this branch of industry can compare with the largest sectors of the economy.

What Is Computerized Informatics?

Computerized informatics is the mechanized or automated process of obtaining, processing, and transmitting information, based on the use of the computer. It is part of the field called social information, that is to say, part of the process of communicating information in which we all are involved to some extent. But informatics is the part handled by computers. In other words, it is the industry, based on computer technology, whose function is to collect and process information and perform control functions. According to Marx, the use of machines makes it possible to produce increasingly more in a shorter and shorter time. The same effect is produced by the computer in the information handling sphere.

The computer-aided information industry came into existence quite recently, when the spontaneous, limited use of computers for performing specific tasks gave way to their large-scale application in the economy, with most or all of the documentation turnover being handled by the computer. Thus, computerized informatics is a new historical phenomenon as it has only been around for about three decades. All practical human activities have until now been based on non-machine informatics, which used a natural "information capacity" of the human mind. This mode of information handling was based on natural (human memory) and artificial (paper, for instance) data carriers.

Obviously, any kind of human activity has two sides: physical (involving energy and materials) and mental (involving information and control). Both sides of social labour have been and are being mechanized. The mechanization of physical labour began long ago, during the first industrial revolution; it was done using the steam engine, the electric motor, the internal combustion engine, and so on. The mechanization of mental activity is a phenomenon we are witnessing now, in the course of the current scientific and industrial revolution; it is being done using cybernetic technology, primarily the computer. Computer-aided informatics is as much superior to pre-computerized informatics as a modern textile mill is to a spinning-wheel.

Any historical period has its own prevalent methods for collecting, processing, and communicating information. For example, manual paperwork was the predominant technique from the outset of industrial development. A man handed over a direction, order, request, and so on, on a handwritten, typewritten, or printed piece of paper. Now a new technique is taking over, namely a man-machine procedure, and a new kind of information handling, aided by computers, allows immense amounts of information to be processed and communicated irrespective of man's capabilities.

In its fully developed form, the new technological base of administrative and production management will comprise automatic communication lines arranged in a network. The network will include, on the one hand, computer centres of different levels, from those at individual enterprises to the top units in the administrative hierarchy, and on the other, automated workstations for various management and control experts. The computers incorporated in the system continuously renew in their memory the information that reflects the state of the economy at every level and holds the suite of programs which are used to help solve all or most of problems of economic or social management.

Computer-Aided Informatics: a Branch of the Economy?

No doubt, this mode of information handling must operate on an industrial basis, and it is rightly called the information industry.

Why should this industry be regarded as a branch of the economy in its own right? Primarily because it has a high labour content. Take, for instance, the United States. In the mid-1970s, the information handling industry ranked third among the other industrial sectors, following only the automobile and petroleum refining industries. It has recently taken the lead.

Computers provided the basis for all the information handling operations: generation, transmission, and use. Information processes have become feasible to account, plan, and provide for. They are concentrated in special departments at industrial enterprises, namely computer centres, which are equipped with sophisticated technology. In addition, independent information enterprises, such as multi-user computer centres, are appearing in ever growing numbers.

Lenin wrote that the changeover from a manufactory-type production to modern industrial production manifested a complete technological revolution abolishing centuries-old manual skills. Similarly, in informatics a change to computer-aided information handling is making a strictly scientific approach to the information process and its organization essential. Computerized informatics makes use of advances in cybernetics, systems engineering, mathematics, operations research, and information theory. Characteristically, information theory as a scientific discipline developed side by side with computerized techniques of information processing. A remark by Engels seems to provide a good analogy. He wrote that we had learned something meaningful about electricity only since the discovery of its engineering practicality. We have now learned something meaningful about information after the emergence of computerized data processing techniques.

Finally, computerized informatics generates a special product and supplies it to other production enterprises. The demand for this product is growing all the time, as is the number of users.

The question now is whether the information industry has features making it peculiar as a branch of the economy. The answer is yes. There are several such peculiarities that have been theoretically substantiated and accounted for. We can only point out some of them here.

The information industry might be said to form a kind of infrastructure. It serves other branches of the production and non-production spheres, aiding their development. In this sense it can be likened to transport and communications, only its functions are more complicated. It is like a nervous system to the other branches of the economy, corresponding to their current scale, tasks, and complexity.

A most important thing is that computerized informatics is a high-technology industry. Being at the "cutting edge" of scientific and technical progress, it requires the latest and best equipment and methods, which enable it to serve as a generator and mover of that progress.

What Are the Functions of Computerized Informatics?

The importance of automation is talked about a great deal and is without a doubt important. But automation presents problems. Take, for instance, the adjustment of information transfer links in automatic systems. So far this task has been performed by man. As automated systems reach a certain level of complexity, the number of setters, inspectors, and maintenance people servicing these systems grows at an increasing rate, and so complex automated systems can no longer be efficient.

Help has come from electronic automation technology, primarily the computer, which is taking over the control functions from man. The computer can not only handle information, that is, collect, process, and output various data, but can also monitor programmable manipulators, industrial robots, and entire automated production shops and even plants.

A particularly important aspect of present-day automation is its application to the non-production sphere. This sphere employs enormous numbers of people, most of them highly-skilled: in trade and finance; in research and development work for routine data processing, controlling experiments, recording instrument readings, and so forth; in business correspondence; in reading and preparing abstracts; in engineering design for drafting and preparing bills of materials; and so on.

Computerized information science is capable of changing the current situation radically. Information search complexes, automated systems for data readout, recording, and inspection, automatic control systems and mathematical modelling of processes are the powerful, efficient, and dependable tools of information science. They not only save labour in the non-production sector, but also change its quality, upgrading it through the application of the state-of-the art science and technology.

But the most significant function of computerized information science is setting administrative control on an industrial basis. Computers came first to science, than to industry, and then began finding applications in complex control systems. Thus, the computer has turned into a powerful control tool. In time, it will become more and more evident that the revolutionary aspect of the computer in modern development is the radical change it is bringing about in the methods of management.

It is quite natural to ask why.

To answer the question, it is important to apply a systems approach to the development of the economy, namely, to take into account two components: one involving materials and energy, and the other involving organization and information. The first component contributes to the economy through a growth in processing raw materials and consuming energy. The second component increases the efficiency of the use of material and labour resources; information provides a resource for the functioning and development of the economy. Moreover, it serves to make up, in part, for material, labour, and energy resources.

Clearly, the more information per unit time is processed by a system, that is, the higher the level at which it functions, the greater the savings in labour, energy, and raw materials it creates.

The amount of information needed to be processed is enormous. In the mid-1970s, for instance, some 200 thousand million items of data circulated in the Soviet Union's industrial management system. The body of information to be processed is believed to be growing in proportion to the square of the complexity of the economy as it develops. The time will come when the economy reaches a level, attended by an information explosion, at which no improvements in conventional planning and management methods will help.

This information barrier can only be surmounted by introducing industrial methods to the process of management by utilizing computerized information-processing technology. The computer allows for control through planning to be enhanced by several orders of magnitude.

How can the planning methods be radically improved? Only by refining computerized data-processing and developing radically new models that will allow the best decisions to be made and implemented quickly in a man-machine dialogue mode.

A system of such models has been devised at the Cybernetics Institute of the Ukrainian Academy of Sciences. The system was named DISPLAN. The models differ from earlier ones in that they not only tackle top-level planning problems but also provide planning at all levels using radically new methods based on computer-aided information handling techniques. When balancing the plan in order to achieve an optimum, DISPLAN is capable of making the requisite modifications at GOSPLAN and at every other link in the industrial sector, down to production shop and section level plans. The fantastic volume of work involved does not pose an obstacle: the models are based on computer networks of an incredibly high information output.

It should be apparent that computer-aided information science is very significant to the economy. We could claim that it provides an advance into the key areas of current socio-economic development. Computer-aided information science enriches the country's resources and opens new possibilities for developing the economy.

Is the Computer-Aided Information Industry an All-Embracing Service?

When discussing the computer-aided information industry, it is best to define the area to which it belongs.

As is known, material production includes those sectors of the economy which are directly responsible for creating the national income. Although managerial activities in this area are separated from physical labour, without doubt they are also associated with material production. Marx wrote that because the function of management stems from the very nature of collective labour, it pertains to the sphere of production.

Production management as a function branched from the direct physical labour with the advent of machine production. At present, a second division is taking place: the informational activity is functionally and organizationally branching out of the management function. Nevertheless, it retains its affinity to the function of management and hence to material production. But, as it is becoming industrial branch in its own right as a result of a further division of labour, the information processing industry is becoming inseparable from the process of production and so contributes to the national income.

The computer-aided information processing industry serves not only the production sphere but also the non-production sphere, viz. science, education, government, political institutions, and so on. Therefore the industry can be said to be "all-embracing", taking over control functions in many areas of human activity.

Depending on whether it serves the production or the non-production sphere, the computerized information industry can be identified with one or the other. By nature it is a non-compact, "spread-out" branch of the economy, like the transport or communications industries.

The accumulation of computer capacity, the number of people involved in the use of computers, and investment in complex computer systems have been growing rapidly. It should be expected that by 1990 the present capacity of the information industry in the USSR and a number of other countries will increase eight to twelve times.

More and more information is stored in computers. For example, 90 percent of all incoming data in nuclear physics is sent to computer storage and not duplicated on paper. Encyclopeadias, reference books, the bulk of economic data are also being placed on computer input media. This improves the reliability of keeping the information, reduces its cost, and, what is of prime importance, allows its easy retrieval and better practical use. The trend now is such that enterprises, organizations, and individuals who happen to remain outside the sphere of a computer-aided information service will in future be cut off from the main flow of new information.

The computerized information industry has now become a priority development area and one of the most important tools for economic advance. With the increasing complexity of problems and the desire to look farther ahead into the future of science, technology, and industrial production in order to develop a failure-free strategy of growth, the need to strengthen electronic computer potential becomes ever more urgent.

The Fine Arts and Cybernetics

The scope of this subject it so wide that it is hardly possible to cover it with only three articles. Nevertheless, in the first of these, entitled "Cybernetics and Culture", an attempt has been made to review, though somewhat briefly, as large a number of topics relating to this interesting theme as possible. Of all their diversity, the problems of modelling in music are treated separately. The author of the paper, the mathematician and musician P.Kh. Zaripov, has been most successful in musical modelling research. His works have gained recognition both in the Soviet Union and abroad.

The chapter is concluded with an article by a renowned Soviet fiction writer and mathematician, the author of interesting novels and short stories acclaimed by readers and a well-known expert in systems engineering research, mathematics, and game theory. Her viewpoint—both of a woman of letters and a scientist—is believed to carry much weight in the dispute over the relationship between cybernetics and the arts.

Cybernetics and Culture

B. V. BIRYUKOV and S. N. PLOTNIKOV

The way in which cybernetics has been taking shape as a complex scientific discipline can be seen through its relationship with culture. Early in the 1960s, despite the relatively modest achievements of cybernetics as applied to culture, many workers believed that all the attendant problems had been solved in principle, and all that was needed was time: in a few years a computer would be able to compose poems and music like professional poets and composers. But these overenthusiastic hopes gradually waned as theoretical and practical experience increased. Problems arose that no one had expected and they roused scepticism about the feasibility of applying the cybernetic approach to culture and the arts. Nevertheless, the research went on. Achievements ceased to give rise to illusions, and failures ceased to disappoint. Little by little, the terra incognita named "cybernetics and culture" was explored. A new era ushered in a stage when a scientific structure was erected methodically, a period of the sober assimilation of the ideas, methods, and advances of cybernetics and its related sciences into the cultural field as a whole, and into the fine arts in particular.

The word "culture" in its broad sense can embrace a very wide spectrum of ideas from the evolution of material and spiritual values, the progress of science, education, art, and religion to ideas such as the conditions of labour, human relations, life style, and the like. In other words, culture in this sense is all that has been produced (and is being produced) by man as opposed to all that has been created by nature. More specifically, culture refers to the fine arts, that is, prose, poetry, music, theatre, the graphic arts, cinema, architecture, and so on. It is in this sense that we are going to discuss culture and its relations with cybernetics. In doing so, we single out three areas of research on the application of cybernetic ideas and techniques: the process of creation, the study of the arts, and the planning and management of cultural development.

Cybernetics and the Creative Process

The "cybernetization" of a scientific discipline or engineering can be assessed by the use of the ideas, approaches, and methods associated with the concepts of system, structure, complexity, model, information, control, optimization, and so on; with application of mathematical procedures, computer technology and automation ranging from relatively simple office equipment and calculators to mainframe computers and networks. But if the advent and proliferation of digital electronics is a recent development, quantitative and mathematical methods in the fine arts have been used for centuries.

The idea that there is relation between the arts and mathematics is one of those fundamental human ideas which, having arisen, take root and live throughout history, changing their form and appearance but nevertheless invariably asserting themselves in any major epoch of human history, be it the Greek or Roman civilizations, the Middle Ages, the Renaissance, or modern time. Every major stage of historical development requires a reformulation of the idea that mathematics and the arts are closely interrelated. The Renaissance, for instance, brought forth great scientists and artists rolled into one, such as Leonardo da Vinci and Albrecht Dürer. In architecture, the idea that art and mathematics were united was elaborated by Luca Pacioli in his *De divina proportione* (1509). He described the concept of what became known as the "golden section" principle, which was also familiar to Leonardo, and which was scientifically analyzed by Adolf Zeisinger only as late as 1880s. The principle is drawing attention of present-day researchers as well. Poetry also requires mathematical calculation, this was asserted by another Renaissance artist J. du Bellay .The first attempts to compose music by non-musical methods date back to the 18th century.

These were based on "games of chance" and musicians such as Haydn and Handel used dice to establish notes, tempos, rhythms, and so on. A book was published under the title *A Guide to Composing Polonaises and Minuets with Dice*; another book of this kind entitled *A Guide to Composing Waltzes in Any Quantities without the Knowledge of Music and Composition, using a Couple of Dice* was ascribed to Mozart. This was a background to modern machine music.

The idea of using mathematics in the arts has been quite fruitful in some cases (in architecture and to a lesser extent in the graphic arts), whereas in other areas (such as music) it has produced nothing more than curiosities. This situation—an array of curiosities and real achievements—has remained largely unchanged. In a number of European countries, the United States, and Japan, cybernetics and the computer have given rise to so-called computer art. Computers are being applied to the graphic arts and music. Products of "computer creation" in pop-art, "kinetic art", "abstract" music and painting, "permutation" art, and the like have been displayed at numerous contests, festivals, and exhibitions. This activity was readily sponsored by various funds and promoted by mass media, the inevitable price for "computerizing" the arts. It is important, however, to emphasize the positive side of the computer entry into the sphere of art in order to properly evaluate the phenomenon.

The application of computer technology to architectural design is an undisputable achievement. Working with the computer, an architect can fix the spatial form arising in his imagination by entering it as an image, or sketch, into the computer's memory. He can then obtain pictures of the structure from various viewpoints on a display screen or plotter connected to the computer. This dialogue between the architect and the computer, which has been practised in a number of countries since the 1960s, has produced positive results. It does raise new challenges, both technical and psychological that place new demands on architects who now have to switch over from their traditional working practices to the new and superior techniques.

The computer as an aid to man in creating objects of art has proved fruitful not only in architecture but also in industrial design, in the cinema, and so on. In the cinema, the first steps were to produce animated cartoons. The artist aided by the computer need not draw a long sequence of pictures, each nearly identical to the preceding one. It is enough for him to put into the computer the first and the last frame; the intermediate frames are produced by the computer using a suitable "kinematic" program.

Similar methods are employed to design cloth. At the end of the 1960s, S.N. Kallistratova devised computer programs to design and analyze the weave patterns needed for fabric. This is done by special artists who design the patterns and select the colour schemes. In the first experiments, the BESM-6 series computer working on Kallistratova's program produced over a hundred designs in 20 minutes (with the relevant numerical data) for linen, serge, satin and their derivatives such as textiles with plain twill, and crepe. Several years later, the Oktyabr textile manufacturing association, which makes fabrics in several hundred designs and colours, introduced two automated design systems, Avtocolorist and Avtodessinator. Until then, designers would have spent two to three months developing a weave pattern and colour schemes for a fabric. These systems reduced this work to minutes, allowing the best cloth textures, colours, and weaves to be selected. In effect, the industry was producing textiles designed with the aid of a computer. Zaripov obtained similar results, devising an algorithm for making lace, so that this handicraft can eventually be automated.

Computers can also be used to aid the composition of music. Special computer languages are now being developed for placing musical information into a computer and processing it. The aim is to compile a catalogue of original tunes that can be identified by citing a few notes. However, what is primarily meant by computer music is a new musical text produced by a computer in some form (in a machine code, in a regular musical notation, or directly in sound). The first experiments of this kind date back to the 1950s. Since 1959, R.Kh. Zaripov has written a number of "musical" programs for a computer which composed single-voice melodies. He also demonstrated that a computer operating on such a program can compose a tune to lyrics, whose rhythm (the sequence of strong and weak syllables) has been fed into the computer in a suitable form, and thereby a song results.

Research on computer music has shown that modelling the composition process does not result in professional-quality music. Hence composers only resort to the computer as an aid helping them by carrying out all the routine tasks. In particular, a computer can be utilized to prepare musical "blanks"—individual combinations of notes, chords, sequences, tempos and so on—for the composer who then picks out what fits into his ideas.[1] This is often done when composing music that has a "non-traditional" structure. The Soviet musician L. Astvatsatryan describes the action of a computer in creating series of tones, or excerpts—specially arranged sound combinations he used in composing a symphony: "... the series I had in mind was extremely complex and time-consuming. In this respect the computer is an ideal aid, in no way limiting our musical imagination. Moreover, the computer enables a composer to approach the mystery of what is hidden in the unity of interval, rhythm, and thought"[2]. Zaripov notes that the computer-aided techniques are also applicable to the more "traditional" musical forms. For example, the Italian mathematician E. Gagliardo composed a musical piece which was made up of tunes put out by a Ural-2 computer running one of Zaripov's program; an accompaniment to it was arranged by a formal method proposed by E. Gagliardo.

Zaripov's early computer programs synthesized a tune from individual sounds following patterns that had been found by analyzing human melodies (songs by Soviet composers). The greatest difficulty was to obtain melodious musical intonations. At present, Zaripov is working on a new and totally different method of composing: the melody is to be arranged from intonations found in musical literature. In doing so, a natural frequency distribution of intonations is picked out from a musical-intonation frequency dictionary compiled from a collection of tunes (the same Soviet songs). This should imitate the musical arrangement of a composer who unconsciously selects the intonations already existing in his musical memory, which was formed as he developed as a musician. Zaripov believes that in this way the computer will compose a melody which (with the proper instrumentation that can also be assigned to it) may be performed in public.

An inalienable part of creation is the collection of "primary information". This lays the groundwork for creativity of an artist, and as he presents his final product to its "consumers" their response comes back to the artist to influence his later artistic work.

Within the framework of these "sociodynamic cycles" of culture[3], a key role is played by the distribution of art and this includes distribution by the mass media. One of the first research projects in this area was conducted at the computer centre of Radio Estonia. The task was to release the staff members from routine functions, including the search and treatment of basic materials for radio programmes so that without limiting producers' intentions they could be used quickly and efficiently. In the course of the project (in the

1970s), the research team described the distinguishing features of thousands of musical compositions, worked out how to assess the efficiency of radio programmes and methods for retrieving the stored material to use it in a radio or TV programme, developed an information system to search for material (referencing by facts, events, and personalities) and a system for arranging the material into shows and concerts at the request of the producers, and devised the appropriate algorithms, computer languages, and programs. Later, the computerized system was used for long-term broadcast planning and scheduling, for processing the news, and so forth. In the 1980s, the use of automated systems and computer technology in the information service of major radio and TV networks has become normal practice. In television, these systems have been used for arranging programmes and selecting illustrative material. The same can be said about the place of cybernetics in publishing, printing, and in libraries. Today, computers are installed in nearly every big library helping to provide for prompt and efficient service in this sphere of culture.

The effect of modern automatic equipment (computers, electronic instruments, and the like) in creating artistic values largely depends upon advances in modelling the informational aspect of art. Here, aesthetically oriented man-machine interaction seems to be a promising trend. One example is the work by V.S. Fain, in which he describes the development of an interactive sculptor-computer communication system. The author designed a mathematical model of variation in the shape to which the surface of the material is to be sculptured, and proposed the structure of an appropriate interactive system. According to Fain, such a system would provide an efficient tool for facilitating and speeding up the mechanical element in a sculptor's work[4].

It is obvious that further "cybernetization" of creative activities will require computers to be applied to the work of architects, designers, graphic artists, cinema and theatre producers, and even to journalists and writers. Man-machine systems in the arts must enrich the creative potential of an artist. We believe that electronics and computer technology will form an organic part of the creative process and the computer will become a companion of inspiration, the quill pen of the 21st century.

Electronics and cybernetics are closely associated with new creation methods and new kinds of art. In particular, we have in mind the new methods of producing a musical "item" and the artistic synthesis of sound and colour. In the USSR the feasibility of use of electrical sound equipment for playing music was studied as early as the 1920s by L.S.Termen, a physicist and musician who invented the world's first electric musical instrument, named the Termenvox. But a real impetus to work in this area has been given by modern electronics and digital computer technology. The old idea of synthesizing music and colour, which was ardently promoted by A.N. Skryabin, an outstanding Russian composer and pianist, has been revitalized. The union of colour and music manifests the significance of scientific methods and cybernetic engineering as a source of new means for artistic creation. It allows creation to interact with electronics, aesthetics with technology, and art psychology with neurophysiology. The integration of colour and sound seen as an aesthetic event gives rise to questions never before confronted by "traditional" art. It stands to reason that the most promising way for art to progress now is to search for a technologically "suitable" and aesthetically justifiable inclusion of man, as the creator and performer of the work of art, into the system.

At present there is already a large choice of colour-and-music instruments: manually operated, automated, "kinetic devices" that automatically produce dynamic shapes and colours, and so forth. The use of laser and holograph technology also holds great promise. The synthesis of colour and musical dynamics is beginning to take an increasingly more organic place in aesthetic relation between man and reality, in the world of emotional expressiveness. Music is accompanied by colour at concerts; concert pieces have been composed using musical themes by Tchaikovsky, Chopin, Wagner, Prokofiev, and contemporary composers. Many people work on principles of composing colour music.

Another application of colour-and-music is industrial design. A number of systems have now been developed using electronics, automatic devices, and laser technology. Experiments indicate that colour and music and "kinetic" art may be quite potent for relieving fatigue and nervous strain. The combination of colour and music finds its natural place in special psychological-relief rooms which have been arranged at some industrial enterprises, and also in an instrument designed by L.N. Melnikov[5] and called the Relaxator.

Cybernetics for Studying the Arts

Research and development in the cultural field is another application of cybernetics. Scientific research of the arts also has a long history. It is interesting to see how the methodology and concepts have changed with time, and how the range of problems being tackled has become ever wider. The first problem to appear and the most significant was how to analyze a work of art.

Artistic creations became the subjects of study as soon as the first aesthetic concepts and theories emerged. Throughout history we encounter concepts of analysis whose aim is to substantiate such traits as harmony, balance, proportion, integrity of composition, and to assess them in quantitative terms. This is to be found in works of Durer, Descartes, Leibniz, Hume, Hogarth, and the researchers in semiotics and art of early this century (A.Bely, G.Shpet, P.Florensky, V.Propp, B.Tomashevsky, and some others). In a sense, the cybernetic methods for analyzing works of art have many precursors.

Today cybernetics is employed more and more for studying, say, literature to define the writer's style and vocabulary, or to identify the author of a text. The reader can find in scientific literature descriptions of a number of computerized methods for identifying literary and musical texts. In the Soviet Union, the emphasis in research is placed on the semiotic aspect as well as on the mechanism of generating literary texts. In the most general sense, this approach is to interpret culture as a single semiotic system playing the part of some sort of collective intellect that possesses a common memory and means for working out radically new texts.

In terms of semiotics, films and plays are special texts, but their semiotic study is not the main aspect of the cybernetic approach. Statistical analysis and computer modelling of art yield more significant results. What can be done is demonstrated by the following example. In a research programme sponsored by UNESCO and carried out by the International Sociological Association, of which the Soviet Union is a member, cybernetic methods were employed to analyze the annual output of cinema films produced in the USA, France, Italy, Yugoslavia, Czechoslovakia, and Poland. The aim of the analysis was to uncover any feature that seemed to be typical of the films of those countries. Similar studies of cinema and theatrical productions have been conducted for 15 years in the Soviet Union.[6] Let us consider in detail a survey carried out by V.N. Dmitrievsky and B.Z. Doktorov as a good illustration of cybernetic methods and their potential.

The repertoires of nine Leningrad theatres were analyzed during a complex socio-theatrical research project called "Theatre in the Spiritual Life of Modern Youth". The method was based on expert estimates of twenty attributes chosen to characterize the plays. These ranged from "comic", "melodramatic", "tragic", "thrilling", and "amusing", and so forth, up to "significant to Leningrad's theatrical life". The questions put to the expert were like this: "Do you think the show is a "comedy" (or "tragedy", or "melodrama")?", and he had to answer with an unqualified "yes", a qualified "yes", a qualified "no", or an unqualified "no" (the answers being rated from 1 to 4 for mathematical treatment). The results were subjected to a correlation and factor analysis. Even though the basic attributes were somewhat vague, the results turned out to be very interesting. For example, the amusing and the comic element were found, as one might expect, to correlate with each other (the correlation coefficient being 0.61), but the relationship of these attributes to the others helped interpret this qualitatively. The nearness of the comic and the amusing element was manifested by similar coefficients with respect to such features as musical and decorative merit, plasticity, synthesis, and the lack of rationalism. But compared to other qualities, the two elements proved to have different coefficients. As the "comedy" element increased, the "melodrama" element fell as did the "tragedy" element, only more so and, strange as it may seem, the "thrilling" attribute rose slightly. "Amusement" seemed unaffected by changes in the "melodramatic" quality, but was negatively correlated to "tragedy" and was more closely related to "thrilling" than "comedy" was. The presence or absence of "comedy" did not affect the appraisal of acting, stage direction, and setting. At the same time higher degrees

13—01169

of "amusement" usually correlated with lower ratings of acting, stage setting, direction, and the overall quality of the play. A good comedy requires good music, whereas a merely amusing play can very well do without.

Although most of these conclusions appear to be quite natural and concur with results of conventional qualitative critical analysis, their strong points is their quantitative certainty and also their forming part of the overall picture revealed in the course of the survey.

What is important is that in addition to these conclusions, the method has brought to light some "hidden" variables that were objectively present in the system of the attributes in question and the possibility of constructing "numerical profiles" for plays and theatres, and the possibility of classifying the theatrical situation. Thus, if you take a two-dimensional space (plane) defined by the axes "amusing plays"-"serious plays" and "modern interpretation"-"traditional interpretation", you will find that the plays staged by the "Bolshoi" Dramatic Theatre in Leningrad fall into the quarter of the chart which corresponds to the modern interpretation of serious plays; a theatre frequented by young audiences stages plays typical of the modern interpretation of amusing plays; while the plays put on by the Leningrad Municipal Theatre occupy the central part of the chart, belonging equally to every quarter.

The conclusions from the study are not absolute of course; they depend on the model adopted, that is, on the set of attributes and structure of the charts. The conclusions should not be placed in opposition to the "traditional" methods of art critics; they supplement and deepen those methods.

The results of this survey could be analyzed for evaluating how the experts received the plays, rather than as described above. We would then be dealing with the task of using mathematical modelling to analyze perception of art. This task also has a history. The perception of art was first studied experimentally and quantitatively in the last third of the 19th century. It was known as Fechner's experimental aesthetics, and his methods have been substantially improved in this century. Observations and experiments similar to Fechner's were conducted in Russia by Ts.P. Baltolon between 1896 and 1898. At present, studies of the perception of art form a separate area of the psychology of art. They are based almost entirely on the application of computer technology and are closely associated with the analysis of the concept of art information. This concept is considered in relation with the other concepts used in aesthetics, art studies, and similar disciplines. The aim of an analysis is to determine the scope, subject, and features of art information, and its difference from other types of information (for example, scientific, managerial, commercial, and the rest).

Analysis of artistic productions was one of the first applications of information theory, although the area had hardly anything in common with communication engineering which had brought about those ideas and methods. The prompt adoption of information theory as a tool for studying art can be put down to the fact that the theory appealed to many researchers, both art experts and mathematicians, by it capacity for defining and measuring "aesthetic substance", that is, the quality which gives vitality to any work of art and produces the aesthetic effect. Many scientists were convinced that this "substance" was similar to information at some level of abstraction, since it could be reduced neither to form alone nor entirely to an aesthetic-communication content. This was despite the fact that in a certain sense it was determined (via laws yet to be discovered) both by the form and content of the work of art. The discovery of a connection between the aesthetic effect of a work of art, its elements and the methods of artistic expression on the one hand, and the elements of "unexpectedness," and originality, on the other, was interpreted as the affinity of the "aesthetic substance" to the phenomenon of information (even in its simplest, Shannonian form). Hence followed a search for an information-theory based criterion (or criteria) of aesthetic influence, a search in which some art critics hoped to find a tool for measuring aesthetic phenomena they needed very much, and a search in which information-theory researchers wanted to refine their methods by using them for problems that they were unfamiliar with. Such was the beginning of the collaboration between cyberneticists (mathematicians) and art critics, a collaboration which has resulted in many papers dedicated to the informational significance of art and to the quantitative evaluation of art in general. The researchers included such scientists as G. Brikhoff and A.N.Kolmogorov. Actually, the problems turned out to be more difficult than was first thought. It became obvious that success may only be achieved through persistent joint efforts of mathematicians, art critics, and sociologists using methods elaborated on a mathematical and cybernetic basis.

Experiments on uniting information theory and art studies were not all for nothing; the informational approach to aesthetic perception has taken root. One of the concepts that reflect this approach, "informational aesthetics", has already been treated in many articles and books, in particular, in Moles's monograph[3].

Informational aesthetics usually has as its point of departure the statistical theory of information developed by C. Shannon. The formulae of this theory, when properly applied, make it possible to calculate how much "new information" (in the Shannonian sense) there is in an aesthetic communication, that is to say, how "original" it is, and how much "superfluous" data it contains. Moles, who is developing this approach, believes that owing to superfluous information the form of a communication can be varied without changing its content. The aim of informational aesthetics is to find out how the author of an artistic communication has used its superfluous information. In other words, this line of research studies the way in which texts are written rather than their content.

Informational aesthetics as such covers a rather narrow understanding of art. In other approaches, such as the semantic one, the concept of art proves to be more significant. Thus, many researchers of poetry conclude that the signs and symbols expressing aesthetic values undergo a "desemantization". In their view, the desemantization in a work of art collides with the opposite desire to comprehend all elements of a text, and hence a "tension" arises between the poetical and non-poetical aspects of texts Poetical information is carried by another kind of information, namely factual information to which it is opposed. And there is no other way to communicate poetical information.

The tension can be sensed, as it were, when we compare "machine poetry" and human poetry in which verses are very close to one another in terms of their factual content. Given below are six verses, of which some were written by an eminent Russian poet and the others were "composed" by a computer. We leave it to the reader to identify the authorship.

The pearl-grey ornament at daybreak,
Slender, misty, ghostly, and pale...
A glance is cast upon the lake,
Sad and forlorn like a distant wail.

The bush is tired of groaning
The birds dart o'er the dyke
The bare-legged dawn wades, roaming
The marshes, heron-like.

The dwellings lost all hope for healing
The poppies fell deep in a swoon,
The rye, inflamed, swayed madly, reeling,
And God, delirious, blamed the moon.

What dismay has seized the dying!
Flickering lights throw shades around.
But the soul, away from crying,
For infinity is bound.
Mortal moan is close, unsteady,
Eyes in crystals gleam like coal.
Whisper, sickly smile: I'm ready,
Heaven is my awesome goal.

Mysterious ditches hide under the huts.
The air has breathed in too much coke at the stations
And flared up. But night, having just killed the sunset,
Glows rosy again. And the fence is astounded
By this paradox.

Here's a sweet bird,
Here's a soft look.
My quaint adornment
Flows like a brook.
Quick, sparkling, and bold
Feels heavy to hold.

We think that the reader will find it difficult to place these verses. This is not simply because they have been translated into English by a human translator. The identification is equally difficult in the original Russian. The main point is that these verses lack "extra-artistic", primarily factual, information. The predominance of the imaginative and metaphorical, or "poetical", over the factual and "extra-poetical" is so overwhelming here that these verses, being emotionally expressive, need for their comprehension the imagination of the reader to make up for the lack of clarity.

This example distinctly shows that a work of art carries with it a specific informational relationship between its aesthetic and non-aesthetic aspects. Hence it is important to develop mathematical models of perception based on information-theory principles and to explain some of the features peculiar to the structure of a piece of art.

Studies of aesthetic perception using mathematics and computers allow us to group distinctions in "the sense of the beautiful". In surveys[7] of this kind a method earlier applied by V.V. Nalimov[8] was used in which a group of people (experts) arranged pictures (realistic paintings) according to their appeal—from the "worst" to the "best"—without any comments. A mathematical treatment of the results by the non-metric multidimensional scaling method showed up what was most attractive in the pictures. In particular, the figure and the age of the model proved to be the principal attraction in the portraits of women, with specifically "masculine" and "feminine" preferences being revealed. A similar technique was used to analyze music and literature. We shall describe one of them.

The people in the test were presented with excerpts from writings by Russian authors (Pushkin, Lermontov, Gogol, Tolstoy, Turgenev, and Bely) and asked to arrange them with respect to stylistic preference (the experiment was carried out using the same non-metric multidimensional scaling technique). The analysis showed that one of the qualities of prose style perceived by the readers and influencing their judgements was what we call lucidity of style. This can be defined as being directly proportional to the concreteness of the associations induced in readers. In linguistic terms, this att ibute can be expressed as the ratio between the number of the verbs used in a text and the total number of the verbs, nouns, and adjectives. According to the investigators, the results indicated that some readers prefer concrete and material images (the lucid style) while others prefer a certain degree of abstraction. Those liking a lucid style ranked Pushkin and late-period Tolstoy higher while those with the opposite inclination preferred Gogol, Turgenev, and Bely.

These examples demonstrate that modelling provides the basic cybernetic method for evaluating and analyzing works of art. Convincing computer simulations of the creative process have been obtained by Zaripov. His concept of "machine music" clearly shows the orientation towards discovering the patterns (simple though they may be) of which the composer is usually unaware in the process of composition. One of such patterns, as brought to light by this analysis of composition, is the transfer of invariable relations from one piece of music to another.

All that has been said enables us to interpret properly the meaning of "machine music" and "machine poetry". Machine "composes" new melodies using the structural patterns in music that are based on mathematical models. Obviously, the creator of a piece of machine music is not the computer nor the mathematician carrying out the research, nor the programmer, nor even those composers whose music was analyzed for their composition patterns subsequently inserted in the program. Rather, the creator is the whole man-machine system, that is made up of all these constituents.

The same can be said about "machine poetry". Of the six verses presented above the first, the fourth, and the sixth were "composed" by the computer. The mathematical model and the principles used for the program[9] made it possible to imitate the artistic style of a poet and his vocabulary. In our case, the "machine" verses were composed by a computer whose memory was loaded with a vocabulary borrowed from a collection of poems by Mandelshtam (the human verses were written by Pasternak). As the reader could see, the poetry written by the man-machine system was unsatisfactory. It would be opportune to recall a remark by Kolmogorov, who said that in order to make a computer write poetry as well as great poets do, the society in which the poets developed must first be modelled. Apparently Pasternak's verses proved hardly distinguishable from "machine"-Mandelshtam's because first, the verses had been specially selected and taken out of the poem's context and second, the poems are perhaps not Pasternak's best. As to the "machine" verses, the punctuation, which has a great effect on the perception of the written verse, was done by a human.

In summing up our discussion of cybernetic methods as applied to art, let us point out an important trend. The evolution of science or, rather, of a series of scientific disciplines dealing with art, is moving towards a wider aim: from the analysis of "the beautiful", of art and its elements, and of aesthetic perception to the evaluation of cultural phenomena at large. In this paper our emphasis has been on strictly scientific procedures; on reproducible experimental results, including those obtained by computation and modelling techniques; on the accumulation of results, that will allow the addition of more recent achievements in modelling to knowledge already existing; and, finally, on positive orientation towards the practice of planning and management in the cultural field. We shall discuss the last in the next section.

Cybernetics of Culture

Scientists in the Soviet Union and other countries are taking more and more interest in the social processes that occur in modern artistic culture. Systems-engineering and cybernetics approaches and methods are being increasingly applied to the field.

Cultural and aesthetic phenomena in their social milieu have of course also long been studied with the use of mathematics. Mme de Staël in her book *De la littérature considérée dans ses rapports avec les institutions sociales*, published in 1800, proposed a procedure for surveying literature and of the reading public mathematically. In the Soviet Union sociological surveys of literature and reading started at the end of the last century and continued in the subsequent decades. The tastes, interests, and views of the public concerning the graphic arts have been studied in the Tretyakov Art Gallery in Moscow and in the Russian Museum in Leningrad. Meyerhold studied theater-goers, the types and frequency of their response to what was happening on the stage; while Eisenstein introduced strict analytical techniques of surveying cinema audiences (in one instance, he studied how viewers responded to his "Potemkin"). These and other studies of that period were experimentally founded and used statistical methods. A new stage came at the beginning of the 1960s, when cybernetic and mathematical computer-aided modelling methods began to be applied on a large scale. The research has covered every institutional form of culture: the cinema, theater, art exhibitions, musical activities, and so forth. The aesthetic needs of different social groups, attendance at cultural events, the evaluation of plays productions by social and age groups and especially by the young have all come to be the subject of research. The goal was to break down the barriers existing in the study of culture (for instance, the organization of leisure activities in clubs was conducted without regard for the surveys of cinema, television and bookselling, or theatre criticism was not complemented with analysis of the social function of the other arts). It became apparent that only integrated research using modern data-processing equipment is capable of clarifying trends in cultural development, and allows realistic prediction and planning in cultural fields to be made. This research could therefore be termed the social cybernetics of culture. The urgent need for long-term and current planning of cultural development and for a method for evaluating decisions whose implementation demands much time and labour and involves significant restructuring of the existing socio-cultural cycles and institutions, requires intensive work in this field. Today, decisions in the cultural sphere cannot be made by intuition; the object to be controlled is so intricate that the analysis required to plan rationally is beyond the power of even teams of people, to say nothing of individuals, unless they have the modern ways of processing and communicating formal data. It is obvious that the direction of cultural development must be supported by science and technology, which make it possible to take decisions with far-reaching implications.

One of the authors of this paper has outlined the main ways in which the efficiency of directing the development of culture can be increased. These are: orientation towards a goal currently set (upgrading the cultural level of the population, improving the production of works of art, and so on); the effective use of economic incentives; the development of rational criteria for assessing the state of socio-cultural processes; and the introduction of a special service for collecting relevant information using automated information systems with massive data bases. These guide lines should help create a sound structure and adequate methods for monitoring cultural processes. In fact, we are talking about the comprehensive target-oriented planning of socio-cultural processes based on substantiated long-term predictions of cultural development in its various aspects and on the analysis of alternative decisions from the angle of short and long-term effects. This seems to be the only way of tackling such an important problem as the cultural development of rural areas, a task that is influenced by many factors and by the great cultural diversity of different regions of the country.

The development of culture, the need for improved managerial activities and greater efficiency in the scientific research in this area, all make it necessary to work out a cybernetic-based methodology for socially analyzing culture. In effect, this is a systems approach since culture is here being considered to be a single, intricate, stable, and purpose-oriented system, having a definite structure, function and informational process; the working tools to be used are quantitative evaluation and measurement, and the results obtained are clearly oriented towards application for monitoring cultural processes.

It was shown that the cybernetic systems approach to artistic culture can be embodied in the form of a social analysis of culture encompassing general, special, and empirical sociological levels. On these levels, particularly on the second and third, culture is studied empirically, using measurements and mathematics, while practical applications cover the areas of strategic, tactical, and immediate guidance of cultural institutions.

Culture as a system is a structural combination of three subsystems: production of art, which involves a whole range of attendant processes and relations; aesthetic needs; and a social institution (or institutions) of artistic culture. The last subsystem is the "closing link" connecting the other two, because the relationship and interaction between artistic production and consumption take place within the framework of an organizational setup (formal or non-formal) of the social institutions.

Research into the dynamics of informational processes

within the artistic culture system shows that it gives rise to flows of aesthetic, sociological, economic and other kinds of information, which connect individual links of the system and make for its development. The knowledge of trends in informational processes and of the character of socio-dynamic cycles gives insight into the "feedback", that is to say, the effect artistic culture has on society, which is essential for planning and direction. This knowledge is gained in sociological surveys, which are actively conducted in the Soviet Union.

The last few years have seen some comprehensive studies into the various kinds, forms, processes, and phenomena of culture; analyses of activities of diverse cultural institutions; and sociological surveys in many regions of the USSR. As a result, a number of steady trends have been revealed. It has come to light, for instance, that among the population as a whole (without its classification into social groups) most of the leisure time allocated to cultural pursuits is dedicated to literature (reading), to plays on the radio and TV, and to the cinema; a distant second to these pursuits come the theatre, symphonic music, and the graphic arts. The notion that the cultural needs of a person are closely associated with his or her education has been confirmed statistically. A large body of data has been collected concerning the character of cultural needs, aesthetic judgements, attendance at various cultural institutions, and other forms of attitude to artistic culture shown by people belonging to different social groups. It should be noted that socio-cultural surveys do not always cover different sociological phenomena equally well. Thus, for instance, more attention should be paid to studying the relationships between the different arts and their social function, to their relationships with the media, and to finding out the attitude of people towards the relics of history and their preservation. To solve these questions, it is necessary to overcome such difficulties as the problem of comparing data obtained through different procedures and from different samples, dissimilarity of socio-demographic characteristics, and so on. Without this solution it will often be difficult to apply mathematical methods and computer technology, an application that ought to strengthen links between socio-cultural research and management of culture.

Of great significance for socio-psychological surveys of artistic culture are the various canvassing techniques (questionnaires, interviews, and so forth) and Delphi methods, content analysis as a source of information treated by correlation, factor, dispersion, and some other analytical methods. For example, a treatment of public opinion on dramatic performances by semantic differentiation made it possible to predict the effect of certain plays on certain audiencies. Another example is provided by the development of a "social portrait". This work was based on the statistically processed results of a sociological poll, which gave answers to a number of questions initially formulated as qualitative hypotheses. These answers confirmed a methodologically important point that the participation in amateur artistic activities not only reflects a person's attitude to art and not only is governed by one's aesthetic needs, but also correlates with the scope of the person's general cultural interests and socio-cultural activity[10].

The research programmes run by Research Institute of Culture under the RSFSR Ministry of Culture are interesting from the socio-managerial point of view. One of these attempted to quantify such an intrinsically qualitative phenomenon as the culture of a rural district. A system of parameters was devised, and they were grouped into a relatively small number of factors relating to two sides of rural culture: its material base and consumption for the year under study.

Computer processing of a large body of data yielded a finite number of integral characteristics, which were used to make comparative analyses of the cultural levels of different districts.[11] In another paper, a new computer-aided approach was developed to evaluate the efficiency of cultural institutions[12]. This approach was based on the comparison of two blocks of data: "measurements of the activity of a cultural institution" and "measurements of the effect of these activities". The two blocks were compared within a dynamic-system simulation model that combined the ability of a human expert to think non-formally and the capability of the computer to simulate a complex process with subsequently analyzing its numerous variants. The effect of activity of a cultural institution was assessed by a "personal culture index" calculated by the computer. Basic data for this index was obtained by socio-psychological tests of a sample group of respondents taken from the people who "consumed the products" of the given institution.

We believe that quantifying such qualitative phenomena as aesthetic needs, interests, tastes, preferences, and the like, is an important task in order to ensure a prompt and reliable service for collecting social information in the cultural field; this service must be an indispensable element in developing management information systems for culture. Such a service, upgraded to the level of computer-based information-search systems, can considerably facilitate cultural guidance.

Experience gained at the Computer Centre of the RSFSR Ministry of Culture has shown that both the methodological and organizational problems of collecting and analyzing the relevant socio-economic and socio-psychological information can be successfully tackled.

By having a system of measurable characteristics of culture, adequate mathematical data processing methods, and experience in developing computer-implemented models, it is possible to solve the difficult questions concerning the relation between prediction and plan and to work out a single concept of cultural development more efficiently. Such a concept must outline: the spheres of planning—the object (culture in its various guises) and the subject (cultural administration) of the study of culture; the levels of planning—strategic (a nation-wide programme for cultural development), tactical (culture as a branch of the economy), and immediate (plans for cultural institutions' activities); methods of planning—extrapolation, normative, and goal-oriented; kinds of planning—territorial, sectoral, inter-departmental, and comprehensive; and finally planning in terms of time—long-term, medium-term (five-year), and short-term (one-year). This concept should serve the purpose of transition to a comprehensive goal-oriented planning in the cultural sphere. Such planning should take into account the structure and aspects of culture as a large system in the cybernetic sense. In a socialist society culture manifests itself on the one hand as administration (embodied in a group of ministries and departments) and on the other, as an infrastructure encompassing and penetrating every part of social life, since the cultural level of the people irrespective of their occupation is of great importance. A target-oriented approach can take account of both of these sides of culture, translating prognostications into the language of plan targets (covering the material basis of culture, cultural workers, the study of culture, cultural administration, and the cultural level of the people as a whole). The plan, based on the optimum (within given time limits) variant of the forecast, should schedule the achievement of the targets, should allocate the necessary funds, and should establish the geography of culture. Success in research based on this approach largely depends on joint efforts of scientists, administrative workers, and planners. What was said many years ago by G.M. Krzhizhanovsky, the first head of GOSPLAN of the USSR, holds true today: "I think that the science of planning, like any other science, will come into being as theory develops in response to practical needs".[13] A significant contribution to satisfying the practical needs of today can be made by cybernetics, which appears to be the most practical of all theoretical scientific disciplines.

References

1. Зарипов Р. Х. Музыка и искусственный интеллект. *Число и мысль*, вып. 3. Москва, 1980, 176-177.
2. Аствацатрян Л. Роль ЭВМ в создании серийного материала симфонии. *Материалы первого всесоюзного семинара по машинным аспектам алгоритмического анализа музыкальных текстов*. Ереван, 1977.
3. Moles A.A. *Sociodynamique de la culture*. Paris, La Hoye, 1967.
4. Файн В. С. Человеко-машинный диалог в художественном творчестве, Москва (Научный совет по комплексной проблеме «Кибернетика», АН СССР), 1977, 15.
5. Мельников Л. Н. Комнаты психологической разгрузки, *Машиностроитель*, 1978, I.
   Мельников Л. Н. Светозвуковой релаксатор, *Машиностроитель*, 1978, 9.
6. Дмитриевский В. Н., Докторов Б. З. Как измерить театральный репертуар. *Число и мысль*, вып. 3, Москва, 1980.
7. Петров В. М., В. С. Грибков и В. С. Калинский. Проверить гармонию... экспериментом. *Число и мысль*, Москва, 1980.
8. Налимов В. В. *Вероятностная модель языка* (Москва, 1974).

14—01169

9. *Автоматика и телемеханика*, 1978, 8.
10. Михайлова Н. Г. Социальный портрет участника художественной самодеятельности. *Социология культуры*, вып. 3, Москва, 1976.
11. Мучник И. Б., Г. С. Новиков и С. Н. Плотников. Об одной статистической выборке, обусловленной специфическими требованиями социологического исследования культуры. *Социология культуры*, вып. 3, Москва, 1976.
12. Измерение и прогнозирование в культуре. *Труды НИИ культуры*, 71, Москва, 1978.
13. Кржижановский Г. М. *Проблемы планирования*. Соч. т. 2, Москва-Ленинград, 1934.

Modelling in Music

R. Kh. ZARIPOV

Perhaps no topic of cybernetics attracts as much attention or arouses as much heated discussion and controversy as the relationship between cybernetics and art. Most of the interest in this problem is stimulated by its seeming simplicity: many people tend to believe that no special knowledge is required to evaluate machine art. In fact, the situation is much more complicated.

Any lack of a thorough understanding of the problem, and a superficial approach to the assessment of machine composition, often leads to misapprehension and confusion, especially when human and machine creations are compared.

Computer Simulation of Creativity

The advent of electronic computers has given rise to a new, objective method of studying creativity, namely computer simulation (modelling).

Simulation is the artificial reproduction or imitation of the object being studied (a process or condition), or more accurately, an imitation of those properties that are of interest to the investigator. The need for the object to be artificially reproduced in the process of simulation leads to an understanding of its essential properties and so contributes to acquiring knowledge about it.

Modelling creation by computer in the various arts, such as painting, dancing, poetry or music, holds great appeal.

It helps elucidate the nature of intuition, this actually existing, but still incomprehensible, mysterious entity, vital for any creative process.

The general laws of creativity can be studied on different objects, but it is essential that the results obtained in a simulation should be manifest and similar in form to the respective human productions and elicit the same response.

Music is an ideal object for investigations of this kind.

With regard to the feasibility of simulation, music stands out from other arts. Music, in a sense, is an expressive and not representative art. A musical composition reflects reality without showing its specific visible features. This facilitates the computer simulation of musical composition. This should be taken to mean that when simulating simple forms of music the results should be comparable with the product of professional composers and, according to listeners' evaluations, be indistinguishable from them. In contrast, the computer simulation of other types of artistic creation (for instance, dance, poetry, or painting in the forms that are accessible to an average audience) is either less spectacular than analogous human productions or requires special knowledge and experience in order to be analysed and evaluated.

The Computer Simulation of Music

The research into music using electronic computers is conducted along four lines both here and abroad.

1. The development of special programming language for inputing, processing (for instance, analysis), and retrieving musical information and for generating programs.

2. Analysis of musical compositions (structural analysis, comparison of style, and so on) in order to clarify the internal formal relations (largely statistical) between elements of composition. The American mathematician and musician M. Kassler devised an algorithm for identifying dodecaphonic melodies[1].

An interesting topic in this respect is finding the parameters that change from one style to another but remain invariable or alter insignificantly within the same style. Thus, the West German physicist W. Fucks[2] has found musical parameters that characterize the evolution of some formal structural elements in Western music over the last five centuries.

3. Sound reproduction by means of computers having an acoustic output in order to synthesize timbres that imitate the sound of both traditional instruments and new instruments. This, in particular, opens a possibility of investigating some problems in the psychology of perception.

This line of research also includes investigations connected with pianola-type problems, that is, using a computer to generate sound sequences given by a musical notation. These experiments are based on the assumption that the score of a musical composition is a system of instructions for a musician, which designates primarily the pitch, duration, and volume of each sound. It also contains indications of the timbre and various suggestions on dynamic accents and performance peculiarities. Evidently, a score may be regarded as an algorithm or a program a musician executes during the performance.

Hence, such a "program" can be entered into a computer with an acoustic output. By using a digital-to-analogue converter, the computer synthesizes sounds according to a specified program, the sounds corresponding to notes written in a digital code, that is, the computer "plays from the music". The computer can imitate the polyphonic and polytimbre sound of an orchestra.

It is noteworthy that the computer as a musical instrument overcomes the limitations that have so far been imposed by physical and mechanical factors on the performance capabilities of conventional instruments.

To date, all the research programs in this field have not gone much beyond the mechanical reproduction of a score, which of course is rather far from a real musical performance.

4. Experiments on the synthesis of musical compositions by the computer are conducted in order to find or prove the laws of composition which are commonly used by composers unconsciously, that is, by intuition.

The computer can also be helpful as a generator of "semi-finished music", that is, preliminary variants of various combinations of sounds. This has proved to be especially convenient when composing music of "a non-traditional structure". Out of a host of "semi-finished" pieces, the composer chooses (without the computer) the best variants and includes them in his composition. This is an example of a man-machine system in music. The composer may also use computer-made fragments to compose music of a traditional structure, as the Italian cyberneticist and musician E. Gagliardo does.[3]

Below we consider the simulation of musical composition with the electronic computer, in which the computer synthesizes a complete piece of music without human intervention in the process of composition.

Man-machine systems and computer simulation are two main ramifications of the problem of creation of artificial intelligence, a line of research which has recently been extensively developed both in this country and abroad.

Two methods of simulating musical composition with electronic computers are known.

(a) The first method rests on the principle of exclusively local interconnection between sounds. Homophonic compositions alone can be synthesized by this method, which draws upon the theory of Markov chains. This form of analysis was developed by the Russian mathematician Markov in 1913 for investigating poetry. The experiment is based on the assumption that the number of related adjacent notes is not large statistically. This number varies with different researchers from zero to seven. While very attractive in form, this technique relies solely upon a local interrelation of sounds and does not yield and, more than that, cannot yield satisfactory results. This is the method that was mentioned by Academician Kolmogorov in his article *Automata and Life* as an example of the simplistic approach to cybernetics in the field of the computer composition of music. The fallacy of the approach is that it ignores some of the important properties of music. These include the system of harmonic intervals that is based on the tonic and non-tonic notes of the scale, and the structure of a composition, in which the rhythmic and melodic figures in the melody are repeated and which divide it into its separate components (bars, phrases, and themes). In listening, these characteristics of music contribute to an easier appreciation of the various intonations and themes. These laws are more critical and definitive for music than local interrelations. This is especially manifest in experiments on modelling music of a certain type, where the melodies generated by the computer by this method are compared with human-composed reference melodies. The results of these experiments testify (obviously, against the intentions of their authors) to the fact that all the notes in a melody are interrelated and not a few adjacent ones.

Moreover, the method fails to clarify any interconnection between the various elements of a musical composition, and the presence and formalization of the principles, rules, and laws by which musical compositions are arranged. But this is the most important aspect for the theoretical science of music and for understanding intuitive activity.

(b) Another method, which we call the structural method, appears to be more promising. It rests on incorporating the rules and laws of musical composition which have previously been found into the program.

How a Computer Composes Music

In what follows I am going to discuss a method of devising algorithms that I have synthesized and the "structural" technique for simulating some of the functions of a composer and musicologist. Various programs to be run on a computer have been compiled and it can now compose tunes, homophonic musical pieces. The rhythm of a verse (the sequence of stressed and unstressed syllables) can be fed into the computer, and it will compose music for this verse, that is, produce a song. The computer can also imitate some of the learning activities of students at musical colleges and conservatories, viz. it is able to solve, and without errors, problems to do with the harmonization of melodies. Students tend to make errors in such problems and if given a solution containing a mistake of this kind, a computer will indicate it. Such a program serves the function of an examiner and is a prototype of a teaching system*. In addition, a computer can compose single homophonic variations on a given musical theme.

The structure of the computer program is of paramount importance for conducting experiments in the simulation of creative processes. Obviously, the chief purpose of such a program is experimentation and continual improvement rather than the mass production of computerized music. Therefore, the program should be easy to devise and handle and capable of being changed within certain limits. To put it another way, the program should be flexible enough to accommodate experiments of various kinds, and the structure of the algorithm should meet these requirements.

The principle of devising an algorithm for a musical composition is as follows.

Different elements of the composition (a note, a chord, the type of structure, the random distribution of note values or intervals, and so on) are sampled using a random-number generator by an appropriate coding technique.

A composition is synthesized according to a set of the programmed rules of composition. The random number generator produces one note after another. If a note meets the set of rules, it is placed onto the stave. Otherwise, the note is rejected, and another is considered. The process continues till the composition is completed and recorded in a coded form.

Now let us consider how the algorithm is arranged. Any musical composition is characterized, both syntactically

---

* These programs are described in detail in *Cybernetics and Music* (Moscow, Nauka, 1971) by the author.

and semantically, by a set of parameters that reflect the rules, patterns, and elements of its structure and development. The range of pitch, the time, the distribution of interval frequencies, the number of tones in the octave may all be used as parameters. Each of the parameters can have several values. The value of a parameter is a number or a set of numbers, a law of distribution of the frequencies of an interval, a set of chords, and so on, taken out of the multitude of the values admitted by the program.

What we mean by the type of composition is a characteristic of the music that is peculiar to a number of compositions (e.g. style, genre, emotional colouring, and the like). Dance music, waltzes, Strauss waltzes, loudness, melodiousness, variability and so on, may all be referred to the type.

Simulation is based on the assumption that any type (characteristic) of a composition is defined by a number of parameters contained in a set of the permissible values.

Thus, a formal and quantitative characteristic (a set of parameter values) is assigned to each qualitative characteristic (the type of a composition). Accordingly, in order to model a composition of a certain type, the coded values of the parameters are loaded into the computer memory. In this way, the computer is given a set of rules that should govern the future composition. The program is formed, or "tuned", automatically by these codes. Here, a single specified value is selected out of the programmed values of each parameter. If the value of a parameter was not specified, then when forming the program it is chosen randomly.

It is now apparent that only some of the rules are used to synthesize a composition. This part is given by the set of parameters that determine the type of composition. Programs using this principle illustrate how quantity (the set of parameter values) is converted into quality (the type of music).

The computer composition is recorded together with the list of rules that were used for its synthesis, that is, the structure of the composition is indicated. This makes possible various psychological experiments, for instance, in musical perception. In this way, a relationship can be found between the structure of music and its emotional effect on the listener.

The method we have described can also be helpful for analysing musical compositions, when the mechanism of composing certain types of music needs to be clarified. Here, a direct analysis of a musical piece is replaced by a formal analysis of the synthesized (computer-generated) music which is near in type to the given piece.

How to Evaluate Computer Music

We have already noted that the object of the experiments is to investigate the laws of artistic creativity rather than to compose music.

An analysis of a phenomenon commonly gives rise to various hypotheses about the laws governing it and a computer simulation is a powerful method of testing such hypotheses. When modelling music on a computer, the music is bound to be machine music whether we like it or not—such is the nature of simulation. Computer compositions are, in a way, "by-products". But the "by-products" are still worth discussing.

The fact is that the criterion of the quality and perfection of the program from which the computer operates and composes music is the degree to which the computer music and its human counterpart are similar. What is important here is not the absolute quality of computer music, but that it should resemble as closely as possible the music we investigate.

In this sense, a computer capable of closely simulating the programmed types of composition, individual styles, genres, peculiarities of folk music, and so on, can play a key part in studying the laws of composition and musical creativity. The development of such a computer, or rather such a program, would define the extent of knowledge about creativity, that is, the level of knowledge that a computer is able to reproduce at the time. Computer compositions serve as a criterion of how thorough our knowledge and formal objective description of the mechanism of creativity is.

However, a problem arises as to how computer compositions can be evaluated and compared with works by human composers. They can only be evaluated by listening to them. The problem is connected with listener psychology. For this reason, an objective comparison of music composed by a man and by a computer calls for a special experiment, to overcome the psychological bias of listeners. It is essential that they should not know beforehand what they are going to assess—computer or human music. In addition, the experiment should provide an objective evaluation of computer compositions as compared with human ones, that is, to show their quality.

What music should then be chosen for comparison with computer melodies? Obviously, we may not compare incommensurate things, for instance, a song and a monumental concert composition like a symphony. The compositions must have similar durations, structure, and syntactic complexities.

For my experiment I chose melodies by notable Soviet composers from published song anthologies and the same number (eight) of melodies composed by an Ural-2 computer. All of these melodies were played in an arbitrary order unknown to the listeners. The listeners were to mark each of them using a five-grade scale and to put the grades down on a special questionnaire. The experiment had to be staged on a large scale to exclude random factors.

Several different groups with approximately equal levels of musical knowledge were formed among the participants. They included students at the Moscow Electrical Energy Institute, students at the Gnesins Musical Education Institute, participants in a symposium on the problems of musical perception, secondary school students, mathematicians participating in a methodology seminar sponsored by the Steklov Mathematical Institute and the Computing Centre of the USSR Academy of Sciences, artists from the Bolshoi Theatre, and people working for various cultural organizations, in all over 600 participants.

In addition, a similar experiment was conducted on two national radio programmes on 25 August, 1973 and 29 June, 1976.

The results of the experiment were varied. As in any sociological study, conclusions were based on averaged marks.

The procedure of the experiment proved itself since it helped the participants to overcome the psychological bias we mentioned earlier. The listeners failed to differentiate between human and computer music although they believed they had. Thus, one of the participants wrote on his questionnaire: "All computer music is not real music, it lacks feeling...", but he nevertheless gave preference to computer melodies. The table of his evaluation marks clearly shows this.

	Mark	5	4	3
	Computer	2	3	3
Composer	Human	0	1	7

5 = excellent
4 = good
3 = average
2 = poor
1 = terrible

The experiment showed that every group gave the computer compositions better marks by various criteria than they did to human compositions. Here, for instance, are the results of the poll of the students of the Gnesin Institute (70 questionnaires):

	Mark	5	4	3	2	1	
Composer	Computer	76	253	204	22	5	$S_c=3.67$
	Human	61	213	247	31	8	$S_h=3.51$

The table shows how many marks were received by the melodies composed by the computer and human composers (S_c and S_h are the respective averaged marks).

This experiment has been conducted several more times including a musically experienced audience. All these results showed that the computer simulation of simple musical forms (song or dance melodies) is capable of producing compositions that are not only comparable with human ones, but that excel them in a number of instances.

It is noteworthy that the melodies by composers used in the experiment (independent of their quality or listener approval) are the result of a human activity considered to be a creative one. If these human compositions are works of art, it is only logical to rank the computer compositions which were appreciated by the listeners still higher as works of art, too.

A reader familiar with *Computing Machinery and Intelligence* by Turing[4] will be aware that the experiment we carried out is an "imitation game" (the Turing test) applied to music. The Turing test ascertains the presence of "intelligence" by the results of an "imitation game". The play involves a human expert and two systems A and B, one of which is a person and the other, a machine. The expert asks the systems questions, and by analyzing their answers, must determine which of the two systems is the machine. If he fails to do so in a specified length of time, the machine is considered to be "intelligent".

The results of our experiment indicate that our program composer has passed the Turing test.

Computer-Plagiarist

When simulating compositions of certain type, a computer generates a variety of melodies having some common characteristic. This phase of modelling confirms the general laws of the given type of composition. The following phase in furthering our knowledge about musical laws is to create a program that will make the computer synthesize melodies that exactly match a composition being investigated.

Here, of a great interest is what we call borrowing in music. Borrowing and the ensuing artistic treatment, that is, the transformation or variation of the musical themes is not plagiarism in a general sense of the word. Many composers have deliberately used popular melodies, mostly folk songs. For instance, Rimski Korsakov used the tune "Chizhik-Pyzhik" in the aria of Tsar Dodon in his opera "The Golden Cockerel" and the theme "Vó polye berézanka stoyála" is used in the final movement of Tchaikovsky's fourth symphony.

One of the most striking examples of this kind is Tchaikovky's use of the theme "Rococo" for his famous cello variations. H. Stein cites a talk between the composer and his friend, the cellist W. Fitzenhagen: "Do you know what rococo is?" Tchaikovsky once asked. Fitzenhagen nodded. "I think," Tchaikovsky said after a pause, "that it is light, undisturbed joy (schwebende Heiterkeit)...", and he sang a short tune resembling a gavotte[5].

Light, undisturbed joy is indeed a surprising association, considering that the melody of the bubbling folksong "Along the Piterskaya" was being transformed into "rococo" form in the composer's mind at that time. That the rococo theme originated from this melody can be seen from a comparison of the two themes. However, the ear does not always hear what the eye sees, and the likeness of these melodies is not easy to feel when listening.

Very often, as we listen to a theme and its variations, we perceive intuitively their similarity and interrelation. This occurs because a variation retains some invariable elements.

They are, however, thoroughly masked by changeable elements, such as rhythm, time, scale, and the melody line itself. These masking elements often transform a theme beyond recognition.

What Is in Store?

The future application of computers to music could well be the subject of unbridled conjecture. But we have limited ourselves to a discussion of some problems that are likely to be solved in near future.

Although research on the application of computers to music is conducted along a number of different lines, the results that have been obtained have been virtually unused in practice. The obstacles to this are engineering rather than fundamental ones in nature. The results of laboratory experimentation have failed so far to catch on. However, we are not a long way off from the day when computers will be essential teaching aids at conservatories (as they are today in many engineering colleges) for, say, checking solutions to problems in harmonization or fugue compositions.

Music students are not accustomed to the coded notation of tones in the form of numbers, but computers already have output devices capable of recording results in the form of graphs or notes. If an automatic music reading device is added, the important problem of the machine copying of music will be practically solved.

We have just discussed a program that composes variations on a chosen theme. An attractive idea is to attempt to solve the reverse problem, namely, to reconstruct the initial theme from a given melody. This may be either some kind of "simplification" of the melody or a search for its original that is, establishing the fact that it has been borrowed. (This would be similar to the program for analysing harmonization problems and finding errors in students solutions).

The first variant of the problem is the simpler because of its ambiguity. The second variant requires not only a gigantic computer memory to store an enormous quantity of possible melodies, but also a fast method of comparing melodies (like the one man uses).

Similar problems arise when retrieving data from memory. Thus, a chess program that plays "at grand-master level", which is at present much discussed, is inconceivable without taking past experience into account. It is evident because thinking over the next move reminds the chess player of similar positions he has chosen (mostly unconsciously) from the immense number of games both he and other chess masters have played. Accordingly, a good chess program should not only store a great number of games, but also (and here lies the greatest difficulty) be capable of quickly retrieving a game that is relevant for the position in question.

We need to learn to identify melodies not just to be able to establish the fact of "plagiarism" and "denounce" the plagiarist (these will again be unavoidable by-products) but in order to compile a catalogue of melodies and their variations or a "dictionary" of musical themes, and to clarify other problems associated with the creation of a musical library of the future.

Let us take a look at the prospects of reproducing sound

with a computer. The simulation of the polyphonic sound of an orchestra will help a composer working on an orchestral piece listen to rough variants of his symphonic music that use new and uncommon timbre combinations. Not all composers can hear mentally their compositions in orchestral sound, and faults detected when listening to a piece of music played by a symphony orchestra are difficult to correct.

The simulation of a musical performance is another very interesting field of research. Here the problem is to see how performance style changes with different performers. When listening, we instinctively feel this difference in personal style. Indeed, the unique touch of Daniil Shafran cannot be confused with the performance manner of any other cellist. Our intuition implies that there are laws which can be made manifest.

As for verifying hypotheses about these laws, the same method of testing, that is, computer simulation of the performance process, can be applied.

The problem of the impartial assessment of musical performance is also essential. Here is the opinion of a prominent pianist and piano teacher G.G. Neuhaus[7]. In an article dedicated to the preparation for the Tchaikovsky International Competition in 1962 he wrote: “Perhaps, in our age of cybernetics, the day will soon come when highly-organized... electronic computers assisted, of course, by human musicians will play the foremost part in the judgement and evaluation of individual performance at musical competitions. And I expect from those future computers the accuracy and freedom from error of which people are not capable.”

Discussions on the prospects of composing music with a computer often give rise to the opinion that a computer can only imitate known musical structures and styles. It is even admitted that the learning capacity of the computer can be brought to the point where it will be able to reproduce the styles of known composers. But the computer, it is argued, will be no more than a "good craftsman": it will be beyond its capability to create anything new and original or somehow to prefigure the styles of future composers. These views are erroneous because they ignore the capabilities of some types of computer programs. Using the method of devising algorithms described earlier in this article, a computer can go beyond the bounds set by prescribed rules. It can, for instance, complement the set of values permissible for a parameter that was obtained beforehand as it is creating the piece by new values not found during the initial analysis and therefore not included in the program. The resultant composition may differ substantially from the analysed one and contain features that were not at first envisaged.

To make this point clear, let us consider simple examples of parameters with their sets of values, initial and additional, which can thus generate structures unknown in musical practice. Suppose the analysis revealed the parameter "time" and its two values 2/4 and 4/4. Let us assume that as it was synthesizing a composition, a computer added another value, 3/4, to the set. Then, the set will consist of three elements: 2/4, 3/4, and 4/4, and the resultant composition will also be in three time signatures: 2/4, 3/4, and 4/4. It is important that the 3/4 time signature was not initially identified and entered into the program. It is known, however, that music in 3/4 is a new structure and is quite different emotionally from music in 2/4 or 4/4, that is, a waltz or mazurka differs from a march or a charleston.

Thus, novel syntactic structures and orders can arise from a mere increase in the range of the values of the initially specified parameters. The following parameters may be varied: "the number of notes in the offbeat", "the number of tones in the octave", and many others. It will be recalled that as regards the parameter "the number of tones in the octave", the i teger 5 corresponds to the pentatonic scale (Korean, Tartar, Hungarian, and other music), the integer 7 to the diatonic scale (common European music) and the integer 12, to atonal music and, in particular, to the dodecaphonic scale. And these three structural arrangements of musical sounds produce quite different impressions on the mind of the hearer.

These examples show the feasibility (in principle and in practice) to extend the number of classes of compositions, initially chosen for analysis, within the predetermined rules. Hence a computer is able not only to imitate known compositions, but also to create novel musical structures and thus to anticipate the techniques of future composers.

Computers may prove useful for carrying into effect and elaborating the musical ideas of composers, who for instance could choose one of the compositions produced by the computer. It is possible that in the not so distant future, computers will be capable of composing musical ideas themselves. Leaving this question aside, we should like to note that the selection of promising styles seems to be a more vital and considerably more complicated task than the creation of new styles. Incidentally this is also an important problem in other branches of cybernetics, for instance, in evaluating theorems.

We now approach a problem that might be called "the problem of the masterpiece", that is, the problem of creating a composition that will outlive its creator. This is not a technological problem because a musical masterpiece is selected, speaking figuratively, by time and not by the composer.

Let us recall Saglieri, who in his time was an outstanding musician, both composer and teacher. His pupils included Beethoven, Liszt, Schubert and many other famous composers. His music was perhaps no less popular than Mozart's, and his operas were staged by many European theatres. This all seemed to predict that the immortal fame of a great composer would be his. But time decreed otherwise: you can hardly hear Saglieri's music anywhere nowadays, and even his name is usually mentioned only in connection with the well-known legend.

References

1. Kassler, M. *The Decisions of Arnolde Schoemberg's Twelve Note-Class System and Related Systems.* Princeton, 1961.
2. Fucks, W. *Nach allen Regeln der Kunst.* Deutsche Verlags-Anstalt. Stuttgart, 1968.
3. Gagliardo, E. Introduzione all'edizione Italiano. In: R. Ch. Zaripov. *Musica con il Calcolatore.* Padova: Muzzio, 1979.
4. Turing, A. M. Computing Machinery and Intelligence, Mind, 59, 433-460. Reprinted in E. Feigenbaum and J. Feldman (eds.) *Computers and Thought.* McGraw-Hill Book Company, New York, 1963.
5. Stein, R. H. *Tschaikowsky.* Deutsche Verlags-Anstalt. Stuttgart, 1927.
6. Зарипов Р. Х. *Машинный поиск вариантов при моделировании творческого процесса* (Москва, 1983).
7. Нейгауз Г. Г. Желаю удачи! *Советская музыка*, 1962, 3.

Polemics and Its By-Products: About the "Machine Creativeness" Controversy

I. GREKOVA

Can the machine think? Is it capable of creating on its own?

This topic has already become a commonplace. From time to time the disputes quiet down and then flare up again. Well, there is nothing wrong in it. Arguments about the feasibility of "machine thinking" each time give us reason to reflect on what the process of reasoning is. The important thing here is to cast off the conventional opinions and overcome the triteness of the accepted stereotypes. Perhaps, it is for this reason that consideration of heated debates concerning this subject appears to be interesting. Such debates, as a rule, come to nothing: both sides come away from these verbal clashes each all the more convinced (if possible) that its view is right.

So what is the controversy all about, anyway?

At first sight, the topic may seem far-fetched, even pointless. The very formulation of the question brings to one's mind a well-known medieval proposition: "Can Almighty God create a stone too heavy for him to lift?" At one time, this question was the subject of animated disputes.

Many people see the reason of the argument in that the concepts under discussion are insufficiently clear: once the opposing parties have come to an agreement about what is "the machine" and what is "creativity", everything will be put right.

However, it is not definitions that matter here. When it comes to widely known and often used notions, rigorous verbal formulas are not very helpful. Take, for instance, the definition of the word "table" given in a dictionary: "a piece of furniture in the form of a wide horizontal board with long supports called legs". It is doubtful whether this definition can refine or enrich our idea of a table. In general, a concept's real meaning is formed not by its definition, but by all the experience one acquires in his social life and practical activities, and by an entire system of associations, images, analogies, and even emotions having to do with the object or phenomenon. This entire system may briefly be called a concept's "associative basis".

The question arises: is not the content of memory and the range of images different for different people? Does this imply that the meaning of concepts may not be the same for them?

Precisely that! There are not two people, and never were, who would attach exactly the same meaning to one and the same notion. We can talk only of a rough general coincidence of meanings. Such coincidence can be encountered in a group of people with a common psychology, culture, and range of information. If a common associative basis (common model) is absent, one and the same word may mean quite different things.

This is also how things seem to be in the disputes over "machine creativeness". It is no accident that the disputing parties represent two schools of thought: that of art and that of science. On the face of it, clear-cut and definite opinions clash, but actually, what comes in conflict is the distinct associative bases that gave rise to them.

In the process of society's historical development, concepts, too, do not remain unchanged: they are transformed, taking a new meaning, or die away. For example, the idea of a "machine" has quite a different meaning and content for us than for people of the last century. The same thing has happened right in front of us with the idea of space: quite specific, down-to-earth associations have taken the place of hazy, philosophic abstractions.

Thus, the meanings of words, expressions and concepts imminently change in the process of historical evolution. And obviously, priority in mastering notions belongs to those who face them more often and work with them. As the English saying goes "The proof of the pudding is in the eating". Undoubtedly, an engineer or a mathematician ascribes a fuller and more updated meaning to the notion "machine" or "automaton" than, say, a literary critic or an historian. On the other hand, it is doubtless (although, less apparent) that a scholar in the humanities has a certain advantage over the engineer or mathematician: the notions "reasoning" and "creativeness" have more profound significance for him because he thinks over them and makes use of them more often.

If we frequently encounter in art quarters a narrow, one-sided, and obsolete idea of "machine", then a superficial, primitive, and nihilistic attitude towards the notion "creativeness" is just as frequent among engineers. Some enthusiasts of engineering technology rashly declare that the first (and altogether modest) achievements in simulating certain creative functions of man are mature productions on the verge of replacing man as a creator or organizer. It is just these woeful enthusiasts calling for the immediate mathematization and automation of all human mental processes who are to blame for a great deal of misunderstanding that emerges around the problem of "the machine and creativeness".

Naturally, a discussion, held without mutual understanding is senseless. The only way at present to find an achievable approximation of truth, if not truth itself, may be an expansion and amplification of the associative bases of notions, and not for one side, but necessarily for both sides. The question is not, as some people think, that humanities-oriented people who are "behind the times" should be given the right notion of what a modern day machine really is, but that the two sides should, as far as possible, discuss one and the same thing, without polemical excesses and mutual accusations. We must try to get to the roots of the contradictions and bring the opposite points of view closer together on the basis of mutual understanding. It is much more useful to understand where the opposite side is correct rather than where it is wrong.

Let us get back, then, to the subject of the controversy. The question we raised at the beginning in a rather naive form, "Is a machine able to think?", can be developed into a somewhat detailed and rigorous proposition of the sort: is reasoning, creativeness, and so on, the prerogative of the human mind alone, or is the existence of intelligence possible in principle, in other forms, for instance, those artificially created by man.

That such a question should come up in our time is altogether natural. In recent years, machines (or automata, as scientists prefer to say) have begun to master at a fantastic rate some functions related to mental and creative activities which have always been the exclusive prerogative of man. Present-day machines control production processes and military actions, design engineering devices, execute traffic control functions, play checkers, chess, and other games, derive formulas and prove theorems, and "compose" poetry and music. Machines are being used as teaching aids, for instance, as "tutors" and "examiners". Work is being conducted on machine translation, machine synopsis of scientific articles, and so on. Undoubtedly, the capabilities of machines will grow year after year, and the field of their application will extend. Does this mean that the reasoning functions of man are accessible to the machine? Does this mean that the machine is able to create in the real sense of the word?

Different experts answer these questions differently.

K. Steinbuch, for instance, gives a firmly positive answer. Yes, he says, machines and man-made devices in general are capable of mental activity. He declares the opinion that reasoning is the function of the human brain exclusively to be hopelessly obsolete and harmful for the development of science. The revolution in scientific thought caused by the discovery of other carriers of intelligence, distinct from the human brain, he compares to Copernicus's revolution, which substituted the heliocentric system of the world for the geocentric system.

The prospects of machine creativity are being positively assessed by many other notable scientists, too. For instance, Academician V. M. Glushkov wrote: "... in principle, we see the clear technical feasibility of building a system of machines which could not only solve separate intelligence-related problems, but could also attain complete automation of such high-intelligence and creative processes as the development of science and technology. In the second half of the twentieth century, the task of extensive automation of mental work, apart from being hypothetically feasible has become an actual historic necessity".

Advocates of the opposite point of view are also not lacking. This view appears to be stated most definitely by P. Palievsky in the article, "A Measure of Scientific Approach" and in his other works. Briefly, this position amounts to the following: all things created by nature have an immeasurable advantage over artificial, manufactured things, and all that is genuine has advantage over any imitation. Palievsky sees the root of this advantage in that all natural things are connected with the enormous, inexhaustible complexity of the world, its self-movement and self-development, whereas artificial things have no such interrelations. Supporters of the alternative view are ironically called by the author "the enthusiasts of manufacturability".

Though not so elaborately and categorically, but no less definitely, other scholars of the humanities are also protesting against the invasion by machines of the higher types of human mental activity. They look upon the attempts to reproduce these types of activity by automata as something poor, defective, and inevitably doomed to failure.

It is just these points of view (perhaps put no so definitely) that clash in all discussions about the "machine creativity". Let us call them conventionally "the engineering one" and "the humanistic-oriented one" (conventionally, because the adherence to one or the other view does not always correspond to the profession of its "carrier"). The "engineering" point of view regarding the creative capability of machines varies from a definite "Yes!" by Steinbuch to a less categorical, but quite favourable "Why not?". In contrast, the "humanistic-oriented" point of view fiercely opposes the very idea of "machine creativeness", regarding it as "a sacrilege", a rude invasion into the "holy of the holiest", a sign of the terrific offensive of the world of robots upon the world of man. Many arguments cited in support of this view appear fairly convincing: the phenomenon of human creativeness is very complex indeed (this is not to say—immeasurably complex), and all attempts at its simulation look, at least at present, extremely imperfect and primitive when compared with the original.

The point of view of each participant in the discussion rests on his (or her) associative basis. And the decisive element in this basis proves to be emotions rather than thoughts and facts. The root of the contradictions and of the existing (although sometimes hidden) antagonism of debators lies not in logic, but in the sphere of emotional preferences and repulsions. And the "engineering" view is commonly on the offensive, whereas the "humanistic-oriented" view is on the defensive.

Let us try to comprehend, if only roughly, the emotional sources of this antagonism.

To begin with, the emotional colouring of the notion "machine" or "automaton" is sharply distinct for the debators.

The supporter of the "humanistic-oriented" view imagines

an automaton in a generalized form, as an abstract and foreign entity. The automaton is for him something complex, scarcely comprehensible, powerful, but soulless and vagely hostile to man. The associative field related to the notion "automaton" lies with him somewhere between slot-machines (from which, as is known, nothing good can be expected) and numerous science-fiction robots, who, though being said to understand speech, are heartless, self-willed, and fearsome. In the imagination of some of the "humanities" people, the future will be the purview of mythical robots, just as primitive man saw his world as being inhabited by evil spirits.

For the engineer or the mathematician who deals with automata at first hand, the machine is "one of the boys", without anything fearful or mysterious about it. On the contrary, the automaton sometimes irritates one exactly by its helplessness and "stupidity" stemming, for instance, from a small volume of memory, or inadequate speed—in short, by quite real drawbacks. Knowing these drawbacks, the expert figures out ways to overcome them and sees the difficulties he is likely to encounter in his pursuit. His attitude towards the machine is constructive rather than mythical by nature. He appraises the capabilities of machines soberly and reasonably and, what is important, he is not inclined to set any limits to them. The research engineer simply has no use for the hypothesis that the capabilities of machines are limited. He clearly feels annoyed when someone attempts to impose such limits on him. Here lies the first emotional difference.

Let us note another one. The controversy about the machine and creativeness problem is substantially influenced by one wide-spread prejudice which is worthy of special consideration. This prejudice concerns scientific methodology and is rather common in engineering circles. It claims that sciences should be classified as "genuine", that is, exact ones, and "second-rate" ones (the humanities). Typical of the first category is the quantitative method of research, the application of mathematical techniques and their ensuing indisputable conclusions. In contrast, the second category is characterized by vagueness and qualitative (and hence, unconvincing) methods of argumentation. In this respect, the name of science may be applied only to that which can be expressed by quantitative, mathematical laws, the rest is just "words, words, words..."

Many engineers, physicists, and mathematicians share, openly or hiddenly, this belief. Being accustomed to the laconic and rigorous quantitative form in which truths are expressed in their sciences, they heedlessly brush aside any scientific argumentation expressed in verbal form rather than equations. A certain physico-mathematical haughtiness which often comes out while they are just beginning their studies, is characteristic of many specialists in the exact sciences. There is the story of one well-known scientist who once opened a speech at a party of students in the physical and mechanico-mathematical departments at the Moscow University with the following words: "Physicists and mathematicians share a feeling of absolute mental superiority to students in other departments" (for the sake of fairness, it should be noted that such a feeling is nowadays less frequent among physicists and mathematicians than among engineers that apply mathematical methods).

If we look at things in the cold light of reality, we shall have to say that there are no ground for such haughtiness. While it goes without saying that quantitative, mathematical methods are a powerful tool of investigation into phenomena of the surrounding world, it would be erroneous to declare this tool to be universal and uniquely scientific. It should be remembered that there are no reasons to regard a truth derived by mathematical methods as indisputable. Theoretical ma hematics alone enables one to derive correct conclusions out of arbitrary postulates: what is verified here is not the truthfulness of certain axioms, but the correctness of the chain of logical conclusions that relate the basic premises to the conclusions. In any other science, the situation proves to be more complicated. No mathematical method, however perfect, can by itself lend truthfulness to scientific conclusions. Another thing is essential: is the mathematical model taken as the basis of investigation adequate to reality? If not, the investigation and its conclusions will be fallacious.

Construction of mathematical models and their quantitative studies have yielded, as we know, magnificent results in solving physical and engineering problems. Over the last decades, the field of application of mathematical models has expanded immensely. Mathematical models offer a valuable aid in biology, medicine, linguistics, economics, and military science. It should be borne in mind, however, that each of these sciences deals with incomparably more complex phenomena than the subject of study of classical mathematics and physics. For this reason, mathematical models play an auxiliary, not fundamental, part here.

As regards branches of learning that deal with the most complex social phenomena—say, the arts—mathematical modelling methods are just beginning to make inroads. Mathematical methods have so far played a more than moderate part in the classical humanities (aesthetics, literary criticism, and so on), and the results they have produced do not compare to those obtained by traditional descriptive methods.

It is also not likely that the humanities will develop along the way to full formalization and mathematization in future. The apparatus of mathematics (at least, in its present state) is not sufficiently flexible to express a number of essential categories, such as "similarity", "acceptability", "importance", "pithiness", and others. Attempts to render these categories in purely quantitative language, in terms of "greater or lesser", often lead to oversimplification and distortion of reality. Verbal description, which is seemingly a rather unreliable and inaccurate tool, actually proves more accurate and more flexible than a mathematical formula. Nevertheless, representatives of the exact sciences often look at the humanities as something to be conquered. As one of them put it, "there are no branches of learning that are not amenable to mathematization; there are only those which have not yet been mathematized". Such a position can only elicit a defensive reaction on the part of the humanities people.

Aside from the main, emotional, roots of the "machine creativeness" dispute, mutual misunderstanding also rests on some common fallacies, the cause of which is simple lack of knowledge.

Let us consider some of the most frequent objections as to the feasibility of machine creativeness.

One of them is the following: creativeness involves bringing something new into existence, whereas the machine is capable only of actions that were programmed beforehand by its creator, that is, man.

This objection does not follow as it is based on the obsolete, naive conception of the automaton as a device all of whose actions are predetermined by a program. Indeed, at the outset that is what automata were, but today highly organized devices capable, like man, of learning and self-learning in order to improve their program by experience are under development (and already in use). The automaton, initially provided with a primitive and imperfect program, interacts with the environment, receives information from it, and accordingly corrects its actions, elaborating an optimal program for the situation. It is exactly these automata, which can both be taught and teach themselves, that will prevail in future; they alone will be able to reproduce the higher functions of the human brain.

To maintain today that the automaton is not capable of independent actions and creation of anything new is like saying that no man can ever create anything new because all his actions are predetermined by the combination of genes inherited from his mother and father.

A curious question may arise at this point. Does it then follow that the automaton possesses a freedom of action, a freedom of will?

Yes, we should think that it has a certain freedom of action (the freedom of will we had better leave aside because here the analogy is doubtful at present).

In disputes about the machine and creativeness, the above statement on "a certain freedom of action" is often subjected to sharp criticism. It is regarded as virtually idealistic. Just think: an automaton and freedom of action!

In fact, the matter is very simple: the ability of the automaton to act unpredictably (arbitrarily) is provided for by entering into the program a "generator of random steps". Suppose, for instance, you need to choose between two actions: go to the right or go to the left. As you have no experience of how to behave in this situation, you are bound to choose the direction by chance. You toss up a coin and if it comes up heads, you go to the right, if tails, you go to the left. Gradually, by repeating the experiment, you may become oriented in the situation and see for yourself that going to the right is on the whole more convenient for you than going to the left. Then you can play your game so that the result "to the right" is more probable:

for instance you spin two coins, and if at least one of them shows up heads, you go to the right, but if both show tails, you go to the left.

A similar, though much more complex, mechanism is used as a basis for random, unpredictable actions by the machine. Taking analogous actions and following the response of the environment, the machine, as it were, orients itself in the situation, feeling its way to the correct action. Under the influence of signals from the environment (or a teacher), the initially chaotic, pointless behaviour gradually changes into rational, meaningful actions. Note that an analogous procedure, known as the trial and error method, often underlies the process of learning or self-learning with man.

A supercilious attitude towards chance as a source of novelty is rather frequent. Such an attitude is unjustified. Chance in one form or another is the source of many new phenomena. The role of random mutations is well known in biology. It is exactly mutations that start new forms of living organisms, a process indispensable for progress in living nature. Selectionists also make use of controlled, artificially induced mutations for breeding new species.

A great deal of scientific discoveries originated from a random concurrence of circumstances (the legend about the Newtonian apple is unlikely to be true, but it is characteristic of the role ascribed to chance in science). Chance also manifests itself as a creative force in the arts. Recall the kaleidoscope, an elementary "machine" designed exactly for creative activity, although a very primitive one. Pieces of coloured glass are mixed up randomly in a tube with glass partitions: reflected from mirrors, they form fanciful, sometimes very fine, patterns. There exist methods of cloth manufacture by which patterns on the cloth are formed in a random manner. It is known that some painters (Leonardo da Vinci among them!) derived the images of their paintings from random patches of mould on the wall, a random accumulation of clouds, and so on.

The same holds true for literature. Every writer knows what a striking effect can sometimes result from a mere slip of the pen or the tongue.

Obviously, creativeness is not just a matter of chance, but, chance is undoubtedly one of its constituent elements. Any creative activity is likely to be a fusion of random factors with orderly, systematic elements.

Roughly, any creative process may be conventionally broken down into two stages: a preparatory one and a selective one. The first stage is used for creation of "semi-finished pieces", or variants. At the second stage, the variants are "sieved", inadequate variants are rejected, and the best one is finally chosen. Beyond all doubt, the tremendously fast computer, which is capable of going over an immense number of variants untiringly and unremittingly, can be of great help to man at the first stage.

Let us consider, for example, the work of a product-design engineer who is developing a special-purpose engineering device. Certain solutions occur to him, but he is not at all certain that he has exhausted them all. Tomorrow (if not already today) he will turn for help to the machine, which will place before him a host of variants (some of them, possibly, very advantageous) that did not occur to him.

Sceptics, perhaps, will find this example unconvincing. The creative work of the design engineer is not, after all, the same as that of the artist. Very well, let us take another example.

Every writer is familiar with moments when he gropes for the "right" word, the one word which absolutely fits in that context, but the word eludes him, and other words which are very close in meaning but, nevertheless, not quite right, come to mind instead. But what would be wrong with having the opportunity to turn to a machine which could momentarily give him a string of words close in meaning to those coming to his mind? The machine could also issue another string of words closely associated with the sought word.

Of course, turning to a machine for advice will occur like sacrilege to some writers, but did they not resign themselves to replacement of a feather-quill pen by a steel nib, a steel nib by a fountain pen, and a fountain pen by a typewriter?

I personally find nothing wrong or sacrilegious in using a machine-handbook or a machine adviser, provided, of course, the handling of the machine is sufficiently easy and convenient. Experience shows that any introduction of technology into the realm of creative work is at first strongly resisted by adherents of the old Pegasus, but then the novelty becomes widely accepted and does its business.

Hence, the machine can undoubtedly help man in the first, preparatory stage of creative work. But what about the second, selective, stage?

Obviously, things are much more complicated here. To choose the best, the unique, variation from a multitude of variations is much more difficult than to prepare these variations. Selection, discarding of the superfluous, is the genuine function of a creator. The famous sculptor August Rodin described the process of creating a sculpture this way: "I take a block of marble and chisel away all that is redundant." Leo Tolstoy also sees the creative process as "the rejection of the needless", "the removal of covers". Remember how the artist Mikhailov in the novel *Anna Karenina* works on a drawing of the figure of a man in a fit of anger. A chance spot of stearin suddenly animated the drawing and gave the man a new posture. "The figure was alive, clear, and definite. The drawing could be corrected in compliance with the figure, the feet could and even should be parted in a different way, the position of the left hand changed altogether, the hair thrown back. But in doing so he did not change the figure, but only cast off what was hiding it. He was as if removing the covers behind which the figure was not seen; each new trace revealed the figure ever more in its energetic vitality, such as it showed up to him out of the spot of stearin."

Hence, real creativeness means selection, "casting away all that is excessive", "taking off the covers".

This suggests the conclusion that at the second, selective stage, the machine cannot be helpful any longer. And yet, this is not completely so.

First, the process of selection may vary in complexity. In the simplest cases, it amounts to discarding variations that do not meet some formal requirements, out of a body of random variations generated by the machine. In this way, for instance, modern computers "compose" music. At first, the machine generates random sequences of sounds, and then automatically rejects those which do not follow the rules of harmony, counterpoint, or the specified stylistic demands. Incidentally, musical productions obtained in this way are not devoid of artistic value and may well compete with ordinary compositions by professional composers.

The following fact is a good example to confirm the above statement: one TV program dedicated to "machine creativeness" was from the beginning to the end accompanied by music "composed" by a digital electronic computer according to a program compiled by the musician and mathematician R. Kh. Zaripov. The viewers were not told beforehand that the music was composed by a computer. As a result, no one noticed in it anything suspicious or "unhuman" (likewise, no one indicated that it had any special artistic values).

At any rate, the music was perceived as something quite normal, and not differing from the usual musical accompaniment of TV programs.

So much for the use of machines at the selection stage in the simplest cases, when selection criteria can be formalized, that is, reduced to a system of rules.

In more complex instances, typical of artistic creativeness, the selection criteria are obscure and not amenable to formalization. Here, the selective function is much more critical and has so far been the prerogative of man alone, with his insuperable capacity for solution of unclearly stated, non-formalized problems. Does this mean, however, that in such situations the selective function is in principle beyond a machine's reach? No, it does not.

After all, it is not present-day, imperfect automata that are in question, but tomorrow's machines capable of learning and self-learning. Here, as in all poorly formalizable problems, so-called heuristic programs can be of help, by which the automaton which is being taught reproduces to some extent man's selective function, imitating its teacher, and taking similar procedural steps. These techniques are already being used to teach automata some kinds of human activity, for instance, the work of a controller. Heuristic methods hold an immense potential. A curious facet of theirs is that, starting with a mere imitation of man, an automaton can, over some period of training, improve its program and even, in principle, excel its human teacher. There are even now some examples of this kind of "man vs. machine" competition where the taught machine beats its teacher. True, they concern relatively simple kinds of mental activity, but it is the first step that counts.

It is evident that devising heuristic programs is enormously difficult and the difficulty of the task sharply grows with the complexity of the mental activity which the program is to reproduce. But fundamentally, the feasibility of teaching the automaton certain kinds of non-formal activities seems doubtless.

Among objections to "machine creativeness", one close to the philosophic conception put forth in the afore-mentioned article of Palievsky is found rather often. It states that no artificial thing, no imitation, can be essentially as complete and sound as the object being imitated, because it will always lack "something" that is present in a natural, non-artificial thing.

This point is difficult to refute precisely because it is extremely indefinite. How can one prove that there is that elusive "something" in his artificial creations? The situation is reminiscent of a certain fairy-tale demand: "Go I know not where, and fetch I know not what". The only possible way to dispute such a position is to provide a convincing analogy.

Mankind, we know, has created an artificial device, the airplane. It was first conceived as an imitator of the flying power of birds, but rapidly outlived its imitator role and began a new life of its own. There is hardly anyone who would question the capability of the plane to fly soundly and do it in some respects better than a bird, although the latter has all advantages of a natural and living creature. The fact is that we are already used to the concept of "flying machine", but the concepts of "thinking machine" or, "creative machine" still strikes us as something wild and incongruous.

One may argue, of course, that the flight of the bird is quite different from that of the plane, and the point is well taken. The term "thinking machine" also implies some alteration in the notion "to think". We are already accustomed to the term "machine memory", as this is a convenient way of describing the processes that occur in the computer.

So, is it worthwhile to object so heatedly to such broad usages of words and, moreover, to lend a philosophic hue to these objections?

Incidentally, a philosophically grounded form of objection in the "machine creativeness" dispute is not so frequent. Another form, which may be called "negation with shifting bounds", is encountered much more often. It amounts to the debater's agreeing to acknowledge as authentic only such examples of thought and creativeness as have not yet been achieved by machine. Once a field of human mental activity is mastered by the machine, the boundary of "authenticity" is shifted further off, and the negation continues.

Two or three decades ago, such "negators" conceded to the machine only the capability of computation; but the creative function of developing the program, they added, was beyond it. The advent of automata capable of generating and optimizing their own programs made them modify their stand slightly; the program-devising function, as it proved amenable to machine, was placed with non-creative functions, and the tasks of devising mathematical models, carrying-out algebraic transformations, logical conclusions and so forth, were declared to rest with man only... So what? Today the machine begins to compete with man in all these areas... The boundary of authentic creativeness is always shifting farther off, but the existence of the boundary itself is defended as ardently as before.

Obviously you cannot keep people from maintaining this "constantly variable" view, but it automatically eliminates the subject of the debate. If authentic thinking and creativeness are only bound up with things that have not yet been achieved by machines, then the answer to the questions: "can the machine think?" and, "is it capable of independent creativeness?" will always be the same: "No".

Let us touch upon one more clearly emotional objection that is often put forward by opponents of "machine creativeness". It may be formulated like this: "whatever you do, the machine will never be able to replace man."

Here, we face a misunderstanding of the word "replacement". As a rule, experiments on the simulation of man's mental and creative functions are not aimed at replacing man, at whatever cost, in carrying out these functions. The object of these experiments is to gain a better understanding of the processes being simulated.

It is reasonable to replace man by a machine only where the machine performs some functions better than man does. In these cases, also, replacement is not forced as a result of the aggressiveness of "enthusiasts of manufacturability"; it proceeds peacefully, by itself, dictated by convenience and economic benefits. In this way, for instance, man has been peacefully phased out by machine from the field of complex numerical computation. Last century and at the outset of this one, computing virtuosos, who were capable of precise computations with the aid of seven-digit logarithmic tables, were held in high esteem. Where are those virtuosos today? And where are the seven-digit tables? Life has passed them by. In the near future, such may also be the fate of complex transformations of mathematical expressions with letter-designated quantities (this is now an art which has outstanding performers). The formal proving of theorems is next, and so forth. The first attempts to use computers in these areas are being made right now. For instance, the computer carries out identical algebraic transformations of expressions given in letter form; from the possibilities obtained, it chooses the one which is simplest ("most elegant") in some respect (the number of letters, a single-term or multiple-term form and the like). What a relief it would be for mathematicians, particularly absent-minded ones, who are not able to perform a more or less complex transformation without an error in the sign or a loss of a factor of 2.

Experiments are also under way on applying computers to the formal proving of theorems. I should like to note a curious fact: in the process of trying out a program for executing logical actions, the computer was assigned the task of deriving a number of theorems relating to one of the branches of geometry. Not only did the computer accomplish the task, but also derived additionally two new theorems hitherto unknown to the developers of the program.

Thus, the replacement of man by machine is made in a smooth and timely manner where the machine is more capable than man. As regards the higher forms of creativeness, man has so far been better fit for them than the machine, and there is no question of "replacing" him either today or in the near future.

Enthusiasts often point with glee to some effective computer-aided artistic productions, for instance, musical melodies, or pieces of poetry, which are sometimes difficult to distinguish from those created by professionals. Although such productions may look fairly impressive, they are not convincing enough. What in fact is demonstrated is separate elements that, along with other elements, can be found in creative works by man. The far more difficult task of general composition, of combining the elements and harnessing them so that they work for a predetermined conception remains so far unresolved by the machine. It should also be kept in mind that not all machine creations are displayed for the public but only the best in the view of the researcher. This means that the function of choice and rejection is carried out by man anyway. Such is the situation in the field of music, where "the creative machine" has scored the most notable success. As regards "machine poetry", the achievements are still more modest. Experiments on "machine composition of poetry" have proved at best that by using a certain vocabulary (that is, essentially, a set of cliches), the machine can create something looking like a piece of verse where all rules of the game are observed: the phrases are grammatical, the metre is correct, the rhymes are appropriate... However, even the best (specially chosen) pieces of "machine verse" look, at present, like a parody of a second-rate versificator's writing rather than authentic verse. Besides we are acquainted with translated, not original, pieces because the number of machine verses produced in this country is negligibly small. But the work of a translator can "humanize" the original text beyond all recognition.

Does it signify that experiments on simulating creativeness are meaningless and useless altogether? By no means, because the chief purpose of such experiments is to try to comprehend, as far as possible, the mechanism of the creative process. The "artistic" productions obtained by computer simulation are its by-products rather than its aim. However, it is a remarkable fact that some of these by-products have an independent (although up to now not great) artistic value.

Our popular-scientific literature (let alone science-fiction) places a great emphasis on the possibilities of science and technology, but says almost nothing about their limitations. The public is virtually ignorant about serious difficulties involved in the imitation of some of man's creative functions, and not even the most complex ones. Few people are aware that present-day and near-future automata are not able to substitute, say, for a doorkeeper who sits on duty at the door and checks the identity of visitors by their photographs. There are automata that read typed texts but those capable of reading handwriting do not yet exist. There are automata which obey simple vocal commands but none can execute a complex sequence of commands uttered in a usual speech form because people's voices, peculiarities of pronounciation and rhythm of speech vary too widely. All these tasks relate to pattern recognition, which is one of the cardinal and most difficult problems of present-day science.

The real mastery of machine technology will come about when we teach automata to recognize patterns as man does. Here we are encountered with a peculiar ability of man, not yet reproducible by machine, to assess a situation as a whole, ignoring insignificant details and taking into account the essentials alone. For instance, the most slow-witted person is able to recognize an object named "house", whether it be large or small, painted red or white, side or front lighted, and with trees or a fence as a background. At the same time, the most sophisticated present-day automaton cannot solve this simplest problem and a number of similar ones. The automaton cannot be given a command like "acquaint yourself with the situation, assess it, and act accordingly". It must be instructed in minute detail how to proceed in each case. Under such conditions, man cannot even be slightly approached by the automaton: he is able to solve so-called informal problems. To teach automata how to do it would mean a great achievement in the imitation of purely human functions; we should see clearly, but without despair, that this step is tremendously difficult.

Awareness of the difficulties generates a sense of admiration for what has already been achieved. To appreciate something, one needs to know at what cost it was obtained. Today's layman reared on science fiction often tends to underestimate both what has been done already and what still needs to be done. Some people think robots that speak, understand, stand guard, and eavesdrop are tomorrow's, if not today's, reality, and that there is nothing surprising in it, because science is omnipotent. This is a purely philistine outlook. "A philistine", the writer A. B. Raskin once said, "typically combines a blind faith in the omnipotence of science with a deep conviction that nothing good can come out of it".

One sometimes cannot help wondering at how easily some people lose a natural human sense of amazement.

Is it not amazing, for instance, that our extremely imperfect machines of today are capable of composing music which can be listened to without aversion? Are the experiments in automatic design of engineering devices and the automatic deciphering of ancient texts not astonishing? Is it not wonderful that after ten to twelve hours of training, the machine unfailingly beats at checkers the man who has created the program for it?

But what of that? Our sceptic can neither marvel nor admire. He can only criticize. He concentrates on finding faults and shortcomings with current products of "machine creativeness". Here he can score an easy success because the shortcomings and faults are numerous and readily identifiable. And the critic triumphantly declares: "You will fail anyway". "Don't forget" such a critic ought to be told. "Better take into account that the electronic-computer technology is very young, and the cybernetic simulators of human mental activity are still younger. It is not very gentlemanly to reproach a child taking the first steps that he is a poor walker..."

But, on the other hand, one feels a desire to cool down such enthusiastic engineers who having achieved the first success in the field of "machine creativeness", hasten to announce that the problem is already solved. We tend to forget that the first spectacular attempts and demonstrations are a long way from a real, "industrial-scale" application of automata in a given sphere of mental activity.

Let us remember the state of affairs with machine translation. The first successful attempts at such translation were demonstrated in the early fifties. It seemed then that it would take but a little bit more effort to solve the problem. Those hopes were not realized. The first, rather primitive algorithms of machine translation proved to be too local, too dependent on the peculiarities of the text under translation. More general methods were needed. This need gave rise to a new independent scientific discipline, mathematical linguistics, which studies different types of linguistic models. Regardless of great progress made in this field, the actual problem of machine translation remains practically unresolved. Machine translations of special, mainly technical texts (productions of rather poor quality which require editing) are the maximum that has been achieven. The editing function remains to date a prerogative of mad.

Thus, we can see that every stage in the development of science and technology produces a temporal division of labour between machine and man. The machine is assigned functions that it can perform faster and more cost-effectively. No clear-cut boundary exists between "creative" and "non-creative" functions of man. Do not let us become offended by the words "the thinking machine" or "the creative machine". We should not set any limits to capabilities of the machine. Such restrictions have never borne fruit, but do not let us be hasty in declaring "the replacement" of man by machine in functions which he still performs better. Man still has things he can do!

From a New Angle

Interaction between man and machine is a problem of great importance today. In analyzing this concept, we must outline not only its scientific and technical aspects, but also its social implications. We must show not only the limits of computer use, but the ethical problems involved, as well.

This chapter throws light on these issues and gives examples of the application of cybernetics in history and law, and for resolving marriage problems and coordinating efficient collectives.

Regrettably, for various reasons, we cannot here consider some other interesting topics, such as variations in the functioning of scientific collectives, the role of structure of collectives, and so on. However, the articles that follow expound the basic ideas necessary for a first introduction to these complex questions.

Man-Machine Interaction

G. L. SMOLYAN

The development of cybernetic concepts and methods and their application in different areas of engineering, economic planning, and other sectors of the economy have tangibly transformed the informational basis of society. The hypothesis advanced by A. A. Kharkevitch in the 1960s that the amount of the information to be collected, processed, and transferred grows at least in proportion to the square of the industrial potential is being confirmed today. And, of course, computer is the most important tool for data processing. The population of computers is rapidly growing, and the production of telecommunication and data handling equipment quickly expands. This ensures efficient solution of problems by the aid of computers. In general, this leads to changes not only in the economy and management of the leading industrial sectors—mechanical engineering and instrument making—but also, and this seems to be more remarkable, in the whole system of providing information for social life.

The growing capabilities and extending application of computers in the 1970s-80s may with a good cause be regarded as "computer revolution". The term is widely spread and, on the whole, represents a major (if not the principal) trend of current scientific and industrial development. It also reflects an overall effect of automated (man-machine) control and information handling systems, these new tools of cognition and social management, on society. The "extended" interpretation of the "computer revolution" concept is justified, because only these systems can effectively combine human and artificial intelligence.

The "computer revolution" primarily involves the integration of informational (communication) and control processes. The computer is a powerful tool by itself, but it acquires importance in systems that gather, store, process, and transfer data by means of telecommunication. This concept is essential, because we may look from a new angle at the "man-machine" world in which we live, and appreciate in full measure its enormous productive potential.

We want to demonstrate that the current "computer revolution", as the main achievement of cybernetics in the late 1970s, more obviously than ever before embodies in concrete forms the idea of man-machine interaction. Most of all the computer cannot be regarded as a machine intended only to perform mathematical operations, for which man has no time, ability, or patience. The computer is the most powerful means of human communication, providing direct access to human and machine sources of information.

It should be pointed out that changes and trends in computer application for only three decades give a special meaning to the "computer revolution", making it a qualitative "leap forward" towards the development of integral communication-computer systems of man-machine interaction. In fact, these trends have prevailed in all areas of mental activity that undergo automation.

Here are a few examples. In control, these trends are effected in automated systems combining the functions of production and administrative control.

The integrated MIS's (management information systems) are a new type of practical cybernetic systems. In the area of cognitive activities, man-machine interaction provides a means for solving problems in systems engineering and forecasting, for instance, by simulation, that is, by means of "flexible" models and iterative procedures, including the evaluation of results and modification of input data by a human operator. In computer-aided design, interactive graphics is finding an ever increasing application, where human and machine methods of the design and engineering of complex objects are integrated in a single process. In information handling, users receive information through a direct interaction between man and computer.

There is good reason to believe that the dialogue between man and computer is a creative process. The computer-aided design systems operating, for instance, on a real time basis, produce not only objects of familiar physical reality. The computer easily produces new images and situations that substantially extend our traditional concepts of the properties and functioning of real objects. In this undoubtedly creative process man and computer are closely connected. The computer is somehow psychologically "implanted" into the human brain. This forms a single creative and aesthetic system, where man has the leading organizing role. Although considerable psychological and linguistic barriers in the path towards effective dialogue systems still exist, the prospects for their development are certainly promising. And indeed, it seems hardly reasonable to place equal demands on a man-machine dialogue and on a human dialogue.

This allows the boundary line between the functions of man and machine to be shifted and defined anew.

And, of course, our current understanding of man-machine interaction has resulted from long and hard work, hot debates, and the tortuous development of cybernetic ideas.

Now, let us cast a look at the sources of the man-machine interaction concept. The past of science, as A. A. Lyubishchev put it, is not a graveyard of ideas buried forever under tumbstones but, rather, a collection of unfinished architectural assemblies. Most of them were left uncompleted because they were conceived too much ahead of their time and not because they were basically unsound.

The concept of man-machine interaction evolved from a conjecture that the processes of control and communication in man and machine are similar. Although in early works, and most of all in Wiener's *Cybernetics* (New York, 1948), it looked rather like a simple analogy based on guesswork, this conjecture was formulated with such an immense conceptual potential, that in only two decades the idea developed into a profound methodological concept, which unlocked a new path to cognition of informational processes in nature and in human society.

Wiener made a remarkable progress from practical tasks to the philosophical aspect of the problem, from a simple analogy between man and machine to the informational concept of the functioning of society, including the rise of the need for information and the informational provision for control functions. Here are some conceptual milestones on this way as seen by Wiener: analogy between digital computers and the human brain, a mechanism for effecting a target-oriented action based on a negative feedback, formulating the thesis that communication and control are inseparable both in machines and living organisms and revealing the informational probability basis of this inseparableness, adapting digital computers to production control and realizing the historical significance of this stage of automation.

It is worth mentioning here that cybernetics from the very start regarded man and machine as data processing systems. New problems—self-learning and self-organization, the assessment of intelligence and creative abilities, pattern recognition, the use of bionic principles, and many other problems—implied a direct or indirect transfer of qualities from man to machine and from machine to man. This paved the way to computer simulation of organization and control processes.

Wiener in *Man and the Machine* considers the man-machine interaction as one of the three basic problems of cybernetics (the other two are self-learning and self-reproduction of machines). The interaction between man and machine has found wide application and has drawn, therefore, special attention. The reason for it is that the concept fits well in the scientific and technological advance, in the move-

17—01169

ment towards greater optimization of human activity in organizational and technological man-machine systems.

There is yet another factor of a general methodological character which determined the leading role of the interaction concept. The very logic of development of relations between man and machine necessitated conceptualizing both the overall picture of informational processes and its component objects. The work could be started only with reorientating all cybernetic problems towards man and with introducing the human element into the technological world of cybernetics. Therefore, the relations between man and machine as seen today point first of all to the interaction, a direct dialogue between man and the computer.

Already at its early stages, cybernetics faced the task of describing the content of the goal-oriented system concept. By disclosing it through the human ability not only to perceive, judge, and act, but also to intend and foresee, cybernetics began to shape its theory. Those human qualities were simulated in computer models, and hence cybernetics began turning into the science of man-machine system models oriented to practical application in the systems optimization area. Naturally, the models have been updated and enriched by refining the methods and means of problem solving. This way of development has proved to be the most adequately fitting to the socio-practical aspects of control optimization that were posed by the economic, scientific, and industrial development of the 1970-1980s.

Today we are concerned with the objective-aimed (semantic) interpretation of the man-machine interaction. The methodology of this interpretation, however, is also exceptionally important: it signifies a change from "automation-oriented" to "activity-oriented" cybernetics.

There is an objective logic of the evolution of cybernetic

systems: from general-purpose information to decision making oriented systems. It is this evolution that paves the way for the current cybernetic methodology. It accelerates because cybernetics comes to grips with problems pertaining to natural sciences and humanities, most of all, with activity-oriented problems. Theory and practice merge, and this is a distinguishing feature of the present-day scientific and technological advance in the sphere of man-machine interaction. Remarkably, cybernetics owes its "optimization" character to the analysis of human activity. It is precisely the activity-oriented approach that carries the necessary normative element, and, as a result, an "evaluating" function is added to a "natural" understanding of processes. Cybernetics more than any other scientific discipline has contributed to the formation of the applied normative sciences. This took place because its engineering problems turned out to be naturally connected with the optimization of organizational, managerial, and informational activities of people.

It should be emphasized that progressively extending and deepening interaction of man and computer makes organization and management a powerful productive force of modern society. And as this, it greatly influences the spiritual life of people. The consequences, like ripples in the water, move farther and farther away from the initial point, Wiener's *Cybernetics*, revealing new social and humanistic, in a broad sense, aspects of the interaction concept. It is just for this reason that our time can be described not only as the initial stage of a cybernetic civilization but also as the time of a developed cybernetic mythology. The latter has a particularly solid foundation, since cybernetics, unlike other scientific and engineering disciplines, from the very beginning had to do with the subjective factor and, hence, with the possibility of boundless speculations.

These speculations, these myths of modern science, whatever form they may take—the intriguing science fiction or the dry, statistically substantiated predictions—expose new unexpected facets of the eternal problem, the problem of man and his attitude towards the world he lives in.

It is now nearly a commonplace that the scientific and technological revolution radically changing physical and mental labour gives a new starting point for philosophical and social outlook. What is less evident is that man-machine methods of production and, in a broader context, social organization (including the production of spiritual values) give rise to a scientific and technical fetishism with its dubious conclusions and controversies.

Talking about automation and the introduction of computers into the sphere of administrative control, it is usually stated that work becomes more and more intellectual. This issue is far from being simple, and the danger of alienation of the human content of labour from man himself and of a concrete person from man as an abstract productive force in a modern man-machine world appears to be quite real. Objective conditions have made some kinds of labour tedious and devoid of a creative element, requiring no exertion of intelligence and emotion in any appreciable degree. As we see it, many disquieting and critical tendencies in modern society stem from man's alienation from his work.

The alienation changes its character and form in accordance with the changes, principles, and scale of use of productive forces, their technological and human components. Technotronic utopias and elitist theories of the cybernetic era do not come from nowhere. Their proponents are scientists and engineering professionals, whose increase in importance has largely been due to the advent of electronic computers. The computer-based informational control systems of the 1960-80s have a considerable influence on the social outlook not because of their qualitative and quantitative growth but rather because of the sharp rise of the social prestige of new professions engaged in the development and application of man-machine systems. It would be no exaggeration to say that cybernetics professionals are exactly the main group of people who preach "scientific and technological chauvinism".

"Ideologists" of the man-machine civilization, irrespective of what they believe to be the centre of philosophical thought—man or machine—all have to work through various schemes of analysis and synthesis of the man-machine interaction concept. The principal question concerns the role of man in the "computer revolution" epoch, and the answers to it are closely associated with different, primarily ethical, aspects of the interaction concept.

When considering relations between man and machine, Wiener pointed to serious moral traps. The practice of the last decade has not eliminated them. One of the traps is whether a machine that fully understands a human language acquires some human traits. Apparently the development of man-machine systems as such leads to a change of the social status of human beings in such systems, and that necessarily gives rise to new moral problems. The history of moral problems shows their special inconstancy and perplexity, for standards and ideals of human activity continually change with a rapid technological advance.

Three tendencies can be pointed out in establishing the moral imperatives associated with application of computers. The first describes the world of automata as a tool for "triggering a nuclear war". Wiener singled out the "machine worshipers", and his antimilitaristic *Man and the Machine* cautioned against the error of the "machinal solution". Born also expressed, in a vivid essay form, his moral judgement of political and militaristic horrors, which he believed to be necessarily a consequence of the scientific development. He wrote that even if mankind were not obliterated by nuclear war, it might degenerate into a race of stupefied speechless creatures, living under the tyranny of dictators and driven by means of machines and electronic computers. In these and many similar warnings typical of the early stage of "computerization", automata were regarded as a "new symbol of evil", rather abstract, having a single, but destructive quality—triggering the mechanism of the world's calamity.

The second tendency reflects the progress in creating computerized informational systems. They may tighten control over society, which will inevitably lead to great moral losses. The computer, which is the main element of an informational system, is considered as a definite and powerful force opposed to man. According to R. Cassin, an expert in international law, computer-aided data transfer and treatment can infringe on privacy and individual freedom. He also states that accumulation, long-term storage, and easy retrieval of information about all personal aspects, health, social activity, political views, associations, and so on, are dangerous.

The third, perhaps the most common line of criticism expresses the general humanistic tradition, which rejects the machine as an impersonal thing which is indifferent to man but makes decisions for him. The computer is identified with a "mechanical monster".

The pessimistic notes are typical of humanistic literature as a whole, repeating in general the pathos of the 1920s or bringing to the fore the dramatism of the conflict in a milder and implicit form. "The machine does not require court painters or poets; it wants the transformation of the living flesh into wheels, nuts, screws. Freedom and individuality must go in the name of mechanization of the entire life"*. This sentence of Julio Jurenito does not differ too much from what is stated by modern opponents of computer culture. Paul Valéry wrote that the machine does not tolerate the situation where its power is not absolute, where there are individuals for whom it means nothing, who are beyond its sphere. It tends to eliminate people whose role it cannot comprehend, and to reform others in its own way caring neither for the past nor even for the future of humankind.

The "unemotional" approach looks different. It is focussed mainly on the political side of the responsibility-sharing problem as a direct consequence of realizing new aspects of man-computer relations in the current administrative practice. The proponents of this approach assert that "... the computer scientist, like anyone else, is responsible for his actions and their consequences. Sometimes that responsibility is hard to accept because the corresponding authority to decide what is and what is not to be done appears to rest with distant and anonymous forces. That technology itself determines what is to be done by a process of extrapolation and that individuals are powerless to intervene in that determination is precisely the kind of self-fulfilling dream from which we must awaken".

The wave of criticism, the emotional or unemotional denounciation of political, social, and moral consequences of a "computerized" civilization result from the fact that people are becoming aware of the various aspects of the man-computer interaction problem.

As follows from the above, the instinct of self-preservation gives rise to fears of the "too automated world". These misgivings are especially manifest in certain illusions and myths surrounding the man-machine interaction

---

* Эренбург И., Собр. соч., 1962, т. 1, стр. 69.

problem. Even if these myths have been partly or fully dispelled in theory or practice, their significance is large enough, for they lead beyond the sphere of the matter-of-fact understanding, show the problem from a new angle, and draw the attention of researchers to dangers hidden in the current trends. They reflect the first reaction to the principal problem of our time: science and technology—the individual—the future. Moreover, in the atmosphere of the universal scientific and technological fetishism any striking idea that sounds credible induces a resounding response in public conscience. Unfortunately, ideas, as they become subject to a far-and-wide propaganda, often tend to be distorted. Mass media generally place emphasis on unusual and spectacular machine applications, especially if they contain the creative element, be it control problems or chess games.

Let us mention the main concepts treated in scientific literature and science fiction. They can be arbitrarily classed into two categories: (a) political and ideological and (b) technical. Here are the most deep-rooted views, the peculiar stereotypes of political and social thinking.

1. Computers already exercise or will exercise absolute control over political, economic, and social life. The "wise" and "impartial" computer takes on full responsibility for all decisions it makes. This is the guarantee of a "stable" society in conditions where social processes run quickly and unpredictably. In another variation of this myth, a full "electronic" democracy is provided for, judicial errors are excluded, public opinion is absolutely impartial, and so on.

2. Computers not only perform and will perform all routine tasks but also release people from work altogether, leaving them to indulge in hedonistic pleasures. The computer is "the soul of the arts", "the morality", and "the embodiment of the collective mind's creative power".

3. Computers eliminate the intelligensia, turning it into a class of programmers, computer servicing personnel, and administrators. Machine instruction also eliminates "the institution of human teachers". In this context the most frequently mentioned prospect is complete bureaucratization of society in accordance with Parkinson's law.

These myths are often accompanied with speculations about the need for powerful social safeguards against "the computer takeover" and "the total programming of life". They are often pessimistic. In this connection, Wiener is often referred to. He wrote shortly before his death that a reasonable understanding of the principle of a machine may come long after the machine has completed its tasks. That means that although in theory machines can be subjected to human criticism, it may so happen that when this criticism becomes possible, it will be long since irrelevant.

"Technical" myths also have definite ideological implications.

1. A "symbiotic" society is established, which is based on the transmission of signals from the computer directly into the human brain. In such a society, control over the human mind is a natural function.

2. A single global linguistic and cultural communication is effected via a computer that performs the encoding and decoding of languages. All scientific and cultural values are translated into the computer "esperanto". Collection and exchange of knowledge are fully computerized.

3. Diverse intimidating scenarios of the world's catastrophe due to a failure of "the supercomputer" are envisaged.

4. The independent and uncontrollable development of machines takes place on the "self-reproduction" principle, and they move along the lines of the "human evolution".

Such are, in general, the outlines of the modern cybernetic

mythology. Analysis of cybernetic myths can not only reveal the focal points of social and technological development, implying a definite solution of the man-machine interaction problem, but can also point to a way in which control over scientific and technical evolution may prove to be most effective.

The changes in different spheres of social and economic life due to the "computer revolution" are really large and difficult to foretell. For this reason, analysis of the already obvious trends in computerizing seems very timely. Humanistic aspects of the "computer revolution" pertaining to the interaction between man and machine make up today an organic part of methodological cybernetic thinking. And that is what this article has been all about.

Reference

1. Weisenbaun, J. On the Impact of the Computer on Society, *Science*, 1972, No. 4035, 614.

Man and Machine: The Limits to Computer Application

V. M. GLUSHKOV and Yu. M. KANYGIN

What Causes Concern?

The man-machine problem has turned into the major present-day philosophical problem. It reflects the distinguishing feature of the current revolution in productive forces.

The classical machine is intended for doing physical work. Therefore, its aim is to release man of arduous and hazardous labour.

The situation is quite different when we speak of cybernetic automata. Coupled with machines and apparatus known before, they may serve as transport vehicles operating without human drivers, or may be manufacturing plants and offices doing without human workers, or they may conduct chess tournaments without human players. Electronic technology produces means of sensory perception. This allows man to receive information from hostile environments, e.g. outer space and deep water. Such things are no longer miracles.

The computer not only supplements, but also tends to replace the human brain like the steam engine once replaced the muscle power. Today, the electronic "brain" processes information and makes decisions sometimes even better than man does. So, the question arises: "What are the limits to the automation of mental activity, if any?"

The outputs of modern cybernetic systems (their concrete behaviour) are not necessarily strictly related with their inputs and depend on the programs introduced into the computer and on its memory. The stochastic element in the computer's behaviour increases, and this behaviour may not always be "virtuous". What if electronic monsters exceeding man in intelligence, lacking its conscience, his notions of good and evil come into being? This prospect is dreadful, and it is evoked not only by science-fiction writers.

The philosophical and sociological problems brought about by cybernetics and creation of artificial intelligence are quite different. Among them two groups of problems should be distinguished: the first includes scientific and technological problems of imitating intelligence, its functions and specific actions; the second includes problems of social consequence of developing and using "intelligent" robots and the historical responsibility that stems therefrom.

The problems are quite different and should not be confused.

Are There Any Scientific Limits to Developing and Using Cybernetic Machines?

Researchers into artificial intelligence realize, of course, that neither now nor in future will the computer be able to work miracles, as man cannot do it either. The functioning of the computer, as well as that of the human brain, is governed by the laws of nature. Man sets the task of making computers and their systems operate as closely to the human brain as possible in terms of complexity and functional capacities. As is obvious, machines will be able to imitate the human brain only in such areas that lend themselves to algorithmic formalization and programming. These areas, however, are widely extending and thus we do not seem to have reached any appreciably positive limits.

The computer takes on not only sensory functions but also mental (and this was always the prerogative of man) such as memorizing, retranslation, and computation, and it often performs them better than man. Moreover, computers solve problems that cannot be solved "manually" because they involve bulky computations. Computers can now self-learn; play chess; modify the program of their operation; process not only numerical data but also letters, sentences, charts; understand human speech; and so forth. These adaptive systems tend to imitate the higher functions of the human brain. Of course, the level of such systems has so far been lower than the average level of human mental activity. But, on the one hand, nobody is trying to create artificial intelligence comparable with the intellect of

Dostoyevsky or Einstein, and, on the other hand, we must not underestimate the rapid advance in cybernetics and electronic technology.

Are there any limits to extending the computer's capabilities, and which are they in nature, qualitative or quantitative? To say—the limits mean that man retains all creative functions and leaves routine functions to the computer—is to say nothing. The limits are too indefinite. A computer is known to have solved a problem that proved too difficult for mathematicians of high calibre, and even to have made an invention for which a patent has been granted.

On the other hand, the so-called routine functions (such as memorizing, for instance) are inalienable from creation. Man should not go too far in transferring these functions to the computer. In administrative control, man-machine methods do not mean to discard the managerial experience and practical knowledge. Managerial skills are the knowledge accumulated directly in the brain and not in the computer. Hence, the border lines between routine and creative mental operations (data processing) are somewhat blurred.

The rational, or "mechanical" component of mental activity may be computer-simulated without qualitative limitations. As mathematics, physics, electronics, cybernetics, chemistry, biology, genetics and other sciences continue to develop, so do the new techniques and methods of data processing and transfer and, hence, artificial intelligence.

But we must not forget the major stumbling blocks in the path towards artificial intelligence. We shall indicate two "complexity thresholds".

The first is the complexity and intricacy of the human brain as a biological phenomenon, the product of two billion years of evolution; and not of the brain alone, but of the whole biological system of the human intellect, where the brain functions as a central processor.

There are rather convincing proofs that mental activity implies nothing more than data processing, and that any functioning which can be logically and positively defined with a finite number of words can be realized by a formal (artificial) nervous system.* True, these proofs, as presented in works of Turing, Von Neumann, and some other authors, are purely theoretical.** There is still a long way to actual models in this area. Although some individual functions of living organisms have been simulated by non-living models, we are still far from being able to imitate artificially the functions of reproduction and development of the amoeba, to say nothing of man. And we are still farther away from creating mechanical models of the human brain and its complex functions.

Can all the processes running in the human brain be described accurately enough, and so be automated or, at least, formalized, expressed mathematically? In principle, it is possible that sooner or later the brain processes will be expressed algorithmically, describing yet undisclosed or partly disclosed phenomena such as intuition, imagination, and surprise. To think that subconscious processes have no structure whatsoever, that they do not obey the laws of nature, and that they are irrational, would mean to have mystic views.

---

* Not every informational process is mental, although every mental process is informational. From this standpoint the following statement appears incorrect: "Any technical system can be regarded as intelligent if it can generate, process, and output information" (Амосов Н. М. Искусственный разум. Киев, 1969, с. 122). But what if such a data processing system operates at the level of the amoeba?

** See, for instance, Turing A. M. *Computing Machinery and Intelligence*. Mind, vol. 59, pp. 433-460, October 1950. Reprinted in E. Feigenbaum and I. Feldman (eds.). *Computers and Thought*, pp. 11-35, McGraw-Hill Book Company, New York, 1963.

Those who are sceptical about the possibility of machine simulation of mental processes usually argue, that although the computer can in principle realize any data processing method, these methods in man do not remain invariable, they are constantly complemented and refined with experience, whereas artificial intelligence is something fixed, unchanging.

This viewpoint ignores the fact that systems of rules (in other words, programs) can be updated with the accumulation of experience. For this purpose changes in the rules are studied and programmed. These second-level rules can in turn be subjected to changes by means of third-level rules, and so on. In short, the computer can in principle be used to program the behaviour of infinitely complex self-learning and self-improving systems. And only the general laws of evolution of the organic world can serve as the ultimate-level rules.

As far as limitations are concerned, they are practical, rather than theoretical. For example, the computer memory is not large enough, elaborate programs are hard to devise, and so forth.

In addition, we must recognize serious methodological difficulties of imitating human intelligence. For its practical solution, we may have to work out new paradigms. In any case, the old principle of reducing the complex to the simple in the process of cognition and modelling is here losing its universal character. Now that we have come to grips with large systems as complex entities (intellect is one of them), we begin to understand that in some aspects the world is complex and indivisible.

Therefore, the first complexity threshold bars the way to cybernetic devices simulating the human brain as a collector of information that is superior by several orders of magnitude to any artificial or natural system. The ability of a system to reflect the outside world depends on its data-collecting capacity. Hence, we need still more powerful computers to bring artificial systems radically closer to the brain. Perhaps specialized artificial intelligent systems will be combined to produce a universal artificial intelligence.

The second threshold is associated with the social nature of intelligence. The most important component of intelligence, namely thinking, contains something that from the biological point of view can be regarded as "irrational". This "something" stems from the fact that intelligence is a product of the historical as well as biological evolution of man.

In order to understand the social aspect of intelligence, one should take into account two points: first, the will and the motivations that determine it; and, second, the "collectivistic" nature of cognition, where society as a whole, and not an individual, is the subject.

The range of volition makes man a system with an unlimited number of degrees of freedom. It is possible, in principle, to build a computer (or a network of computers) with an unlimited number of degrees of behavioral freedom. Some people, however, have doubts on that score. The motivations which shape volition are predominantly social (although some may be animal instincts). They are interests, feelings of good and evil, faith, love, hatred, tastes, and so on. It would be futile to assert that they have nothing to do with thinking (information processing). The motivations make up an intellectual "call", prolonged commands, coming from "inside" the social organism or an individual, or as a poet would say "the languishing of the soul" or "the beautiful flights of the soul". Psychologists have yet to decide what is more important for a personal outlook, rational data processing of outside signals, or this, largely irrational, inner call.*

A Dostoyevsky's character once said: "... if one day they really discover some formula of all our wishes and whims, that is to say, ... a real mathematical formula, man may perhaps at once stop feeling any desire..." And more to this effect: "... volition is a manifestation of the whole life, I mean, of the whole human life, including reason with all its concomitant scratchings. And although our life, thus manifested, very often turns out to be a sorry business, it is life none the less and not merely extractions of square roots."**

A search for truth is not a simple processing of information. The scientific potential we enjoy today has been painstakingly accumulated throughout history. The cry of Archimedes "Don't step on my circles" as an enemy soldier brandished the sword at him; Socrates, who, voluntarily in fact, gave up his life for the sake of truth; and thousands of similar cases have a direct bearing on the tree of knowledge on the Earth. The computer can be programmed for individual deeds, even extravagancies (skin scratching as mentioned above), but how to program the behaviour of a scientist (or, generally, of a thinking person) and his views (and they are inalienable from cognition)? The computer, "intelligent" as it can be made, can so far be only the tool, and not the social subject.

Touching upon the social character of cognition, we can say the following. It may only seem that science advances

* The nature of this "call of the soul" determines the difference between the Cartesian and the existentialist model of man. Pavlov's model and the Marxist model of man reject both models as one-sided and extreme.

** The Best Short Stories of Dostoyevsky. Translated with an Introduction by David Magarshack. The Modern Library. New York. 1955, p. 133.

18—01169

owing to individuals: Archimedes invented the lever, Newton discovered the law of gravitation and Einstein the law of the equivalence of mass and energy, and so on. Science, however, is not a chain of casual inspirations of individuals, it is a social institution that functions under definite social conditions which determine the level of mental activity. If the society is not prepared to receive scientific discoveries, no geniuses and no computers will help. The computer is only a leap forward in productive forces of mankind. And they have always depended on labour relations and social structure.

Thus, the difficulties of the second order arise from the fact that human beings are social creatures. The intellect of every person reflects and assimilates most intricate interrelations between individuals, that is, the system of their interaction. So, if we want computers to be as intelligent as man, we should put all this into them.

But is there any need to put the social component in the computer? This is the major problem. And only historical laws and social responsibility can help answer it.

Social (Historical) Responsibility for Artificial Intelligence

Now we want to consider the following situation: artificial intelligence outstrips natural intelligence, and man may be replaced by robots. It may sound fine; however, no one is sure it will be realized. In addition to the laws of science, the laws of history govern the advance of society. Human society has a great instinct for self-preservation. Otherwise it would not survive.

The social (historical) responsibility arises with every major innovation, and is the more acute the greater the innovation. Modern computers have already generated the social responsibility, for everybody knows the key role the computers play in modern weapon systems. The social-responsibility problems, specifically those associated with computers, arise not only when they present a direct physical threat to society. For example, automation today breeds tedium and, in some cases, strain in mental work. The computer often sets the pace of administrative activity. Man must keep this pace of data handling and decision making (before, he could go slow in some individual operations or even put them off for some time). The situation somewhat resembles the conveyor-belt operation shown by Chaplin in his Modern Times. The informational flow line is good from the standpoint of production; but is it so good from the worker's?

The problem of man and machine as applied to computers is a problem of changing the structure of human activity (mental and physical) rather than that of "liberating" man from labour. Man will hardly entrust the robot with the task of setting problems, considering and making decisions, and bringing up the youth. The robot can only be used as a "hand" here. Lenin said that there were truths of the first, second, and further orders. The part of robots and computers in man's cognition of the first-order truths cannot be the same as in the cognition of truths of the second (and higher) order. Finally, the quest for moral, ethical, and aesthetic truths will always remain purely human.

Nevertheless, what is the guarantee that scientific and technological innovations, be it nuclear weapons or "intelligent" robots, do not get out of hand and turn into the tools of the devil in the hands of some individuals. Man, however, cannot pin all his hopes on abstract humanism.

Man is a product of social relations.

In a harmonious society machines will not take "human" from man. This is so, first, because man that cognizes nature acts not on his own but as a part of the social organism, and, second, because people in such a society consciously control not only scientific and technological but also social and economic development. As for new information-handling techniques, the society gets with computers a tool of practically unlimited power. And this tool must be perfected by all means.

Social Applications of Cybernetics

V. D. PEKELIS

Today we can hardly name a field of human activity where cybernetics has failed to find its way. Some of these areas are highly unusual. Cybernetics is being used in understanding human relationships in their concrete and abstract aspects, as well as the relationships between individuals and social groups. Moral and ethical factors, which never before were expressed in numerical form, have now been encoded and fed into computers.

But is there any need at all to solve such problems with the aid of cybernetics? We believe there is. The current level of accuracy in social-sciences analysis and the concomitant possibility of predicting social development are far from satisfactory. The reasons are that social life is extremely complex, that subjective and random factors in social life are difficult to take into account, and, of course, that scientific research techniques are not yet adequately developed.

The Past Judged by Computers?

For one hundred and thirty years all attempts to decipher Mayan manuscripts proved futile. The Soviet scientist Knorozov carefully studied the texts and hypothesized that the scripts were hieroglyphic. But how could they be read? Then cyberneticists stepped in. Combining man's intelligence with the computer's swiftness, they created a deciphering method. Following their programs for search and selection of words, the computer carried out billions of operations, allowing the canonical texts of the Madrid and Dresden manuscripts to be read. We learned about Mayan astronomical and astrological tables, descriptions of matrimonial rites, trades, myths of the Great Flood and of gods the Mayans worshipped. In less than a year, half of all the discovered texts had been read, whereas before, hundreds of experts had been able to decipher only a single hieroglyph in a decade.

The mountain village of Kubachi in Dagestan is famous for its jewelry and silverware. The handicrafts of the villagers often saved them from enslavement. They redeemed themselves from invaders with the priceless decorations, utensils, and weaponry that they produced. Legend has it that this centre of art was initially established by settlers from France. True, some elements of the local language do indeed remind one of French. Scientists decided to check the legend. They devised a special mathematical model and, using a computer, determined that the legend did not correspond to the facts. The analysis showed that the crafts of the Kubachi artisans came into being in the mountains of Dagestan in the 3rd century A.D.

Numismatists have compiled large catalogues of ancient coins found in the Northern Black Sea coastal regions. The catalogues list the locations of the finds, where they were coined, what metal was used, their value, and various other data. But it is too much for man to systematically process these reams of data for proper historical and economic conclusions. Computer data processing enables historians to formulate an historical theory based on "numismatical" data, trade and cultural exchanges, and political economy of this part of the ancient world.

Historians now have a great deal of information on the initial settling of America. Not only are historical facts available, but there are also materials provided by anthropology, paleography, ethnography, linguistics, and other scientific disciplines. Computers help sort out these vast amounts of facts and their most significant details, which will permit us to move from shaky hypotheses of what happened to a real picture. Computers thus solve the problem of the accurate classification of millions of individual facts for drawing scientific conclusions.

But, strictly speaking, can all these examples form what could be defined as computer-aided historical studies? Certainly not. This is merely the use of high-speed electronic computers for tackling specific, clearly defined problems. The computer performs what it has primarily been designed to do—to handle enormous amounts of information at high speed—something man shirks and stands helpless against.

When we talk about "the past being judged by computers", we have something else in mind. It is history itself, the historical process, as the subject of computer-aided research. And this is a much more difficult problem.

What is a cybernetic approach to history? This approach implies the need as far as possible (and necessary) to formalize history, that is, to reduce historical analysis to specific computer programs. But it is precisely this specificity that makes the problem so difficult. One cannot expect history to be mathematically strict, for it is a science of continuous process. What happens today is already an historical event.

Despite the venerable age of history as a branch of knowledge and its giant accumulation of data, there are still many unknown facts and events. If only history were a chain of events with every link in its place! Alas, the chain is not whole, many links are missing. Furthermore, experiment as a method is not available to the historian. Today, however, he is able to model separate fragments of the historical process and thereby check hypotheses of what happened from records in historical documents, these "links" between the present and the past.

A typical situation the historian encounters is the same event described in different sources in different ways. Such descriptions are often at variance with one another.

One final difficulty in the application of cybernetics to history is history's ethical content.

It was Norbert Wiener who saw the principal difficulties of applying cybernetics and mathematics to historical studies. He wrote that in social sciences, we deal with short statistical samples, and we cannot be sure that most of the phenomena observed have not been created by ourselves... We are too well inclined to the objects of our research to probe impartially. In short, our studies in social sciences, whether static or dynamic (and they should be both) can be accurate to only a few digits after the decimal point, and they will never yield as much meaningful information as we usually expect in natural sciences. We cannot afford to neglect social sciences, but we must not be too optimistic about their possibilities. Whether we like it or not, we should leave a lot to the 'unscientific' narrative method of the professional historian.

Nevertheless, to a certain extent, the use of cybernetics and mathematics in historical analysis is not only possible, but also necessary.

What Is Your Verdict?

That was the title that Professor V. Kudryavtsev, a leading expert in the application of cybernetics to law, gave to his article. Its message was clear. He wrote: "We want justice, humaneness, inevitability, truth, and other juridical categories to become as accurate as though they rested on the same indisputable evidence as data in mathematics, physics, and chemistry..."

Law is an area also concerned with the management and organized regulation of human behaviour. Cybernetics is the science of control, regulation, and self-regulation of complex dynamic systems. It is natural, then, for jurists to try to increase as much as possible the efficiency of the regulation they deal with. The administration of justice, more than any other activity, requires accuracy and scientifically correct substantiation of decisions, and here cybernetic methods turn out to be very useful.

In the opinion of Academician A. I. Berg, "law, which is concerned with the behavior and actions of man in relation to a great number of other people in diverse circumstances and whose actions are motivated by particular reasons, has every reason to use a science basing itself on the study of phenomena and patterns of mass probability".

The non-specialist is unaware of how enormous the number of laws, decrees, and other legal acts simultaneously in effect in this country is. Not a single jurist could give you the precise figure. How can all these acts be organized into a system so that they do not contradict each other and are all consistent with the general aims of legislation?

Kudryavtsev refers us to the work carried out by a team of jurists and mathematicians led by Professor Kerimov. They put legal acts to strict logical analysis with the aid of a computer. They compared all the decrees in one area of law, brought out all contradictions, and simplified the wording of the acts. It became clear that the verbal descriptions in legal documents could be tightly "compacted" into a brief mathematical code, without repetitions or double meanings. This makes a computerized legal information service a real possibility. Here the computer would facilitate the storage and retrieval of facts and precedents from a large body of collected data.

Such a service is very much needed. Ordinary people are not well informed about legal codet. They do not peruse them in their spare time like newspapers, fiction, or poetry. Imagine how convenient it would be to pick up the phone and in a few seconds get an answer about current legislation, about what you may not do and, more importantly, what you may do legally.

However, a computer-aided legal information service is a far cry from having computers pass verdicts in courts, from using them for purposes of legislation and law studies. What can be done in this area?

The question is not clear yet. Here, as with history, we face difficult problems. The computer "knows" formal logic only, it can deal with formal categories. But legal problems involve the juxtaposition of the abstract with reality, with the content of a fact or event. Formal logic is powerless when confronted with their "subjective infinity".

Just see what happens. Suppose we designate by symbols a court decision to grant a divorce and the legal conditions for such a decision. Various combinations of the symbols will signify situations that occur in real life. This is reasonable because according to statistics, grounds for a divorce are quite definite and come with certain regularity. In Czechoslovakia, for instance, of over 15 thousand divorce cases in 1960 three fourths were caused by husbands having drinking problems, committing adultery, or leaving their wives for other women. When the wife was at fault, the main grounds in more than half of all cases was solely infidelity. The similarity of all those cases is purely formal. In real life a breach of marital fidelity, for instance, has so many peculiarities and shades that sometimes it can hardly be so qualified. Of course, all these intricacies are still beyond the scope of the computer.

The legal procedure in a court of law consists of the investigation and the rendering of verdict. The computer could help the judge systematize the results of the investigation, compare testimonies, logically analyze them, and reveal possible contradictions or a lack of sufficient evidence. In this way it would significantly facilitate and speed up the judge's work and make it more accurate.

It would also be easier for a judge to pronounce a verdict and pass a sentence. This is vital to the fate of the defendant. Has anyone ever tried to program these vital stages in the administration of justice? Not because it is trendy to look for new computer applications, but in order to trace in detail, from a cybernetic standpoint, the way the judge arrives at his conclusion, to reveal the mechanism of appraising the evidence, and to describe this complex process in the language of logic.

It Is Up to Us to Decide

While travelling abroad in the spring of 1964, I came across a newspaper with some marriage proposals on the last page.

"A 20-year-old girl would like to meet a nice young man with serious intentions".

"A 26-year-old widower would like to find a childless spouse".

"Young man wants to find a good mother for his little boy".

There were many different advertisements of this kind. I was amazed. Fancy having this in our time! But don't let's jump to conclusions. Let us take an unprejudiced look at the situation.

In the West, matrimonial advertisements have long been an established practice. Computers are now being used to bring together people wishing to get married—being a sort of "electronic match-making service". Clients fill out detailed questionnaires with their vital statistics (age, education, personal preferences and habits, income, colour of eyes, and so on) and state their requirements for the prospective spouse. These data are fed into a computer, whose task is to find a husband or wife for the client. Sometimes the input data contain information obtained with the aid of various instruments, such as encephalographs and the like.

On the average, a questionnaire contains about 80 questions. It is no easy matter for the computer to find the answers, for an incredible amount of sorting out must be done to arrive at an optimum variant.

The task is so difficult that an IBM-1410 computer in Zurich, for example, managed to "foster" only 50 families in three years. True, it also put out matrimonial recommendations to over 1 000 men and 1 600 women.

Students at Harvard University adapted a computer to the task of "electronic adviser" for establishing contacts between male and female students. Note, that it played the part of adviser, and not "marriage-maker". In its first nine months, this service got 90 thousand applications from students all over the United States. Once you have sent the machine your vital statistics and your specifications, you eventually get back five names and addresses. Needless to say, not all young people fall in love in this way. "We don't try to offer something measuring up to real human love", say those who run the "electronic adviser", "we provide everything short of the love spark". The decision is made by a human being, guided by his own feelings, but he may use the information obtained from the computer. It does not arrange marriage, it only brings people together by processing large amounts of data.

I should like to emphasize the fact that the computer submits its recommendations to people. And it is up to them to decide.

What is important is that one can reduce the random element in the "boy meets girl and marries her" situation. The computer's proposal prepares people for contact in advance, giving them a chance to get to know each other before meeting in person. I would even put it this way: in resorting to computer services, in waiting for the outcome, which takes time, there is a significant element of psychological preparation for marriage.

By the way, in Czechoslovakia there is an "Agency for bringing together people who want to marry". This agency does a lot of work. There are 140 thousand more women than men in the country, and about one million widows. In Prague, for instance, there is one widower for every six widows, and one divorced man for three divorced women. Single people include not only divorcees and bachelors, but also many young girls.

The great majority of them want to find a partner. Public opinion is still prejudiced against making contacts through advertisements and computer services. But, according to Czech journalists, this will change in time, and the agency has already received applications from thousands upon thousands of people. The Prague branch of the agency, for example, registered 300 computer-aided marriages in three years. The youngest female client was 18 and the oldest, 81 years old.

The obvious conclusion seems to be that computer recommendations do make the search for a mate easier, putting people on generally the right track. What's more, it has been established that the divorce rate is negligible among couples brought together with the aid of a computer, and for this reason, it is worth looking more closely at this computer application.

Let us consider some facts concerning the marriage and family situation in the Soviet Union. According to statistics, in 1961 we had some 30 million single men from 18 to 60 years old and 35 million single women. Quite a lot, isn't it? We may assume that these people would like to marry. Theoretically, any bachelor of 60 who has finally decided to have a family of his own has 35 million unmarried women to sort through—no easy task.

How can one go about it? Statistical surveys give an answer: 27.2 percent of couples meet each other during their leisure time, 21 percent meet at work; 9 percent have known each other since childhood, 5.7 percent meet at parties, 5.2 percent meet at holiday resorts, and the rest meet through relatives, in hostels, and just by chance, in the streets and public transport.

As we can see, the choice of effective ways to make a good acquaintance is rather limited. Almost half of all relationships are started at work or at places where people spend their leisure time.

But what is the chance of a woman who works among women and a man who works among men? There are many such people. And leisure activities are not much help to those who live in towns with a predominantly male or female population. Many people fall into this category, too.

It has long been known, however, that geographical proximity is one of the most evident factors in making a choice of mate. As a rule, most marriages occur within one city, town, or rural district.

In addition, sociologists maintain that the choice of a partner in marriage is affected by occupation. A close connection exists between the occupations of husband and wife, husband and father-in-law, and both fathers-in-law.

How long do people know each other before getting married? A span of several days was mentioned by only 3 percent, up to six months by over 9 percent, up to a year by 5.6 percent, up to two years by 23 percent, and up to five years by 14 percent. The greatest number of people, 26.6 percent, have been acquainted before marriage for two to three years.

Note that those acquainted for less than a year before marriage account for only 17 percent. All the others are probably unwilling to "tie the nuptial knot" until they have known each other for a year or more. So why should one distrust "electronic" advice or disapprove of computer-aided matrimony?

Excuse me for some more statistics, but it is the best way to prove my point by supporting it with facts.

To arrive at definite conclusions, we need to know what statistics reveal as the main condition for a successful marriage. In 76 percent of cases, those polled cited love, or love accompanied with trust, sincerity, and common views; 13.2 percent, respect and equality; 4 percent, love and decent housing; 1.6 percent, love and good income; 0.6 percent, having children; and 0.2 percent, "a practical attitude to life" (4.2 percent did not respond). Surveys of young people show that 98.5 percent believe love or love combined with friendship and respect to be the principal condition of conjugal happiness.

Thus, the great majority of those who get married seek a similar outlook, trust, sincerity, and other reciprocal qualities. That may account for the fact that people look carefully at each other for two or three years before deciding on marriage.

And a statistical minority will always be in a hurry, whether aided by computers or not.

How many marriages are registered and how long do they last? Unfortunately, the data I have at my disposal are incomplete. But some information available from various publications (*Вестник статистики*, 1975, 11, 12; *Население СССР*. 1973; *Статистика*, 1975) shows the following.

The number of new marriages in this country has been large: two million a year, or 12.1 marriages per 1 000 people. For comparison, this figure in the FRG is 9.4; in the USA, 8.5; in England, 7.5; and in France, 7.

And what about divorce? Its rate is growing: on average nearly every third marriage is legally dissolved, and that cannot be ignored.

Why do marriages fall apart? It is difficult to give a definite answer to this question. But in most cases the reason must be the partners' "incompatibility", which came out because they did not get to know each other well enough before getting married.

It is a fact, though, that many couples separate after living in accord for five or ten years, and even more. But we are primarily concerned with the initial conditions required for a long-lasting marriage, and it is difficult in this context to cite anything other than compatibility of the future mates, their mutual respect, and, most of all, love for one another.

The problem of divorce is extremely complicated. A divorce has grave implications: personal drama, harm to society, mounting social problems.

There are many ways of trying to lower the number of divorces and to strengthen marriages. But these ways should not be limited to psychological, moral, and social influence only. Since 1968, when the author pioneered in this country a proposal to use computers for matrimonial purposes, heated debates have been raging for more than ten years. These debates, which involved psychologists, physicians, sociologists, philosophers, mathematicians, programmers, and other experts, have shown that traditional attitudes still persist. So far sociologists have failed to tackle this problem, no serious psychological analysis has been undertaken, no surveys have been conducted, no modern scientific methods and means have been used in this area.

But suppose a cybernetic approach to this problem should prove helpful, with computers not only providing information for those wishing to find a partner, but also simulating the prospective married life in each specific case. Why not? Today the computer can answer questions of whether a dam not even built yet will collapse or last for centuries, or whether an aircraft to be built will fly or fall apart in mid-air. Let us ask the computer if a particular family will have a solid life together or not. It is probably worth laboring over a mathematical model of the family in order to have as few actual marriage failures as possible.

It goes without saying that the model of a dam with a limited number of well defined specifications bears no comparison with the model of a family life with an unlimited number of factors whose social substance is not quite clear. But science, after all, has now taken up the problem of artificial intelligence. Surely that is no simpler task.

Nobody is shocked by the fact that crews of cosmonauts

preparing for space flights are tested for psychological compatibility. It is clear that an increasingly cooperative and friendly atmosphere is essential for people on a long space mission.

The studies have shown that it is not an easy task to form even a small team which tends to develop, improve, and strengthen ties between its members. The foreign press has reported on the "disintegration" of astronaut crews which in terms of temperament, moral attitudes, and so on, were incompatible.

It is very likely that the typical divorce formula—different personality types—is nothing more than psychological incompatibility. In other words, a married couple can be likened to a couple of cosmonauts setting out on a long and difficult mission—life. This is hard to dispute. Wise, experienced people know how important it is to "break in" to one another, that is, to adapt oneself to one's mate physiologically, psychologically, and socially. So, compatibility in marriage, not compatibility in general, is what matters. Unfortunately, this aspect is often overlooked.

Take, for instance, a seemingly simple question which has yet to be answered: what kind of people get together more readily—similar or dissimilar? The answer could probably be obtained by using so-called quantitative methods. In other words, the usual verbal, psychological characteristics of a person should be translated into numerical characteristics in order to get qualitative personality features.

Perhaps it is possible to develop a method for obtaining quantitative data for making an impartial self-appraisal and for evaluating the "optimal married couple". Interestingly enough, studies of a person in a collective have established a considerable difference in opinions between men and women. Men tend to overestimate their intellectual power and physical appeal, whereas women, on the contrary, are most self-critical as regards these qualities. And an average rating given to women by men proved higher than that given to men by women.

But that is in a collective. How about in a family?

Of course, the reader may say that the author is biased, that he is trying to draw a single conclusion from all these data. And the reader will be correct. The author is all for using computers to aid those wishing to find a spouse. This by no means implies that tomorrow all service agencies must install computers. But why should not science, and one of its most powerful tools—the electronic "brain"—help people?

The "electronic adviser" is unusual and somewhat frightening, as is the necessity to lie on an operating table on the recommendations of a diagnostic machine. But, according to Professor A. A. Vishnevsky, a prominent Soviet surgeon, today not a single patient suffering from a congenital heart disease is operated on without a preliminary machine diagnosis. Can you really say there is no ethical aspect here? But whereas computer diagnosis may be said to leave no options, "matrimonial advice" by the computer is only a way to a free choice.

Let us weigh all the "pros" before voting against such a computer application. This problem should be regarded without self-righteousness or excessive conservatism. And, what is essential, we should not confuse love with the electronic computer: let us give all that is human to man and all that is machinal to the computer.

Foreseeing the Future

In this chapter, the authors venture not only short-term predictions—until the end of the 20th century—but also medium-term (for the foreseeable future) and even long-term (the distant future) predictions. Practically speaking, however, assigning the conjectures put forward in each of the chapter's four articles to an exact period is highly difficult. This is evident from analysis of some predictions given in the concluding part of this book. There we find some exact hits and some obvious misses. Nevertheless, the value of a prediction does not consist exclusively in its absolute reliability; it should also be reasonably bold and plausible.

The Formula of a Collective Genius

V. D. PEKELIS

A collective. How often we use this word in its various senses. A collective is a group of people working together. A collective is a group of people who got together to accomplish a certain task. It is hard to list all its meanings and all the combinations in which it is used. A few come to mind: collectives of research workers, collectives of amateur artists, collective creation, a collective of students.

Today, the notion of "collective" is very common and indispensable.

In a socialist society, it is important that people should be united not only by a common purpose and common labour, but also by a common organization of labour.

Naturally, a collective which uses moderately straightforward machines and a collective that uses management information systems and computers for production control are collectives of different levels. That is why so much attention has been paid recently to collectives of the new type and to new methods of management.

A collective provides an extensive testing ground for new organizational methods and techniques; it gives a lot of promising material for experiments and research programs. It is in a collective that the highest efficiency of creative work can and must be achieved.

Now, the question is, what degree of perfection can a working collective attain? Different collectives perform to different degrees of efficiency: some do better, others worse. But is it possible to work at maximum efficiency? Or, in other words, is it possible to create a collective genius?

The question is so unusual that many people will probably regard it as a joke, although anyone will agree that at present, when most vital problems are solved by collectives, the discovery of an "elixir of efficiency" for collectives would be invaluable.

Experts will say that the life of a collective can be described as a total of more or less successfully resolved conflicts. The conflicts arise in the process of various interactions. What interactions? Man is at the hub of a collective, and therefore we can distinguish three systems of interaction: between individuals, between an individual and the environment, and between individuals and machines.

In team work success depends on each worker as an individual and on all workers collectively. An individual is connected with his fellow workers through hundreds of links. Hence, he must often subordinate some of his ambitions and wishes to the interests of the collective.

What is the basis for interaction between members of a team? How do the attitudes of fellow workers shape collective opinion? How urgent is the need for a favourable psychological climate: relations between colleagues, relations between superiors and subordinates, relations between individuals and the collective as a whole?

Many questions arise in the analysis of relations between an individual and the environment. It is well known that the aspects of the working environment in the sphere of management and control are extremely complex.

And, lastly, what a host of diverse problems face those working in our cybernetic age.

The variety of collectives is practically infinite, and you can imagine how difficult their features are to analyze. For this reason let us discuss only one type—a scientific collective. It is in this type of collective that the problems in question take the most general forms and are dealt with in the light of the latest concepts and views.

Suppose you are appointed the head of a newly established laboratory in a scientific research institute. You have bluntly stated to the administration and the scientific board that you are going to create a collective by using scientific methods...

Such novelties are not yet always and everywhere received with due enthusiasm, and so the response to such a statement is easy to imagine:

"Well, what's this "science of collectives" anyway? Never heard of such a thing". "Are you sure that methods of forming and developing a good working collective can be reduced to mathematical formulas and charts?"

"Do we really need a "science of collectives"? We have done alright without it till now. Built aircraft, split the atom, launched satellites. Collectives did all that, and without any fancy tricks or fads!"

That's right, collectives do work. But with what efficiency?

In recent years anthropologists have often voiced their view that the evolution of the human organism appears to be flickering out. That may be so, but then the "super-organism"—the human collective—is evolving rapidly, almost explosively. We are witnessing and participating in an incredibly complex process of developing a "superbrain" on a global scale. Any observer surveying man's path for the past several centuries will notice that the power and complexity of collectives and their part in solving vital problems have been constantly increasing.

Nevertheless, experience shows that the productivity of most working collectives (industrial enterprises, research and development institutions, design offices, ministries, and so on) falls short of what is possible theoretically. And the more complex a collective, the farther it is from its optimum performance, and the more potentialities remain unutilized. On the other hand, experts in social psychology have long recognized that sometimes collectives get a mysterious surge of working activity. All the members are gripped by enthusiasm, their emotional and physical forces rise tenfold, individuals unite in a single knot of energy and become capable of accomplishing the extraordinary. At such moments, unknown forces gush into the collective as though from unknown depths.

This phenomenon was mentioned by Karl Marx, who wrote that in most productive activities, social contacts induce energy that increases the productivity of each of the individuals.

This astonishing quality of a human collective may be called emergency.

It is well known that potentialities of a system depend on the number of its component elements. When the number of components reaches a certain level, a qualitative change in the system's performance may occur. It is reasonable to suppose that its performance sharply improves as the collective grows larger and more complex. Unfortunately, that relationship has not been confirmed yet. What is the reason?

Some scientists believe that emergency is possible in the sphere of emotions only. As for an intellectual emergency in a collective, it must be specially organized. Experience tends to support this view.

A number of other factors also support the idea that it is both possible and necessary to develop a special theory of collective genius.

Collective: a Cybernetic System?

A possible way of solving the problem of the efficiency of collectives is to consider a collective (for instance, a laboratory) as a cybernetic system (what this is and how it works is described in hundreds of monographs and papers). Each individual member of the collective in certain respects can also be considered as a kind of cybernetic system. Roughly, it consists of a control unit—the brain, and an object of control—the body; these two units are connected with numerous direct and feedback channels—nerves and blood vessels. The control unit contains a program, that is, knowledge and experience, both inherited and acquired through upbringing and learning. The system works according to this program. In reality, the picture is infinitely more intricate, because man is a social as well as biological being.

Carrying the analogy a bit further, we can say that the laboratory has a control unit—its manager, an object of control—the members of the collective, and a system of direct and feedback connections—orders, directives, advice, plans, and so on, that come from management, and reports, both written and oral that come from subordinates to management. Finally, the manager keeps in his memory a certain program used to direct and control the collective.

If we go back to the days before cybernetics, we note that even then people who well understood the nature of a collective like A. S. Makarenko discerned in it "the elements of a living social organism that has 'control centres', 'relations between the parts' and 'interdependence'."*

It would be relevant to note that a scientific approach to the problem of organizing a working collective is not a godsend, and it has not been borrowed from elsewhere. The social psychology of groups and collectives was successfully studied in this country back in the 1920-30s. A general classification of groups and collectives was outlined at that time. Methods and techniques of studying socio-psychological phenomena were devised, and experiments were conducted on groups of students and scientists. The researchers observed changes in perception and associations and determined the degree to which efficiency of memory and levels of creative thinking and imagination could be raised.

Makarenko came on the scene as an innovator of that time; he not only worked on the theory of organizing collectives, but also proved their possibilities in practice. He proposed a classification of collectives and demonstrated the stages of their development. We can say without any exaggeration, that the Makarenko pedagogy of the

---

* Макаренко А. С. Собр. соч., 1958, 5, 353-356.

collective is still valid today and can be used as a source of ideas for current socio-psychological research on groups and collectives.

Let us return to the discussion of a collective from our somewhat simplistic point of view: a collective as a cybernetic system.

The "organism" of a laboratory pertains to the class of hierarchical cybernetic systems. The head of the laboratory controls the behaviour and mental activity of all laboratory workers taken individually and collectively. He directs the heads of the sections, they direct the researchers, and so on.

To set up an optimal laboratory collective is a task that is somewhat similar to the task facing the designers of a computer which is intended to handle problems of a definite class. The difference is that the designers first create the "body" (hardware) and then, at the programming stage, the "soul" (software) of the computer. The director of a collective must perform both functions at once.

The objective experience of evolution of "thinking systems"—man, the social collective, the electronic computer—shows that the most advantageous structure for them is a pyramidal hierarchy, (with the pinnacle up). But how many elements should this structure have? How should their hierarchy be arranged? How should these elements be linked?

Wise and slow-paced nature solved all these problems by the centuries-old method of trial and error. This pace does not suit us today.

Designers of electronic "intelligence systems" can calculate fairly accurately what amount of information can be processed by every element of the computer they are developing. Given the range of problems the computer is designed to deal with, it is possible to determine the overall volume of information the computer will handle, and hence, the number of the elements required and their hierarchy.

Alas, it is impossible, at least today, to apply such an approach to a research worker. The point is that the information flowing through his brain in the process of work is characterized by two attributes: quantity and quality (or value).

True, the mathematician and engineer Claud Shannon, one of the founders of cybernetics, developed a method for computing the amount of information passing through a communication channel. But the method is not universal. As to the quality of information, it has so far not lent itself to calculation. One could, for instance, find a detective novel containing as much information as *War and Peace* by Leo Tolstoy, but the two novels will not compare, of course, in terms of informational value.

None the less, we may make some recommendations on how to organize an optimal working collective from the perspective of information theory.

We might recall a well-known maxim: there are no people without any talent, there are only people employed in the wrong jobs. In effect, this is the principal law of occupational orientation—the science of search for vocation.

Occupational orientation experts claim that each human being has a special vocation. If it has been revealed and used, the person will serve the society in the best possible way.

Applying this principle to collectives, one can say that a necessary condition for the working team to be optimal is the agreement between the abilities and duties of each member of the team.

The problem of finding one's vocation is not easy and is a long way from being cleared up. But the agreement condition mentioned above is being partially realized by maximum differentiation of duties, by sparing high-calibre researchers, and by assigning all routine tasks to technicians and assistants.

To determine the optimal number of members in a collective is also very difficult. More often than not people fail to solve this problem in a scientific way. Inexperienced managers tend to take on more personnel than they really need—hardly the way to do things. Norbert Wiener, the father of cybernetics, once said that the redundance of elements in a cybernetic system may be more harmful than their shortage.

At present, the so-called systems approach is being used more and more often in such cases. Its scope embraces such concepts as "system", "structure", "communication", "control", "steady state", "target", "instruction", "isolation", "interaction", and ties them into a single knot termed "behaviour". The systems approach is applied to automatic road or rail traffic control, to complex energy systems control, to city planning, to economic systems, and, what is important here, to research into conditions for optimum performance of human collectives.

The systems approach to a collective makes it possible to determine its optimum size, to see its complex organization, inner activity and dynamism as well as its integrity, and to observe its behaviour, development, and all aspects of its functioning.

Who Is to Be in Charge?

Imagine you are appointed to put together a new scientific research facility. Such facilities are usually divided into departments which, in turn, are divided into laboratories. Your task, as director, is to find suitable heads for these departments and laboratories. The collective-forming principle described above applies here, too, but at a somewhat different level.

In managerial schools which enroll people with higher education, an elaborate system of tests is used. There are detailed lists of the qualities a manager should have.

In an experiment, a questionnaire was distributed among members of a small collective of scientists. The questions were all aimed at finding out who they would like to have as their chief. He was to be selected not abstractly, but from the candidates participating in the experiment. The collective voted for the person who scored highest in intellectual qualities. It was pointed out that in addition to intellect he was attractive in appearance, although all the other contenders had good managerial abilities and intellectual qualities, too. Optimism and a sense of humour were also highly valued in a superior. In the view of the collective, these qualities could even make up for some of his weaknesses.

Directing a collective nowadays requires, in addition to everything else, great skill. This skill is a matter of talent, training, knowledge, and experience.

Psychologists believe that a manager must use diverse, seemingly opposite ways and methods of dealing with subordinates: he should be gentle but firm, exercise absolute control but let people have a say in important matters, make them meet his requirements but also satisfy their requirements, check their work and yet trust them, be formal in his manners but friendly and comradely with people, give orders and make requests, persuade and reprimand, smile and frown—in other words, use the whole array of attitudes that make up effective communication.

An executive must always remember that authority is a moral and psychological category; authority does not always coincide with administrative power.

In this age of growing complexity of research work and complex structures of research collectives, it is particularly important to study the ways in which they are directed. It is only recently that we have begun to fully appreciate the significance of the emotional side of relations between people. These relations are active in any group of people; their sphere involves both the superior and his subordinates. It has been found that the superior must spend sixty percent of his valuable time on maintaining good relations within the collective, which is not a simple matter.

A human being has a strong tendency to imitation — the wish to be or act like someone who has captured his imagination, whether it be a fictional character, a movie star, or a great military commander. The person we want to copy must have the qualities—beauty, fame, intelligence, nobility, courage, and so on—that appeal to the masses. Certainly, some of those qualities would come in useful for the head of a collective of research workers.

The position of, say, head of a laboratory differs substantially from that of a rank-and-file researcher, and not merely in terms of salary. The head of a laboratory must meet specific requirements to suit the job. In most of his qualities (level of knowledge, creative capacity, skill in dealing with people) he should be a model for his subordinates.

Most of his fellow workers, in trying to imitate him will move steadily "up" to the model. And there is the danger that at some point they may reach his level and even overtake him (which often happens).

Hence, one of the main requirements placed on a leader is that he should have an unflagging desire to improve.

As to the gap between the levels (intellectual and ethical) of the chief and his subordinates, experience has shown that a sound principle of setting up the administrative hierarchy of a research facility is to work from the bottom upwards, that is, to place people in such a way that every administrator of a higher rank is a head above his counterpart on the next lower rank. The opposite way is no good: if you first appoint a director he will then find a deputy who, naturally, will be a bit lower in calibre, the deputy director will select heads of departments on the same principle, who will, in turn, choose heads of laboratories, and so on. It is one thing if the director is a prominent figure...

If the selection is done from the bottom, the level of the director will be determined "automatically", depending on the collective already formed, whose hierarchy has been established in accordance with the complexity of the problems to be tackled.

Some readers may, at best, feel annoyed at such notions. How can you select people, and highly skilled people at that, as though they were parts for a machine?

But I can see nothing wrong with candidates for director of a scientific research facility or an industrial enterprise undergoing, in addition to the usual checks, psycho-physical tests similar to those used in selecting cosmonauts.

How can the productivity of a scientist, design engineer, institute director be raised? How can the work of a research institution be organized for maximum efficiency? How can we create the best conditions for the research worker to apply in full his talent, knowledge, and energy?

These problems can be solved only by improving the organization of research and development activities and by employing people with a talent for directing these activities.

That is why the questions discussed here are so germane today.

But is it really so difficult to be in charge? Yes, it most certainly is. Just look at it yourself. Suppose you have passed all the checks and tests and are now sitting in the director's chair. What will your first move be?

From the cybernetic standpoint, the process of controlling a collective consists in the director's orienting and modifying the program "stored" in the heads of his people. In the laboratory, the main work on implementing his ideas is done by the rank-and-file research workers, who process data in accordance with their knowledge and, of course, with the program given to them. As scientific problems arise, they are solved in the course of processing the data. The director guides, coordinates, and checks this process.

But, as it happens, most people instinctively resist such a process, because tendencies opposing imitation are also at work within our minds.

A director has several ways to weaken this resistance and gain access to the emotional part of the worker's mind so as to exert an emotional influence along with a rational, verbal influence—persuasion and order. One of these ways is to use authority. The human brain is wary of an outside influence if its "program" sharply differs from that the director wishes to introduce into it. This trait of our ego has probably been felt by everyone: we are more willing to agree with and are easier influenced by a man whose opinions and views are closer to our own.

During prolonged interaction one can, by using logic and personal appeal, introduce a part of his program into the mind of another. The stronger the will of the persuader, the more convincing and reasonable his behaviour, and the greater his ability to induce enthusiasm, the more effective this process is. These and some other qualities make up what is called authority. The influence of a superior grows with his authority because the gap between his program and that of his subordinates gets smaller.

The understanding of this powerful mechanism of influencing people leads to an interesting conclusion. Leaders should be changed as rarely as possible (as long as they satisfy definite requirements, of course). From the cybernetic point of view, a collective must have a permanent "model" man, who establishes a strengthening informational connection with his fellow workers, who produces a constantly increasing influence on them, and who controls and trains them with better efficiency.

"What is training?"—cyberneticists ask. Their answer is: "Training is a typical control process in which the instructor controls the mind of the pupil". The task of the instructor is to form in the mind of the student a definite model of behaviour and a set of rules and skills necessary for solving various problems. To use a simile, the teacher builds in the student's mind an edifice of his future behaviour in life.

Isn't it too bad we have to spend nearly a third of our lives learning, that is, mastering what other people already know? We can reconcile ourselves to this fact, though because if we want to create, we must have knowledge, and knowledge must be acquired. But the problem is that the time needed for learning takes an increasingly greater share of our lives, and this trend is not likely to slow down.

Until recently teachers were glad to put the principal blame for this on the imperfection of our brains, which have hardly changed in the last three thousand years, whereas the amount of information to be absorbed has gone up hundreds of times. Our brains are choking on information.

True, according to anthropologists the main characteristics of Aristotle's brain (capacity of memory, speed of action, reliability) were in no way second to those of the brain of, say, a contemporary student of physics. But the latter, in addition to what was known to Aristotle, must learn the laws of Newton, Einstein, and Bohr, as well as thousands of other theories.

This is what was believed before cyberneticists joined in the analysis. Special studies have demonstrated that with present-day methods of training, only one tenth of man's brain is used for thinking.

Cybernetics holds that for a control unit to ensure efficient control over some object, it must regularly and rather frequently receive feedback signals from this object.

For example, scientists have calculated that for optimal learning in school every student in classes of his native language must send the teacher three hundred feedback signals within forty-five minutes. Usually, the student sends a single signal at best: when he is summoned to the blackboard or when he submits his essay.

In general, the principles of teaching can be applied to the processes of directing a collective. These principles have been fairly well elaborated, and each administrator can master and use them in practice.

By the way, the feedback principle as applied to collectives has been around for a long time. The wisdom of Lenin's definition of democratic centralism consists in that it implies what in effect is the principle of a double feedback.

The problem of setting up feedback connections in a collective has some other implications. It is important that these connections be strong, that methods of directing be well suited to the collective and allow efficient operation in the absence, as well as in the presence, of the administrator. A curious experiment by an American research firm comes to mind. The heads of laboratories were sent on leave all at once. When they returned, management made an unexpected decision. Those whose laboratories floundered in their absence were dismissed. Those whose laboratories functioned normally got a considerable raise.

20—01169

The activity of each person in a collective somewhat resembles the work of a musician in an orchestra. The way the orchestra sounds depends on every musician and on all of them playing together. The overall effect of an annual activity of, say, a laboratory engineer is dependent on his qualities, such as initiative, the desire to extend the scope of his scientific interests, the ability to generate original ideas and to work at a steady pace, and so on. All these qualities can be directed by the head of the collective for maximum efficiency. This necessitates differentiated control and differentiated stimulation.

A member of a working collective should be aware that each aspect of his activity is monitored and at some moment will correspondingly be stimulated by a plus or minus sign.

The Collective and the Individual

A group of sociologists has carried out an interesting survey. They tried to apply quantitative analysis to studying relations between an individual and the collective in a scientific research collective. They quantified such subtle qualities as degree of talent, diligence, and orderliness, and obtained self-estimations of every member of the collective, the collective estimation of every individual, and the individuals' estimation of the collective. The opinions of men about men, women about women, men about women, and women about men were studied separately.

The intricacy of the analysis, accomplished with the aid of mathematical statistics, can be characterized by the list of personal qualities which were considered: intellectual qualities (talent, depth of knowledge, range of intellectual interests, creative imagination); business qualities (capacity for work, ability to attract people); volitive qualities (reserve, emotionality, endurance, will); moral qualities (kindness, modesty, loyalty to friends), motivations (altruism, truthfulness, ambition), attitudes to everday situations (optimism, humor); and so on.

The work was conducted by a fairly large group of investigators, and it necessitated elaborate calculations, although a relatively small group (13 people) was studied. One can only imagine what this work would be like in terms of volume if, for instance, an institute or a big design office had to be studied with a view to obtaining quantitative data on qualitative characteristics of an individual within the collective and the collective as a separate body.

The investigators put a question: when do different people happen to be compatible or incompatible for joint work?

Do you recollect the crew of four headed by Papanin, the people who lived and worked in perfect accord at the "North Pole" station, and in nine months completed much research and experimental work? And this while drifting under severe conditions in the Arctic Ocean.

But history has quite a different case on record. The famous Fridtjof Nansen and his navigator Johanssen left their ship Fram heading for the North Pole. They failed to reach their coveted goal and it took them about one and a half years to get to Franz Josef Land. All that time they hardly spoke to one another, and when addressing each other, which happened only in cases of emergency, they were strictly formal. Ice, silence, hunger, cold, loneliness—all the hardships of that journey were nothing in comparison with the ordeal of mutual dislike.

One might think that could happen only under extraordinary conditions of hardship and isolation, but is it so with radio, television and other means of communication at our disposal? As it turns out, something similar goes on today, too. Leningrad-based sociologists have revealed that twenty percent of people leave research institutes and design offices for reasons of psychological incompatibility!

A rather common point of view is that like persons get on well. On the other hand, the opposite characters are fairly often said to get along, too.

Which is correct? This is no idle question. According to the Myasnikov Institute of Therapy under the Soviet Academy of Medical Sciences, eighty percent of heart attacks follow either acute psychic traumas, or a period of prolonged psychic stress, or exhaustion. Physicians bluntly state that a comradely atmosphere in a collective not only creates favourable working conditions, but also reduces the possibility of cardiovascular diseases.

Unfortunately, we cannot present the survey's large volume of illustrative material in a small article like this, so only some data will be discussed. Self-evaluations and ratings of the collective were studied. This is a very delicate matter. Mutual evaluations may affect extremely sensitive sides of a person.

In one experiment, the collective rated itself above the average in all qualities. The highest rating was given to qualities characterizing attitude to life, and the lowest to those showing manifestations of will and impulse. Curiously enough, the collective judged intelligence and will power to be equal in men and women.

Self-evaluation in men and women was found to differ substantially. The men overestimated their intelligence and physical appeal in comparison with their rating by the collective. The women proved to be more modest and exacting to themselves in regard to these qualities. And altogether, the women's self-rating proved to be more modest that the men's.

I should like to point out that these results were obtained in a single study of a small group, and they cannot be regarded as universal in character. Nevertheless, it is interesting to know that the women, while fully appreciating the men's intelligence and ability to work efficiently, gave a lower rating to their moral qualities, motives, and physical attractiveness.

Frankly, I was surprised by the claim of the investigators that, on the average, the men rated the women higher than the women rated the men.

What is the main conclusion that the sociologists came to as a result of their work?

They assert that people for scientific collectives should be carefully selected with regard to their mutual compatibility and their personal qualities. And so we must repeat: defining criteria of biological, psychological, and social compatibility is of great significance not only to cosmonauts on a mission to Mars, but also to scientists remaining on Earth.

An interesting investigation was conducted in Leningrad. Methods of cybernetic analysis were used for determining the optimum administrative structure for Leningrad University. Structures for managing complex systems of this type have been evolving for hundreds of years, drawing on the experience of universities in many parts of the world. It turned out, however, that in this case many units and links of the structure had been arranged without regard to elementary cybernetic principles. Many information channels worked at hardly one half of their capacity, while others were overloaded. Redundant links in the administrative structure were exposed.

A scientific arrangement of collectives has tremendous potentialities for increasing the productivity of research work. Unfortunately, this sphere has not yet been given enough attention. More and more thought is now being given to the problem of organizing and managing complex scientific collectives.

There are scientific methods that can be used as efficient tools for solving this problem. But more scientists should be involved in this important and complex work. It is necessary to establish criteria of psychological compatibility of individuals for work in a collective, to develop a typology of people working in collectives, to devise optimal models of various types of collective, and to seriously consider creating a pedagogy of scientific administration. In short, a unified approach is needed to the whole problem of organizing and developing scientific collectives. It is worth bearing in mind that a search for the formula of a "collective genius" is one of the paths towards improving methods of administration and management, and so it is primarily a task of social significance.

How to Create an Artificial Brain

F. G. STAROS

Cybernetically, a brain is a system that receives, processes, stores, and retrieves information. Our experience of developing electronic data-processing systems indicates that the quality of such a system is determined by two key characteristics: the quantity of the information stored, and the speed at which it is processed. Whereas the modern electronic industry has already reached the required information-processing speeds, its reception, storage and delivery, particularly in the volume needed for artificial-intelligence systems, are still extremely difficult engineering problems.

Let us at first calculate, if only approximately, the

memory capacity of a human brain. It should be noted that depending on the calculation method the results may vary by many orders of magnitude. The simplest way is to try to determine the capacity of a memory by the number of elements in it and the quantity of information stored in each element.

The number of neurons in the brain exceeds 50 billions. According to some investigators, each neuron accounts, on average, for a thousand synapses (connections with other neurons) and for about ten glial cells. At present, it is still unclear where exactly information is stored—in the neurons, the synapses, or the glial cells—and how much information is stored in each element. That is all we can say in the way of a direct, "brute-force" approach to the calculation of memory capacity.

Let us attempt to find the memory capacity by another method, namely, by counting the number of signals entering the human brain. For the sake of simplicity we limit ourselves to the information that gets into the brain through the eyes, which amounts to 85 percent of all incoming information, according to some investigators. The retinas of both eyes have two million receptors (nerve endings); each receptor generates 14 pulses per second and operates for 1.26 billion seconds (16 hours daily for 60 years). As a result we have 3.5×10^{16} bits (a bit is a unit of information, or the simplest "yes" or "no" signal).

This is a theoretical estimate, but there are experimental data showing that the average speed of perceived information is only 25 bits per second, which gives 30 billion bits per life time. Finally, making allowance for the fact that not all information is retained in long-term memory, we reduce that figure to one third and have 10^{10} bits.

It is interesting to calculate the volume of an electronic information-storage device needed to store this amount of information. To do this, we choose three values of memory capacity: 3.5×10^{16}, 10^{13} and 10^{10} bits. Microelectronics today requires $10 \times 10 \times 1\,000$ μm for each memory element, and we assume the volume of connections in a circuit to be thousand times the volume of the memory elements. Then resultant volumes will be 35 million m^3, 10 thousand m^3, and 10 m^3, respectively.

If we could reduce the volume of a single element and its connections by 5 to 6 orders of magnitude, then the smallest model would take the volume of a cigarette pack, the medium model the volume of a television set, and the largest model the volume of a room. Such sizes are acceptable for practice, but can anything be done in order to reduce the volume of memory by a factor of 100 000 (better still, a million) as compared to the volume attainable using the latest microelectronic technology?

This task is so difficult that such an improvement appears to be impossible at first sight. A careful analysis, however, reveals a fundamental drawback in present-day microelectronic integrated circuitry, the elimination of which would improve the state of affairs considerably.

A circuit essentially lies in an extremely thin surface layer of semiconductor crystal. The total thickness of the layer is about 1 μm. What is still worse is that connections between the elements lie in the same plane and take 99 percent of area for the "simplest" integrated circuit containing a thousand elements. Assume that the memory of an artificial brain requires 10^{13} elements, and a million elements (a thousand times as many) can be obtained on each crystal with an area of 1 cm^2. Then one of our memory devices will need 10 million crystals. But how should the crystals be connected with each other? The number of inter-crystal connections adds up to a such gigantic figure that unfeasibility of the project becomes apparent.

Hence, the two-dimensional design proves unworkable. What about a three-dimensional one? Let us begin with a thin crystalline plate, a square of 1×1 cm. We build up on it a layer of elements 1 μm thick, then apply several layers of connecting circuits in succession, so building up the vertical connections, and then again apply a layer of elements. We shall proceed in this way until a cube with a height of 1 cm is obtained.

Using only 10 thousand layers for the memory cells and 90 thousand layers for the communication channels, such a memory cube can accommodate 10^7 memory cells. A cell measuring 3×5 μm could store about 10 bits of information. Thus, one cube is capable of storing and accessing 10^9 bits, ten cubes, 10^{10} bits, and a thousand cubes, 10^{13} bits of information. Since each cube would have a mass of 3 g, the mass of the artificial brain would range from 30 g to 30 kg.

Hence a layer-by-layer buildup of three-dimensional structures can solve the problem of creating a memory for the artificial brain.

At this point, microelectronics engineers probably shrug their shoulders: "That's just a fantasy! We go out of our way to have a single layer with a thousand of good elements, and you propose 10 thousand layers with a million elements in each! It's out of the question!" Indeed, microelectronics, with all its technological splendour, has no way of building up circuit layers.

Obtaining one circuit layer by the planar process, which is the one used extensively in microelectronics, takes five days; hence, the production of a memory cube would take a 100 years. Any substantial shortening of the manufacturing cycle is barely feasible. The planar process has yet another serious disadvantage. It produces numerous step-like projections of dissimilar materials on the crystal surface, and this will not allow the application of a second layer, let alone thousands of layers. So, even this up-to-date microelectronic process is not suited to producing artificial-intelligence devices.

Some scientists have proposed that all the achievements of semiconductor technology be shelved and that a solution which imitates a natural process is sought. But the main programs governing the growth of natural memory elements are stored inside the growing cells and, hence, the size of elements storing these programs is bound to be many orders of magnitude smaller than the size of the memory cells proper. If the latter measure micrometers, then the size of the elements that store the growth programs must be angstroms, and here, even the present-day science fiction has so far been powerless.

But why not to pursue a more moderate and more real approach, namely, to develop a technology that does not have the disadvantages of the planar process and to build in it a three-dimensional memory cube? Let us take as the basis the process of epitaxial building of semiconductor films, in which a thin plate of a monocrystal semiconductor, heated to an elevated temperature, is placed in a reactor filled with a mixture of gases. The atoms of one of the gases are deposited on the plate with the result that a layer with the same crystalline structure as that of the semiconductor film is formed. By introducing additives into the gas, we can obtain a different concentration of additive atoms in the film, and hence a variety of electrophysical properties in the built-up layer.

We could also obtain a variety of successive layers each having specified electrophysical characteristics and, what is essential, a smooth surface without any "microprofile". This elegant process has only one thing wrong—the microgeometry of each layer cannot be controlled. To produce micro-circuitry, the electrophysical characteristics of each minute feature in each element of the circuit rather than the characteristics of the layer as a whole need to be controlled. We call this pattern the microgeometry, and modern electronics is already able to create it using a micro-image.

It has long been known that light can selectively activate individual atoms or molecules to chemical reaction. Colour photography is a classical example of the process of selective activation of molecules by light. Light beams form a micro-image and the atoms of the base substance and the additive substances "adhere" to the surface of the growing crystal. Light of a certain wavelength "prepares" the atoms of the crystal lattice to receive atoms of specific chemical elements. As a result, thin contours of image projected by laser beams of different wavelengths turn into the various elements of an integrated circuit.

But even a brief consideration of the problem concerning the development of an acting reactor reveals a number of potential difficulties. For example, this method of layer buildup only gives a smooth surface at crystal temperature of about 1 000°C, and unfortunately this temperature causes the crystal itself to glow, blurring the image of the circuit.

If the layer is built up at low temperatures (several hundred degrees Celsius), results unsuitable for integrated circuitry are obtained. At the high temperatures, atoms rapidly glide over the surface taking up vacant places on the preceding layer, while at the low temperatures the gliding is much slower and the new atoms fail to reach their "legitimate" places at the edge of the growing layer and adhere to the builtup areas to form second and third layers before the first layer has formed. Hence, the low-temperature process requires a new type of device, namely a "smoothing ray" that can quickly sweep across the crystal surface after each mono-atomic layer is deposited. Unfortunately, such a device has not yet been available. At the same time, deposition of atoms on the working surfaces of optical and laser apparatus as well as on the growing crystal may prompt switchover to the method of the sharp-focused pulse feeding of the material to the surface by a controlled ion source.

We have indicated only a few of the problems, but assume all of them, both those mentioned and not mentioned, have been solved, and the memory cube is manufactured. Will it be workable? If workability calls for the normal function of all its elements, then we can say with certainty: "No". The process of manufacture produces a large number of defective elements. Hence, the cube must be designed to perform normally with a number of its elements being inoperative. To this end, duplicate physical elements must be present for a single circuit element and be so interconnected that the operation of only one of them ensures the performance of the whole circuit.

Theoretical calculations have shown that when the number of duplicate elements ranges from two to four, the output of operational cubes will be very low, and only five elements at least can give a satisfactory result. These data were obtained assuming that 99 percent of the physical elements are good, though this is a somewhat lower percentage than that provided by modern integrated circuit production techniques.

The dependability of these cubes can be enhanced by loading information into an unoccupied and operating cell rather than a predetermined cell. In this way, we shall be able to use cubes with more inoperative cells, although losses of information due to failure of individual cells in service will not be excluded. To prevent such losses, the information will have to be entered into several separated cells simultaneously, or distributed like visual information is in a hologram. This excellent method is such that the imperfection or failure of even a large number of cells will have no adverse effect on the information stored in the memory.

Having discussed all the difficulties and how they can be overcome, it is interesting to conjecture how things will proceed. Suppose all the difficulties have been eliminated. A sophisticated production complex can then be built: ten reactors and digital control systems including several minicomputers and a large high-speed computer. A well-designed smoothing ray sweeps across every monoatomic layer in several microseconds, and the general rate of crystal build-up is 3 μm/min. Then each reactor will grow its cube in 50 h, and the system as a whole will produce one artificial brain in two days. Operating costs for such a system may be about 200 roubles/hour (the cost of materials is negligibly small). Thus, a failure-free brain capable of doing the work of a specialist may cost about 10 thousand roubles.

This will make this "intelligent" product cost-effective in a variety of production applications.

A final note about the productivity of future artificial-intelligence systems: electronic elements today operate in nanoseconds, whereas the cells of a native brain need milliseconds. This means that an artificial brain can in principle work and remember a million times faster. Perhaps, an artificial brain will "attend school" not for 10 years, but for 5 minutes, and will then be immediately set to work.

How to Create an Optical Brain

V. M. ZAKHARCHENKO and G. V. SKROTSKY

Neurophysiology has in recent years largely clarified the working of the brain, the most complex and mysterious of all known natural phenomena. According to the American scientist D. Hubel, neurobiology has been developing so quickly over the last decade that there has been a veritable explosion of discoveries and insights.

On the other hand, the last decade has also seen the rapid development of microelectronics, optoelectronics and optical data processing techniques. This has naturally prompted attempts to use this modern technology for simulating the operation of the brain and for developing radically new information processing systems. Thus, the combination of optoelectronics and some of the methods of optical information processing is at the basis of a new idea, namely the optical brain.

The brain consists of nerve cells, or neurons, which are connected together by their processes (axons and dendrites) meeting at interneuron contact sites called synapses. According to the latest estimates, the brain contains no less than 5×10^{10} neurons. Although there is a vast number of neurons, they only take up 10 percent of the total volume of the brain. The rest is occupied by the inter-neuron bonds, nerve fibres that are a micron or less thick. The number of nerve fibres arriving at a neuron is breathtaking. Thus, every neuron in the brain's cortex has several tens of thousands of connections each of which conveys signals from other neurons. If the total effect of these signals exceeds the threshold level of the neuron, it becomes excited and generates an output signal. A neuron has only one output connection, its axon, but this branches out into a multitude of connections going to other neurons. The conductivity of all the connections, and hence their "weight", differ in magnitude and sometimes in sign; therefore, other neurons receive totally different signals. Neurons may be likened to control points that receive and distribute signals incoming along the inter-neuron connections. There are more than 10^{14} such connections in the brain. Understanding that synapses are major structural components of the brain and determine its functional characteristics was one of the most essential conclusions made by neurophysiologists. Many neurophysiologists believe that the unique properties of every man—the capability of feeling, thinking, learning and remembering—are contained in the orderly networks of synaptic bonds between the neurons of the brain.

The cortex is the largest part of the brain, approximately 1 000 cm^3 out of 1 400 cm^3. The cortex is folded and is 3 mm thick. The whole area of the cortex breaks down into functional zones that are responsible for visual, auditory, motor, and other types of information. The functional zones are in turn divided into modules with areas fractions of a square millimetre in extent and heights equalling the height of the cortex. Each module processes a certain type of signal coming from particular receptors, for instance, from a section of the retina.

The variety of information on the environment that comes into the brain from the sensory organs is perceived by a great number of neurons in the cortex. Certain regions of the cortex become excited depending on the characteristics of the incoming signal and its position in space. Vertically, the cortex is arranged in layers. Each neuron in one layer is connected predominantly with neurons in another layer. A ganglion of excited neurons in one layer send signals to another layer, exciting a corresponding ganglion of neurons in it, and so forth. Every module of the cortex is essentially a local neuron network which transforms the information, sending it from its inlet to its outlet.

Developing an artificial analogue of this extremely simplified model of the brain can be divided into two problems. First we must have artificial neurons, and then we must set up a three-dimensional structure with trillions of inter-neuron connections.

There is a variety of the electronic models of neurons, and present-day IC technology can manufacture them in sufficient quantities. Creating bonds between them is enormously more difficult. Sophisticated as it is, microelectronic technology cannot yet make systems in which every element has many thousands of connections with other elements in the system, each connection having an individual conductivity. Building a complex three-dimensional structure out of a solid mass of innumerable intertwined connection fibres requires fundamentally new techniques.

One real, practical way to tackle this problem is to model the neuron structures optically. Light rays do not interact and therefore are not subject to limitations on the density of optical communication channels and their spatial arrangement. This optical modelling could be achieved by using holographic memory in practically all its present-day varieties modified to suit the task. For example, the first experimental model of a neuron network was based on a common holographic memory device using a gas laser, a light-beam deflector and a rectangular array of holograms. As the application of integrated microelectronic and optoelectronic technology holds the greatest promise for developing optical models of neurons systems, we shall consider, by way of example, an optical neuron network using a holographic memory based on arrays of semi-conductor lasers.

Information is recorded in such a memory on a light-sensitive medium so as to form holograms 1 mm in diameter which are assembled into arrays. An array of semi-conductor lasers is placed in front of the hologram array. A laser beam passing through a hologram is split into a multitude of light rays. The direction and intensity of these rays depend on the information recorded on the hologram. An array of photocells that detect light signals is located some distance behind the hologram array.

Let us now assume that each laser is the outlet of a neuron. Its output signal, a beam, is split by the hologram into a host of light rays arriving at the inlets of the neurons in the next layer, that is, the photocells. Each light connection has its "weight", determined by the intensity of the ray. All the light connections coming to a certain neuron are added up in the photocell, and the output signal from this cell is proportional to the total signal. Thus, the inlet of a neuron is a photocell, and the outlet is a laser plus a hologram carrying a recorded fan-like pattern of the connections between this neuron and all the neurons in the next layer. Finally, to obtain the model of a neuron, we connect the inlet with the outlet by placing a threshold element between them. Let us now place a holographic memory, identical to the memory described above, behind the photocell array in such a way that the signals from the photocells of the first memory control the radiation of the semiconductor-laser array of a second memory. Behind the second memory, we put a third memory, and so on in sequence. As a result we have a periodic structure equivalent to the succession of neuron layers in the brain. Here, just as in the brain, the incoming information is transferred from layer to layer, being processed all the finer. The processing program is determined exclusively by the structure of the connections recorded on the holograms. The density of these connections is equal to the density of the information recorded on the holograms and makes up about 10^4 connections over 1 mm^2. In order to change the system of bonds, it is sufficient to change a block of holograms, and replace it with another block. A natural brain does not have this advantage, though it does have another asset instead. All of its inter-neuron bonds are flexible; they can be changed as man learns and gains experience. But the optical brain is a pre-instructed brain whose knowledge is contained in the interchangeable hologram blocks and in the structures of the synaptic interconnections recorded on them. If we were to create a perfect analogue of a human brain, these features would be an obvious drawback. But for engineering applications, for instance robot operations, under batch production conditions that require fast changeover to other types of behaviour, this drawback of the artificial system turns into an advantage.

The system has another advantage, namely its modular design, one module being formed by a holographic-memory block. The recording density of inter-neuron connections on a hologram may reach 10^6 connections per cm^2. This means that a plate of 1 cm^2 area can accommodate 10^3 holograms, each with 10^3 connections, joining 10^3 neuron outlets in one layer to 10^3 neuron inlets in the next. Present-day technology is capable of making an array of 10^3 lasers over an area of 1 cm^2. And an array of 10^3 photocells over 1 cm^2 area is an accomplished fact for modern integrated-circuit technology. The task is simplified by the absence of external electric connections, except the supply of current, in both the laser and photocell arrays.

Thus, our module, which we shall call an opto-neuron module, is equivalent to a layer of a thousand neurons and a million inter-neuron connections. It contains an array of a thousand semi-conductor lasers, an array of a thousand photocells and has a form of a cube with sides 1 cm long. The response time of the elements in such an opto-neuron module is below 10^{-6} s, and the number of elements roughly corresponds to the number of neurons in one layer of a human brain cortex.

Let us see what an opto-neuron model of brain having 5×10^{10} neurons and 5×10^{13} inter-neuron connections would be like. Such a brain would require 5×10^7 modules, each containing 1 000 neurons, with a total volume of 50 m^3. The volume of a contemporary electronic computer with its set of peripherals is roughly the same. Obviously, in comparison to a human brain, which has a volume about 1.4 dm^3, an optical brain is approximately 3×10^4 times bulkier. But on the other hand, it could be 10^4 to 10^5 times faster in operation and hence larger in computing power.

Let us now calculate the cost of an optical brain. Proceeding from the costs incurred in high-volume manufacture of integrated micro-circuits, we may expect the cost of one opto-neuron module to be about 1 rouble in the near future. Fifty million modules would then cost 50 million roubles. This is roughly the current cost of a high-capacity electronic computer with a speed of 10^7 to 10^9 operations per second. But the computing power of an optical brain is much higher, as we shall see below.

Consider now another problem. It is not sufficient to manufacture an electronic brain. In order to make it operative, we must load it with an informative substance, that is, to determine the structure of its light ray communications. The brain will become "alive" and will perform the task set for it in accordance with its connections, e.g. to translate from Russian into English, control a spacecraft, or recognize visual patterns. However, determining the structure of the communication pathways in the brain is much more difficult than building the artificial brain itself. Here we can see a direct similarity with computer technology where the software is several times more expensive to develop than the hardware.

There are two chief ways of developing information-processing algorithms in artificial neuron systems. The first is to study information processing in the brain neurologically and such work is now well under way. An example is the investigation into the principles of processing visual information conducted by the American researchers Hubel and Viesel, the Nobel prize winners for medicine in 1981. Another way is to derive algorithms that describe separate brain functions analytically. Algorithms for information search by key words, which are used in most of the current information-search systems, are the simplest algorithms of this type.

Let us consider a variant of such an algorithm, which was developed and used in an opto-neuron systems of recognition of a document's pattern. Although simple, it is reminiscent of the mental operations a human goes through in the course of a search for information.

Suppose you are searching in a library catalogue for literature on a particular subject, say the design of a transistor radio receiver. Let us follow your steps. First of all, you should read the text of the request form and, as you are reading, convert the sequences of letters into words that stand for notions. This is the first stage of processing the information. Then you remember words that are close in meaning. As a result, your conciousness registers not only the words written on the request form, but also many other words and associated notions. For example, if, in the process of looking through the catalogue, you come across a card about a book entitled *The development of portable radio receivers*, you retain it even though it does not contain the words written on the request form. The reason is that the word "development" is close in meaning to "design", the word "portable" most likely means that the equipment is transistorized, and so on.

Thus, elaborating the request is the second stage of information processing that draws upon your knowledge in the field. Finally, the third stage is the assessment of the nearness of catalogue cards in meaning to the request. Here you sum up the number and weight of associations, and if the total is sufficiently large, you retain the card.

We have analyzed the process of searching for information by man and singled out three main stages from it. Now we try, proceeding from this analysis, to develop a structure for a neuron information-searching system. The information-processing sequence will be as follows: letters—words—groups of associated words—cards with bibliographic data. So we have four forms of information and three processing stages between one form and another. In the neuron system, the information is transformed from one layer to the next. Therefore, our opto-neuron system should have four neuron layers and three hologram arrays with inter-neuron pathways, which fill the three inter-layer spaces.

The first layer is letters. Each neuron in the first layer corresponds to a letter in the alphabet, with allowance for its place in a given word. The second layer is words. Each neuron in the second layer stands for a word in the vocabulary being used. The third layer is also words. And, finally, the fourth layer is the subject of search, that is, catalogue cards. Each neuron in the fourth layer corresponds to a card in the catalogue.

Now consider the inter-neuron communications. First, the communications between the 1st and the 2nd layers. A neuron in the 2nd layer is connected to a neuron in the 1st layer if a letter is contained in a certain word. Optical connections between the 2nd and the 3rd layers reflect the associative bonds between words in the human brain. If an associative bond exists between two words, a neuron in the 2nd layer is connected by a light pathway with the appropriate word in the 3rd layer. A third group of connections between words and the subject being sought reflects the set of key words contained on the cards. If a card carries a key word, then the neuron in the 3rd layer that designates this word is connected by a light ray with the neuron standing for this card in the 4th layer.

By recording holograms with the inter-neuron connections, we load the required information into the memory of the system. Now we shall see how it works. Entering the letters that make up the words of the request excites the appropriate neurons in the first layer. As this takes place, the lasers at the outlets of these neurons are set off. The holograms split the laser beams into a multitude of rays going to the inlets of neurons in the 2nd layer in accordance with the pattern of inter-neuron connections. Neurons that receive signals with a level exceeding the threshold of response are excited in the 2nd layer. The group of excited neurons in the 2nd layer corresponds to a number of words in the request. Light signals from the neurons in the 2nd layer come to neurons in the 3rd layer and excite some of them. The group of the excited neurons in the 3rd layer corresponds to a set of associatively connected words. The group of excited neurons in the 4th layer corresponds to the catalogue cards that meet the request. The lasers excited at the outlet of neurons in this layer denote found cards. This is the principle behind information processing in an opto-neuron system.

Now, let us compare the capabilities of an up-to-date computer technology, a human brain, and an optical brain. We shall compare them in terms of two key characteristics: the speed of the information processing and the memory capacity. For a digital electronic computer these characteristics are determined by the number of arithmetical operations per second and the memory volume in bits. For a brain, which operates on other principles, these characteristics are not defined. For this reason, we shall assume the computing speed of a brain to be the same as that of the electronic computer required to simulate its operation, and the memory capacity to be equal to the capacity of the binary memory of a computer that is large enough to accommodate all the information stored in brain s neuron connections. This is the most natural approach because computer technology is nowadays the main tool for modelling neuron systems. A computer memory is loaded with the addresses of the end and beginning of every pathway between the neurons, its "weight", the neuron excitement thresholds, and so on. The magnitude of a signal passing along a communication channel of a certain conductivity is equal to the input signal times the channel's conductivity. Therefore, the passage of a signal along an inter-neuron pathway by the analogue method is a multiply operation. The signal is then added to the other signals at the neuron's inlet. Hence, the passage of a signal through an inter-neuron connection corresponds to the analogue operation of one multiplication and one addition. The number of simultaneous addition and multiplication operations in the brain at full capacity is equal to the number of its inter-neuron connections. The total computing power of a brain is equal to the number of inter-neuron connections multiplied by the frequency of repetitions of a signal. In a computer simulation of a brain these operations are all digital. The speed of an electronic computer is not lower than a brain's computing speed calculated in this way. If we assume that the number of inter-neuron connections in the brain is 10^{14}, and the signal frequency is $10^2\ s^{-1}$, then the equivalent computing speed of the brain is 10^{16} operations per second.

The memory capacity is determined by the number of digits in binary numbers which are used for coding the addresses of the connections and by the total number of the connections. With 10^{14} connections, the number of binary digits in the address of the beginning and end of each connection will be roughly 50, and the total volume of memory will be about 10^{16} bits.

The computing speed of an artificial brain built up of opto-neuron modules operating at a signal frequency of not less than 10^6 s^{-1} is approximately 10^{20} operations per second. The normal speed of a computer is about 10^6 operations per second. The speed of some computers is 10^9 operations per second. It is apparent that not only a quantitative difference, but also an enormous qualitative step in information-processing technology separates the figures of 10^9 and 10^{20} operations per second. To execute parallel information-processing algorithms similar to those created by nature, we are in need of radically different technological means that should be hundreds of millions of times as powerful as the existing ones.

The creation of an optical brain, it is believed, can meet these requirements. Why optical? Because holography and opto-electronics are today the only way of modelling the complex three-dimensional structures of the inter-neuron connections in the brain. And also because the development of the optical brain is within the reach of present-day, not tomorrow's, technology.

The Cybernetic Double

I. M. ROSOKHOVATSKY and A. A. STOGNY

The exploration of the moon's surface with the aid of moon rovers started the era of space robots. These moon missions clearly showed that any future study of the planets will be impossible without them.

As the distances to the explored objects increase and the conditions for conducting planetary research change increasingly autonomous robots will be needed. Even a moon rover requires some autonomous systems because a moving robot must act on its own and is naturally exposed to a variety of hazards during the 2.6 seconds it takes for a radio signal to traverse the Earth-Moon-Earth distance.

The distance to Mars and back will take a radio signal from 6 to 40 min to traverse. Hence, designers of planetary rovers believe that a Mars rover cannot be controlled in the same way as a moon rover.

Suppose an operator on Earth watching his TV screen sees that the moon rover is verging on a chasm, by the time he has reached the control board the vehicle will have already fallen over the precipice. Thus, a Mars rover must be self-contained and fairly intelligent. It will probably have a control device on board to assess the situation and make decisions for itself. Intervention from Earth will perhaps be required only in extreme cases. Design engineers think this is technically feasible, and they are certain that in time self-propelling laboratories will be working on the Mars surface.

Work on robots for Mars is being conducted in a number of countries. Computer-controlled systems have been designed in the USA, for example, at the Massachusetts Institute of Technology (an eye-arm-wrist system) and at the Stanford R & D Institute (an eye-cart system, using a cart with a long distance between wheels which is needed for traversing Mars's desert terrains).

Now assume it will not be Mars, but a more distant celestial body, where a signal goes for months. It is quite clear that we shall require totally autonomous robots.

In principle, we can provide a robot with artificial intelligence today. But how should it be programmed if we do not yet know anything about how man himself behaves rationally on an unexplored planet?

Various sorts of autonomous robots have been proposed. American scientists, for example, have thought of a hybrid of an artificial body and a natural brain, which they called a "Cyborg". This is a system in which the brain is taken out of a recently deceased human and kept alive to be used for controlling mechanical devices. We think, however, that cybernetics indicates another way.

On an unknown planet, a robot would have to consider a situation in detail and make a decision independently, often in a split second. In such cases, a man would find a solution intuitively.

Although the patterns of intuitive human behaviour are still unclear, we can assess who, out of several people, is more talented and thus will presumably be able to find a way out of a complicated situation and who is more intelligent and more inventive. Using the "Follow the leader" principle, we can teach a robot to act like a Mr. A, who is more ingenious than a Mr. B.

It is apparent that if a space robot will be endowed with a model of intelligence of an astronomer (or, at least, with a set of models of some astronomer's functions), then such a robot may be called a "cybernetic double" of the original.

The term "cybernetic double" (CD) does not imply a likeness in appearance, it means an information-processing system which, owing to a large suite of programs and a specific structure, produces a model of a personality that enables the system to act like a certain person or several persons. Here, it seems proper to remember that an aircraft obeys the same laws of aerodynamics as a bird, even though it is not a bird because it has not got the feathers that are essential for birds to fly.

It is quite possible that CD robots will eventually prove

not to be the best type of information-processing system in environments hazardous and difficult for man. At present, we believe that CDs will enable us to bridge the gulf of unknowns in the study of human-behaviour models and thereby to create a duplicate without knowing exhaustively what the original really is.

The development of CDs involves many other problems. Let us touch upon some of them.

Intelligent CD robots will pose the problem of their coexistence with man. The significance of this problem is that the first type of information-processing system must be subordinate to the second, which is much slower, shorter-lived, and more vulnerable to environmental change. In our view, this will lead to the inception and rapid development of a new science of "psycho-robotics" (the "psychology" of robots).

The emergence of CD colonies on other planets, unsuitable for human life, from which they will send mineral resources and energy to Earth, and which they will prepare (where possible) for colonization by man, will require that relationships between CDs themselves should be regulated.

Finally, the creation of CDs will cause their developer, man, to review the old question of life and death. Indeed, what life span should we give a CD?

This apparently simple question is not in fact so easy to answer. Will a hundred years be enough? Or a thousand? Perhaps, ten thousand? Or eternity?

In seeking the solutions required for developing or programming CDs, we shall at first have to turn our minds to the answers found by Nature. Not that Nature is the best teacher. But we, humans, know no better one so far. So, what life-spans exist in Nature? It appears there is the whole range from an instant to eternity, eternity being bestowed on the simplest living matter, unicellular organisms. When it has completed its individual life, a unicellular organism (for instance, a bacterium) divides into two, originating two new lives. There are no corpses in such cases because there is no death, only an infinite multiplication of life.

What then determines generally a life span in nature? Apparently, the function of continuing a species so that the fittest descendants survive.

And what should determine the life of a CD? What span of life should it be given?

A CD is not bound to leave descendants. Its "abode of life" is not confined to Earth or to our solar system. It can charge itself with energy and exist anywhere in the Universe. If a CD decides that it is better not to improve or rebuild itself under particular conditions, but have a duplicate or a modified version in addition to itself, it will build it on the basis of its previous experience.

Does this then mean that a CD will have an infinite span of life? No, it does not. The life span of this unusual "organism" will be determined by the task originally set for it by man.

The main object of the living organisms created by Nature is to survive and produce offspring under the conditions of a certain planet, so ensuring their evolution. CDs will progress under the conditions of any planet or another celestial body according to the program predetermined by man, for a CD, however perfect, is only a double. Obviously, CDs will be given a very long life span guaranteed by adequate design principles, such as the changeability of parts, the capability to add on new units and rebuild itself, a system of interchangeable memory blocks, and so on.

But what about ageing? Would a CD be exposed to it? In terms of cybernetics, the process of ageing of a system consists in the inevitable accumulation of interferences and malfunctions. Clearly a CD is also not immune to it.

But man creating CD will apply to it a certain "standard of youth" which will store information on its vital parts. And the robot will be able to "read" this information at any time so as to check the performance of its parts and units against the standard and to replace or repair them if required.

In the process of creating a CD, man will probably learn a lot about himself because he will be bound to look from a new angle not only at the way he interacts with his environment, but also at the very essence of his personality.

Extraterrestrial Civilizations and Artificial Intelligence

I. S. SHKLOVSKY

This article will treat the oldest and most fundamental question of science: is mankind alone in the Universe? Is there anyone anywhere in the Universe who is our brother in intelligence? Is an encounter with artificial intelligent life possible in the Universe? It should be stated that this problem has not yet been solved. More than that, no one knows when it will be solved and whether its solution is possible at all.

This statement of the problem of extraterrestrial civilizations only seems to be clear. The basic concept of what intelligent life is is not at all simple and requires a thorough analysis.

It is not my intention to answer the host of questions that arise in connection with the problem of extraterrestrial civilizations. The aim of this article is more limited, namely, to pose and highlight some of these questions.

Our conception of the evolution of matter in the Universe leads us to the conclusion that it moves at all levels in only one direction: from simple to complex forms. Indeed, during the 10 to 15 thousand million years of the evolution of matter in the Universe, the structure and character of the interactions between material systems as well as those within single systems have been steadily increasing in complexity. Modern astronomy has clearly demonstrated that all the different forms of matter have their history. Stars, galaxies, and clusters of galaxies are historical phenomena. This means that there was time when they did not exist, and there can be no doubt that in time the stars in the observed Universe will cease to exist.

Diffused matter irreversibly condenses into stars. In the interior of stars, hydrogen is converted into helium and heavier elements to yield stellar radiation. When they have exhausted most of their hydrogen fuel, stars turn into "white dwarfs", neutron stars, and the still mysterious "black holes". These forms of matter are radically different from common stars if only because they cease to radiate some time after they have formed.

Whereas the white dwarfs were discovered as far back as the turn of this century, the detection of neutron stars and "black holes" has only become possible recently owing to the progress in radio and X-ray astronomy. The common stars (that is, luminous celestial bodies which radiate because of nuclear reactions occurring in their interior) "live" longer if their mass is small. For this reason, the dwarf stars, whose mass is one-tenth the mass of the Sun, will exist according to calculations, many tens of thousands of billions of years, that is, they will survive into that immensely distant epoch, when the Universe will be thousand times older. It is difficult to predict today what the Universe will look like then. It is likely to go on expanding boundlessly. In particular, the distances between galaxies will increase a thousand times, the interstellar gas will practically disappear, and the luminosity of the galaxies will diminish by a factor of several thousands.

If stars and galaxies are historical phenomena, the same should be said about life in the Universe. It is self-evident that there could be no life during the early stages of the evolution of the Universe. This is indicated even by the primitive chemical composition of the primeval "fireball" which the Universe is likely to have been at that time. Moreover, if we take into account the enormous temperature and the simple fact that no molecules could be present in the plasma of the fireball, our conclusion will become still more convincing.

Our solar system formed out of a nebula of gas and dust about five billion years ago. The Galaxy, like the Universe, was then half as old as it is now, but it was essentially like our present-day stellar system. This does not mean it was identical, though. A lot of stars (for instance, Sirius, Vega) had still not been "born". But a number of the fundamental characteristics of our galaxy, such as its dimensions, its spiral structure, its full luminosity, the composition of its interstellar gas were then about the same as they are now. Life on primeval Earth originated in the simplest form three billion years ago. Will it evolve on Earth forever?

Present-day science is able to give a fairly justifiable answer to this question: if intelligent life does not develop so as to become a cosmic entity, life on Earth must cease to exist at the end of an immense, but finite, period of time, namely five to six billion years. The point is that the Sun will probably exhaust its stock of nuclear fuel at the end of this period, and will then begin to "swell" , its dimensions will increase many times, and its surface temperature will fall. The power of its radiation, however, will rise by a factor of ten and this will be fatal for evolution and more for the very existence of life on Earth because the temperature on the surface of our planet will exceed 1000°C. But if by that distant future intelligent life still remains, and has also substantially developed, mankind will be able to colonize planets and asteroids far from the Sun and transform them artificially. There will be enough time for that because the transformation of the Sun into a gigantic red star is a very slow, rather than a catastrophic, process. True, in "some" hundred million years this red giant, throwing off its outer layer, will turn into a "white dwarf" star. After cooling down, it will practically cease to radiate (the "black dwarf" stage). There will then be no choice left and if intelligent life is not extint by that time, it will have to "emigrate" from the bounds of our solar system. I want to repeat that there will be more than enough time for that. The whole question is whether there will still be intelligent life at that time and what it will turn into. We shall discuss this later on.

So far we have only talked about life on Earth. It is quite probable that our planet is not the unique abode of life, including intelligent life. It seems quite logical that life is also an historical category. As we have pointed out, life could not exist in any form during the early stages of the evolution of the Universe. We also think that it is fairly reasonable to assume that life if it survives for ten billion years will exist in a radically different form.

Now we need to define our notion of life and intelligence. The question is far from being simple. Thus, if we talk about the life not only on our planet but also in the whole Universe, then the well-known definition of life as a form of existence of proteins is insufficient. After all, we cannot exclude the possibility of life existing in distant worlds on a totally different basis. In this situation, the best definition of life, in my opinion, is the "functional" definition given by the cyberneticist A.A. Lyapunov. He said: "Life may be characterized as a stable state of substance that develops preserving reactions by using information coded by the state of individual molecules"[1]. In my book *The Universe, Life, and Intelligence*, I give an in-depth analysis of the definition and so I shall not dwell upon it here.

Academician Kolmogorov also takes a consistently "functional" attitude towards the notions of "intelligence" and "thought". The cybernetic approach to this problem enables us to make the important conclusion that a living "naturally" intelligent being does not fundamentally differ from a specially manufactured artificial device. We see no essential limitation on modelling systems of any complexity, including "intelligent" ones.

Let us now attempt to see how many highly-developed civilizations there might be in the Galaxy. We designate this quantity N. It can be given as a product of several factors (Drake's formula):

$$N = nP_1P_2P_3P_4t_1/T,$$

where n is the total number of stars in the Galaxy; P_1 is the probability of the existence of a planetary system round a star; P_2 is the probability of the origin of life on a planet; P_3 is the probability of the evolution of intelligence; P_4 is the probability of intelligent life entering a technological stage of development, including the cognition of the laws of nature and the active transformation of the latter; t_1 is the average lifetime of a technological era; and T is the order of magnitude for the age of the Galaxy. The factor t_1/T relates N to extraterrestrial civilizations concurrently existing in our stellar system.

It should be stressed that the term "probability" here does not have its conventional mathematical meaning. The usual applications of probability theory always imply the existence of a statistical set. In our case, however, all quantities in Drake's formula are known to be unique. To date we only know about one planetary system with a reasonable degree of accuracy viz. our solar system. We know only one planet that gave rise to a life form which eventually evolved intelligence. The whole history of the evolution of our life is unique and cannot be "played back" anew. Indeed, what can probability estimates have to do with these things at all? Actually, the P_i probabilities in Drake's formula are more or less subjective estimates by competent experts. Hence the term "subjective probability" was heard particularly often at the Soviet-American symposium on extraterrestrial civitizations that took place at the Byurakan observatory in September 1971.

And yet, arbitrary as such estimates are, they are not devoid of meaning. What is most important is that the advance of science will convert these "subjective" probabilities into "objective" ones.

Modern observational and theoretical astronomy has come to a well-substantiated conclusion that there is a multitude of planetary systems in the Galaxy. Accordingly, the quantity P_1 has been taken from the category of "subjective" probability and made into a common mathematical probability. This fact is very essential to us. I estimate P_1 at a value larger than 0.01. It is not impossible that it exceeds 0.1. This means that our Galaxy accounts for at least several billion planetary systems. It obviously goes without saying that a real (not subjective) estimate of P_1 is a most remarkable achievement of present-day astronomy and is very important for the consideration of our problem.

Unfortunately, the matter is rather worse with respect to the other P_i quantities in Drake's formula. Here we must depend entirely on subjective estimates. Great difficulties arise as we set out to estimate P_2, that is the "subjective probability" of the origin of life on a planet. It seems obvious that life cannot arise on every planet. Our planetary system is a good example of that. Nowadays the achievements of space technology we have witnessed enable us to assert with a great measure of reliability that out of all the planets in the solar system, it was only on Earth that life once arose and evolved over billions of years. In the 1960s we were much greater optimists. But the investigations carried out by the Soviet and American interplanetary probes revealed the extreme severity of the conditions on Mars, and the enormous atmospheric pressure, high temperature, and unsuitable chem ical composition of the atmosphere for life on Venus. Meanwhile it was only these planets that were long regarded as being possible alternative abodes of life in our solar system. After all, we cannot consider seriously the existence of life on Mercury, where lead melts, or on the gigantic cold planets saturated with poisonous gases and devoid of solid surfaces and hydrospheres (some over-optimistic scientists, though, have ventured to suggest that life is possible on these planets). It is fairly obvious that a number of favourable factors must combine to make the origin of life possible on a planet. Such a planet must have the appropriate dimensions and mass, a temperature favourable for the rise of life (largely dependent on the distance of the planet from the central star), the existence of a hydrosphere is likely to be very important, and finally the atmosphere must have a reasonable composition.

Therefore it is quite possible that our estimate of P_1 was a bit too optimistic. But all the same, this is not as crucial as it may seem at first glance. After all, there must be a great many planets round Barnard's star, just by analogy with the Earth. It is very probable that some of them will be adequate for the existence of life. Thus, even if there should be a decrease in P_1, it will not be "catastrophic".

In the assessment of P_2, another question should be considered. Assume that there is a suitable planet. What is the likelihood of the most primitive life developing on it?

The trouble is, let us face it, that present-day science is unable to say how life arose on Earth. In order to answer this question, we need a deep insight into the mechanics of life. In my opinion, no serious discussion about the origin of life on Earth was possible before the emergence of molecular biology and the deciphering of the genetic code. To generate life, matter had to undergo a qualitative change in the process of evolution, and this resulted from a long series of quantitative transformations. This crucial aspect of the problem was virtually overlooked in the past. Attention was focussed on the possible ways the organic material (for example, proteins) could be formed naturally. But a combination of organic compounds, whatever their complexity, is not life. First and foremost, an understanding should be gained of how such "building blocks" could give rise to a particular "machine" with its duplicating capabilities, its mutability and the other wonders of living beings. The enormous gap between the most primitive forms of life (for instance, viruses) and the set of very complex but nevertheless inanimate organic substances is not yet understood. For this reason, the probability that the original living substance emerged on Earth by chance or was even brought in from the space in the form of spores cannot be excluded. I do not, however, assert that everything did happen this way. It might well be that the combination of natural conditions on Earth at that time was so beneficial that life was bound to arise. The difficulty of the problem stems from the fact that at our present level of knowledge we are not yet in a position to choose between these two extreme possibilities.

The complexity of the situation is also due to our inability to solve the problem with the means at our disposal in the next few decades if not centuries. This can be seen from the fact that strictly speaking even now, after all these years of investigation, we cannot answer our obsessive question as to whether there is life on Mars with a hundred-percent certainty. But the difficulties of astrobiological investigation on Mars do not compare with those of investigating the nearest planetary systems.

I believe that under the circumstances we should pin all our hopes on vigorously developing modern biology. What I have in mind is the modelling of the conditions on primeval Earth (which, incidentally, are not yet sufficiently clear) and an attempt to obtain artificial life under these conditions. When this problem is put on an experimental basis, P_2 will be estimable.

Thus, P_2 can vary widely. It could be vanishingly small (if life on Earth arose by chance)—this is a "pessimistic" outlook—while with an "optimistic" outlook, it could be enormous, almost unity if life on planets similar to Earth should arise spontaneously. Nothing else can be said about it at this stage.

The estimation of P_3 is less difficult. The general law of evolution in time of both inanimate nature (the Universe) and living nature (life on Earth) is progress from simple to complex forms. It amounts to the conversion of the accumulated quantitative changes into qualitatively new forms of moving matter. For this reason, we should see nothing surprising in living beings who used primitive tools for work and hunt as a means of survival being able to emerge at some stage of the evolution of life on Earth, whose motive force was natural selection and mutation. The further evolution of this species led to the appearance of intelligent beings on Earth. The dialectics of the process was revealed by Engels. The most ancient civilizations in Egypt and India were descended from nearly bestial ramapithecus who lived 10 to

15 million years ago. I believe an estimate of P_3 fairly close to unity (or, not very small at any rate) to be quite reasonable. Of course, this is a subjective probability.

In attempting to estimate P_4, we are confronted with greater difficulties. There are some grounds for the belief that it cannot be very large. Indeed, is the technological development of a civilization inevitable? After all, modern science based on the study and transformation of nature has existed only slightly more than 350 years (it can be dated from Galileo, who was the first to comprehend the mystery of mechanical movement, which was inaccessible to ancient science). Apparently, a technological era of civilization is not indispensable for the survival of our species. Quite the reverse—it can turn out to be dangerous. Remember one of the most acute problems of today, the preservation of the environment. This problem could only arise when given the technological development of human society. That the technological era is by no means essential is seen from the example provided by slave-owning societies of ancient times. The science of that time, for instance, came very close to the invention of the steam engine. However, objective causes, primarily the slave-owning system, put off the advent of the technological era by one and a half thousand years. Another good example is the thousand-year history of China. It appears that over the centuries Chinese civilization considered itself too perfect to develop any further.

It should be emphasized that a civilization ignoring technological development is not necessarily backward and primitive. Culture in such a society may reach superb heights. Recall, for instance, the Chinese art in the T'ang epoch or the art of feudal Japan. Customs may be very refined and literature may create masterpieces.

Thus, it is not at all clear whether a technological stage is unavoidable in the development of intelligent life. This means that P_4 is definitely lower than unity. On the other hand, one feels intuitively that it cannot be vanishingly small. At any rate, the estimation of P_2 is much more indefinite. But since all our estimates are extremely rough, we can safely assume P_4 to be equal to unity.

Finally, we approach a most important problem, the assessment of t_1, the lifetime of a technologically developed and advancing civilization. Along with P_2, this quantity is crucial as we assess the number of highly developed civilizations that are now existing in the Galaxy. The value of t_1 must also be connected in some way with the scientific and technological potential of a civilization, its capacity for radically restructuring its cosmic neighbourhood. It is fairly clear that if t_1 is large, this potential can reach an enormous value. Over the past three centuries, power generation, one of the most important characteristics of the scientific and technological capacity of mankind, has grown exponentially. Such an "explosive" growth will undoubtedly make human society a cosmic factor in the next few centuries, perhaps even in decades.

Mankind has already taken the first modest steps in this direction. An example is the development of the world's television communications, which has produced an unexpected result. The radio waves in the metre wavelength range, which are mainly used for television, escape freely into space, without being reflected by the Earth's ionosphere. Taking into account the number of television transmitters operating on Earth, their power and the relative duration of television programs, it can be demonstrated that the Earth emits about a million times as much radiation in the metre bands as it should emit naturally as a solid at 300 degrees Kelvin. This example gives us something to think about. For some two-to-three decades, our developing civilization has caused such an important "global" property of our planet as radio-frequency emission to grow enormously. The activities of intelligent creatures have made the Earth lead the other planets radiating at the metre wavelengths, leaving the giant planets Jupiter and Saturn far behind and being second only to the Sun. This is just for the present, but wait a few more centuries....

Our very first steps into the space around us have shown the active change-bringing nature of mankind. The Moon, revolving round the Earth, has been its unique "eternal" satellite for billion years. Nowadays, however, hundreds (perhaps, thousands) of artificial satellites revolve round it. Man is beginning to restructure "the general layout" of the solar system. In addition to its natural satellites, artificial satellites have appeared round Mars. True, they will not last very long and, according to calculations, will soon fall onto the surface of the red planet. But it is the first step that counts, and the large planets may follow suit.

What is also noteworthy is that, having once "stepped" into the outer space, man is beginning to come up with bold projects that may appear fantastic. For instance, there is a project of transforming the atmosphere of Venus by sending hydrogen chlorella into it, there are projects for "towing" asteroids, and so on (the projects of Tsiolkovsky were also regarded as fantasies in his day). Still more daring projects are proposed for the more distant future. An example is the project, proposed by F. Dyson, to create an immense circumsolar sphere with a radius of one astronomical unit using the substance of the big planets. According to Dyson, mankind will be able to spread out over the surface of the sphere when the Earth becomes too small for it. Incidentally, similar ideas were voiced by Tsiolkovsky long before Dyson.

There is an impression now prevailing that science and technology developing at the present rate, let alone any accelerated pace, will produce an immense potential. But will it? In the first place, it is not correct to extrapolate current rates of growth in production and in scientific and technological potentials over very long periods of time. It may well be that our epoch is a certain "transitional" period which will be followed by a long "plateau".

And yet, such unavoidable pauses in the process of unlimited expansion of intelligence are not likely to change the main trend, that is, the exploration of space on an ever increasing scale. On the other hand, the evolution of human society may bring other priorities to the fore with the result that interest in the exploration of space will be lost. All this leads us to the conclusion that the problem of extraterrestrial civilizations and contacts with them is a problem of the future.

Turning now to the estimation of t_1, we note two approaches to the task. The first proceeds from a "short lifetime" of the technological stage in the development of civilization, namely thousands or even hundreds of years. This is based on the excessive pace of development of our civilization over the past two centuries, which may lead to crises, exhaustion of material resources, irreversible consequences of environmental pollution and even probable changes in some social interests, in particular, a loss of interest in unlimited cosmic expansion. According to this approach, the t_1/T factor in Drake's formula must be very small, of the order of 10^{-7}. The proponents of the second approach, a "long lifetime", are so optimistic as to assume this factor to be close to unity. It should be noted that most experts, including the author of this article, advocate the short lifetime view. The "optimists" are definitely in the minority. In the opinion of the "pessimists", the total number of technologically developed civilizations in the Galaxy now existing concurrently with our civilization cannot be more than a few hundred. A compromise can, however, be found between both points of view.

As detailed predictions are unavailable, we can take the following approach in the absence of anything better. Let us assume that the developing technological civilizations are faced with various crises, some of which may cause their destruction. There is, however, a probability that some (let it be a few) civilizations will succeed in overcoming the crises and will develop without limit (or rather, practically without limit), exponentially building up their scientific and technological potential and using the enormous material and energy resources of the cosmic environment. If the number of civilizations in our stellar system is sufficiently large, then it will be quite natural to assume that the number of technological civilizations is larger than unity. Such "super-civilizations" can have their own lifetimes t_1 which substantially exceed the average lifetime of "ordinary" civilizations (say, like the Earth's). This means that, with a large value of t_1/T, most existing civilizations may be super-civilizations. The range of their activities must be truly cosmic.

Since the period in which the scientific and technological potential grows is always substantially shorter than any natural cosmogonic time scale, two types of super-civilizations are possible. These are Type II civilizations, which command the material and energy resources of their "own" central stars and planetary systems, and Type III civilizations that command all the resources of their entire stellar system. This classification, which was proposed by N.S. Kardashev a few years ago, classifies civilizations more or less similar to ours as Type I civilizations.

A good measure of the level of the technological civilization is its energy output. For the Earth's civilization, this will soon reach 10^{20} erg/s. Note that the power of radiation coming in from the Sun amounts to 10^{24} erg/s. Should the power generation on the Earth be increased several hundred times its energy balance as a cosmic body would be disturbed. The average temperature of our planet will rise by a few degrees, which will cause very serious consequences (for instance, the Antarctic ice cap will melt).

If it overcomes various critical situations, a civilization of Type II will be able to use up to 10^{33} erg/s and enormous material resources (for instance, the substance of the "useless" large planets should be such in the planetary system). It is self-evident that the carriers of a civilization of this type will settle throughout their planet system and restructure it. Such a situation may appear to be a fantasy at first glance. It is not difficult, however, to conclude that once the restructuring of a planetary system is started and the resources in its space surroundings are developed at a modest rate (say, doubling the material resources and harnessing the energy of the star in a hundred years), the planetary system will be fully transformed in time negligible by astronomic standards—a few thousand years. We have also included in this term the gradual egress of civilization out into space and a relatively slow rate of its use. What then can be said about Type III civilizations, which must control a power on the order of 10^{42} erg/s and restructure their galaxies over periods not exceeding millions of years (such terms are determined primarily by the extent of galaxies measuring hundreds of thousands of light years)?

Fantastic as it seems, the existence of Types II and III civilizations in the Universe cannot be denied logically. This follows from the tendency of our technological civilization to develop and from the "optimistic" assertion that all critical and conflicting situations can be overcome. And yet, we have to note that the logical approach is not pursued in such reasoning to its end because why should we limit ourselves to Type III civilizations? Why not imagine a further, still more grandiose, expansion of intelligence? Why, for example, can we not imagine a cluster of galaxies including hundreds of constituent parts and extending for tens of millions of light years being transformed by intelligent beings? And generally, can this explosive expansion of intelligence embrace if not the whole Universe (it will not have enough time for that), then a considerable part of it, possibly even the part we are in? I do not think that a reasoning man should pass this problem over as a far-fetched one.

Later on we shall revert to the evolution of Type II and III civilizations. But it would now be relevant to touch upon one important consequence of the scientific and technological development of a civilization. This is the advance of radiophysics which even at today's level makes communication between civilizations spaced at interstellar distances possible. The power and sensitivity of modern radiophysical equipment are such as to allow single-direction communication between correspondents spaced several hundred light years apart. According to a pessimistic estimate (the total number of technologically developed civilizations is about one thousand), the nearest civilization must be several thousand light years from us. Of course, an ultra-pessimistic estimate places the nearest civilization substantially further away.

The above assessment of the capabilities of radiophysics for interstellar communications was based on the modern engineering standards in the field. But the situation may drastically change if the technological level of a signal-transmitting civilization notably exceeds our terrestrial level. For example, signals sent by a Type II civilization could be detected with today's terrestrial equipment, even if this civilization were situated somewhere in the Andromeda nebula, a galaxy two million light years away from us. For this reason, a regular scientifically planned search for signals from extraterrestrial civilizations is by no means pointless even at present. Along with a number of technical questions (which are not worth discussing in this article), one very important problem arises in this connection, namely whether these signals, if ever detected, would be understandable to us.

One more aspect of the problem of detecting and decoding radiosignals from technologically developed civilizations needs to be mentioned. According to a widespread belief, particularly among astronomers and physicists in this country, the whole problem of extraterrestrial civilizations amounts essentially to the problem of establishing communications between them. I think such a view is too narrow and does not reflect the fundamental character of this complex problem.

The establishment of criteria by which to determine whether signals are artificial and whether they can (or cannot) be differentiated from signals of natural origin is an important problem. A more general problem is that of the so-called "cosmic miracle". It is stated like this: shall we ever be able, on detecting unusual cosmic objects, to affirm with certainty that these are Type II or III civilizations? What should be regarded as a reliable proof? The recent discovery of pulsars shows that this problem is not at all simple. Everything seemed to point that cosmic radiosignals of an artificial origin had at last been detected. It soon became clear, however, that what had been discovered were uncommon, but still natural cosmic objects—quickly rotating, strongly magnetized neutron stars.

To avoid such errors in future, I proposed at the Byurakan symposium that a researcher should always presume the natural origin of any cosmic phenomenon. In this way, the "artificial" versions may only be considered after all attempts at a "natural" interpretation had failed. Of course, one can imagine an extraterrestrial signal of an obviously artificial origin, for example, a sequence of pulses that give π in binary form with an enormous accuracy. It is reasonable to suppose that the binary system, if not universal, is nevertheless reasonably widespread among extraterrestrial civilizations. On the other hand, signals from civilizations evolved on a totally different biological basis may well be mistaken for natural noise.

We should not exaggerate, however, the difficulties involved in identificating and decoding signals which may come from extraterrestrial civilizations. Although such civilizations may greatly differ in form and have diverse systems of representing the surrounding world, some part of them will be more or less "Earth-like". At first we shall be bound to reckon with such a limited class of "brothers in intelligence" only. This limitation should hardly be regarded as serious if we take into account the extreme subjectivity in our estimation of P_l.

It seems evident that in the transition from a Type I civilization (that is, a more or less Earth-like civilization, which commands all the resources of its planet) to a Type II civilization, the intelligent life itself is bound to undergo qualitative changes, to make a great leap forward. The reason is that the objectives and "ideology" of a super-civilization differ radically from those of a "common" (in our limited view, of course) civilization. Although we are not now in a position to consider super-civilizations, one circumstance, I believe, should be taken into account.

To-date, the development of electronic computers has been tremendous. Progress in this field is a major indicator of the present scientific and technological revolution. And it is significant that this advance is speeding into an avalanche. It is common knowledge that a number of activities which formerly were the privilege of non-manual workers are now being taken over by computers. It can already be regarded as a proven fact that there is no activity, be it physical or, which is particularly important, mental, that an electronic computer will be unable to perform in principle. The vigorous development of cybernetics has opened the basically unlimited feasibility of modelling complex material systems, thereby filling the gap between "natural" and "artificial" intelligent beings. It looks as if intelligence is transcending its biological shell and is becoming a purely functional property of a special, highly-organized matter. The most important property of intelligent life—the ability to develop and improve itself—is already not the privilege of natural biological intelligence alone. It is well known that even today, at the dawn of the epoch of artificial intelligence, electronic computers are capable of self-improvement. Even today electronic computers and computer systems surpass man in such a vital characteristic of an intelligent being as the capacity of memory.

The electronic computer has so far been man's brainchild. Man has created the computer and the programs for it. This process has been dictated by social practice. But even now the computer is able to design other, more advanced, self-learning machines. And how about the future? I believe it will not be an exaggeration to affirm that by the middle of the next century practically all the mental and physical activities of mankind will be performed by cybernetic devices. Such is the main trend of the current scientific and technological revolution, a normal phase in the life of a civilization entering the path of technological development.

We are not going to discuss here if it is good or bad. What is essential is the irreversible character of the process. By the middle of the next century, a reasoning machine will be able to acquire independence in carrying out its various operations, such as space flights, work in outer space and work in environments hostile to man. Indeed, man in space is not a norm, although the world has witnessed the unparalleled feats of cosmonauts. The great efforts of an army of scientists, engineers, and workers have been spent to build an artificial biosphere indispensable for the existence and work of the first pioneers in space. The cost of such flights is very high. Of course, it all proves itself for there is no other way to explore space at first. In future, however, as cybernetics develops, such space exploration will be thought of as an anachronism.

With all his adaptability, man as a biological species is not fit for life and work in space and ecologically hostile environments. Man, for instance, cannot sustain large doses of radiation. And when from individual space flights, mankind turns to restructuring its space environment and exploiting its resources, armies of people will be required. This will be impractical and, what is important, unnecessary. This work will readily be done by specialized cybernetic devices that are intelligent, highly organized, and capable of making independent decisions in unexpectedly changing situations.

A "revolt of robots" has been a predilect theme of science-fiction writers from the time of Karel Čapek (who coined the word "robot"). The contradictions between natural intelligence and artificial intelligence have always been depicted as irreconcilable. But are they really? It seems to me that both types of intelligence will "peacefully coexist" for a long time, and combinations of natural and artificial intelligence will emerge. In fact, this process is beginning to take shape already.

Natural intelligence is not at all bound to be absorbed by artificial intelligence: we as "naturally intelligent" beings care about the preservation of our ecological environment. The emotions that arise as one muses over these things are not new. In this connection, Academician Kolmogorov wrote: "The development of science has repeatedly led to the destruction of deep-rooted illusions, beginning with the soothing faith of man in personal immortality. Half-knowledge and half-understanding turn these destructive scientific conclusions into arguments against science itself, in support of irrationalism and idealism. Darwin's theory of the origin of species and Pavlov's objective study of higher nervous activity were repeatedly presented as debasing the higher aspirations of man to create moral and aesthetic ideals. In our time the fear that man might not prove to be better than "inanimate" automata is converted into psychological arguments in support of vitalism and irrationalism"[2].

Thus, we come to the conclusion that the entities behind Type II and III civilizations are bound to be artificial intelligent beings (perhaps being?!). Among the other advantages artificial intelligent beings must have over natural ones is longevity. This property is crucial in interstellar flights at non-relativistic speeds. We obviously cannot detail how a super-civilizations functioning on the basis of artificial intelligence will exist and develop. Here the only fact that should matter is that the material basis of intelligence is in no way bound to be "biological". The term "biological" should in this case be taken in its broad sense, without being restricted to the biological history of the Earth. One can imagine these radically different phases of evolution of matter in the Universe: non-living matter; living matter; natural intelligent life; artificial intelligent life. According to this scheme, artificial intelligence is the highest phase of the evolution of matter in the Universe. We are at present unable to discuss seriously whether this phase is the ultimate one.

In conclusion I should like to touch upon a very important point. If Type II and III super-civilizations really exist in the Universe, why have they not so far been identified? Remember that the "unnatural" character of an object that belongs to Type III civilization can be detected by existing astronomical means from any distance in the metagalaxy.

Two basic reasons may be put forward: (a) our criteria of "artificiality" are imperfect, and what we assume to be natural objects (for instance, recently discovered quasars) are in fact Type III super-civilizations and (b) super-civilizations do not exist in the Universe.

Alas, I feel like leaning towards the second explanation. Definitely, nothing "super-natural" or "miraculous" has so far been detected in quasars and other objects. A lot of things are not yet understood, but I believe the astronomers and physicists will some day find the answers. I should emphasize, however, that my assessment of the situation is subjective—objective criteria are still unavailable here, too.

If the conclusion that there are no Type II or III super-civilizations is correct, it may imply that either the crises a technologically developing civilization encounters are so serious as to exclude transformation of such a civilization into a super-civilization, or (an appalling thought!) life in the Universe is a very rare and perhaps unique phenomenon.

I repeat, the latter statement is only a precarious assumption. Nevertheless, it would be interesting to ask ourselves: what if we are alone in the Universe. See how careful we should then be of our civilization! And how can our attitude towards it be influenced by this hypothesis? What conclusions follow from this for mankind?

A professional astronomer alone, who is aware of the real extent of the Universe, can fully realize what a monstrous idea it is that we are alone and unique not only in space, but also in time. For what are a momentary 350 years of the technological era against the 10-15 billion years of the evolution of the Universe.

References

1. Ляпунов А. А., *Проблемы теоретической и прикладной кибернетики* (Москва, 1980).
2. Колмогоров А. Н., *Жизнь и мышление с точки зрения кибернетики*. В кн. Опарин А. И. *Жизнь, её отношение с другими формами движения материи* (Москва, 1962).

Cybernetics and the Computer: Some Predictions

V. D. PEKELIS

One of the most fascinating examples of forecasting is the *Chart of the future* compiled by Arthur Clarke in 1960 (1). Full of predictions about technological development in the future, the chart contains a section on the electronic computer and cybernetics. The entry describing what had been achieved in that area up to 1960 reads:

1940-1960 — Electronic computer. Cybernetics. Transistor.

The prospects for development after 1960 were foreseen as follows:

1970 — Translating machines.
2000 — Artificial intelligence. Global library.
2020 — Logical languages.
2030 — Robots. Contacts with extraterrestrials.
2050 — Memory playback.
2060 — Mechanical educator.
2080 — Machine intelligence exceeds man's.
2090 — World brain.

Clarke's most significant prediction was his firm assertion that we are decades (not centuries!) away from the advent of intelligent machines.

V.I. Siphorov, Corresponding Member of the USSR Academy of Sciences, wrote in 1972 that the expectation that the problem of automatic translation could be solved by 1978 was "overly optimistic" but that extensive use of simple teaching machines by 1975 was "quite feasible".

According to Siphorov automated libraries would be developed not by 1976 but somewhat later. The development and application of sophisticated teaching machines was, in his opinion, "actual and feasible", and "seeing" and "hearing" machines, he supposed, would be available even earlier than 1982. Progress in robotics, the scientist felt, could also be expected before 1992, but he admitted that "the demonstration of complete man-machine symbiosis would not be possible until 2012".

In 1968, when one could still read that the electronic computer was incapable of going beyond the bounds of its program, the first suggestions about the advent of the "second computing revolution" appeared (the first revolution had supposedly lasted twenty years, from the mid-1940s to the mid-1960s.

The most important feature of this upcoming "revolution" was thought to be the development of an interface between man and machine. This interface or direct interaction of man with the machine was to be facilitated by two separate trends: first by the automation of computer programming; and second by the development of diverse output devices, including visual devices. This prediction has stood the test of time.

In the early 1970s the West German scientists H. Beinhauer and E. Schmacke made an attempt to collect, analyse, and order the most reliable (non-fictitious, as they put it) scientific, economic, technological, and social forecasts that had appeared up to that time. Their "Digest internationaler Prognosen"[2] considers the world at the beginning of the twenty-first century. The work contains a number of predictions of interest here. Electronic computers, wrote the authors, would form the basis of information-processing technology and by 1980, would number approximately 355 000 worldwide (as it happened, they proved to be much more numerous).

The ratio of performance to cost, an important indicator of computers efficiency was expected to change. Performance, wrote Beinhauer and Schmacke, will improve, and the cost per operation will drop by a factor of 200 over 20 years.

Computers were expected to become one-thousandth of their present size and, especially important, become much more dependable. Speed, reliability, compactness, and cost effectiveness would make the computers indispensable in all spheres of human activity.

Improvements in computer memory and increases in capacity and speed of performance were considered to be of prime importance; and the time expended in retrieval of information stored in the computer memory was expected to decrease by a factor of 1 000 (at the time the forecast was published information retrieval took approximately 1 μs). In computers operational in 2000, according to Beinhauer and Schmacke, this time will be brought down to 10 ns.

The West German scientists also predicted the development of the first electronic computer with optical memory by about 1990. The optical memory was experted to work by recording information directly on magnetic film or with a laser beam on light-sensitive film.

Another prediction concerned a magnetic storage device with the capacity for storage and retrieval of the information contained on 540 million typed pages.

The forecast also notes designs for a computer memory which can store 20 000 book volumes on a piece of nickel foil 20 × 25 cm square.

Memory capacity, the writers predicted, will grow several hundred times, and a few large storage devices will be able to record all the information now stored in the world's libraries.

Encyclopedic data banks were expected, as a result, to function not later than 1980.

The question when the electronic computer can be expected to "see" and "hear" was a particularly important one. The development of machines with the capacity to read texts was begun early in the 1970s and experts assumed that machines able to read any handwritten text at a rate of fifty characters per second would appear by the late 1970s. Machines capable of identifying individual vocal commands were expected to appear by the beginning of the 1980s.

But computers capable of understanding and acting solely on vocal commands were not expected even by 2000.

It is interesting that at nearly the same time estimates were made by Soviet scientists. Academician V.M. Glushkov, for example, wrote: "As soon as the old methods of 'talking' to the computer are no longer suitable, the means necessary to enable man to converse with the machine will emerge immediately... Such a need will be felt sometime in the 1980s, that is, in computers of the fourth or at the very latest the fifth generation".

Data banks, according to Glushkov, were also likely: "The time is not far off when electronic computers will be capable of storing not only technological and scientific knowledge accumulated by mankind, but also all that has been created by man over the long history of his existence; they will become his immense and eternal memory". The complete symbiosis of man and machine, Glushkov believed, will be attained by scientists by about 2020, that is, in less than half a century.

Undoubtedly, the final test of the worth of any prediction is in the accuracy of its forecasts. Anyone who tackles the problems of the future wants to know how reliable his predictions are and how many of them prove true.

And although conjectures and hopes may be far from the hard facts of reality, it is, nevertheless, interesting to look at some of the hopes scientists have cherished over the years about the future of cybernetics and electronic computers.

The expectations, guesses, and conjectures voiced at different times and on various occasions have been numerous. They may be divided into different categories. Classification of forecasts, however, belongs to the province of futurology, which we discussed briefly in the preface.

Here we merely want to survey the hopes of certain scientists working on problems that have so far resisted solution but are not considered insoluble. Such problems usually serve as landmarks in science: inaccessible today, they may be reached in the future.

Scientists' conjectures are no less important. A dictionary of Modern English defines the word conjecture as a guess achieved by thought or reflections, a supposition and, in scientific research, as an assumption, hypothesis (used mainly ironically). Nevertheless, we shall put irony aside. Let us recall Bohr's comment that in this day and age it is difficult to believe in a theory unless it is crazy.

A quarter of a century ago, the British physicist and Nobel Prize winner Sir George Thomson in his book *The Foreseeable Future*[3] made a careful attempt to analyse the prospects for scientific development. Turning to the problems of the application of computers, he wrote that computers in the twentieth century may find holes in many well established theories. In his view, the main use of the computer will be to administer increasingly complex organizations. Computers, according to Sir Thomson will make possible accurate quantitative planning where we now rely on experienced judgement.

The great potential for the computers in the field of automation was predicted by the historian of science Professor B.G. Kuznetsov in his book *Наука в 2000 году*. Kuznetsov also stressed the role of cybernetics, which, in his opinion, "will gradually come to regulate dynamic processes at an increasingly higher level" because modern cybernetic devices allow automation of not only steady-state processes and dynamic processes associated with the re-arrangement of equipment, but also dynamic processes of designing new equipment and introducing changes into manufacturing technology[4].

Regarding the same problem, the American expert George Kozmetsky stated at the Fourth Goddard Memorial Symposium of the American Astronautical Society in 1966: "We have the computing capability necessary to turn on and off switches that will make the assembly lines of 2001 spring into motion with robot-like precision. More important, in the R & D laboratories, work is proceeding on computers which have the capabilities of making automatic decisions based on their abilities to self-organize data rather than on the programmer's pre-conceived sub-routines."[5]

Great hopes were also pinned in those years on the modelling of the human brain and other organs as well as the cybernetic control of the human organism. Thus, the biologist and bio-cyberneticist Professor S.N. Braines wrote in his article "The future of biological and medical cybernetics": "We are on the way towards developing a model of the living brain, though incomplete, nevertheless having many of the brain's properties. The first step towards such a model, namely, research into the systems of pattern recognition, into the simulation of conditioned reflexes, and into the theory of neural networks, has already been taken. Synthesis of these investigations supplemented by the study of active forms of behaviour is likely to be the next step. As a result, a model capable of adaptive, intelligent behaviour will be developed. Such a system may bring to mind the robot of science fiction; its creating on the basis of the research mentioned, however, seems to be feasible"[6]. Braines believed that the primary task of biological cybernetics was the development of an integrated theory of control in the human organism as a constituent part of the general theory of medicine.

Specialists in radio held similar opinions. A.F. Plonsky, a Doctor of Engineering Sciences, whose research concerned electric oscillations of high stability, thought that an electronic prototype of the mythical "guardian angel", which continuously keeps track of the state of your organism by sensing and interpreting bio-electric signals, is feasible. On detecting the slightest trouble in your "functional system", it establishes automatic communication with a medico-mathematical computing centre. If required, urgent and effective remedial actions will be taken[7]. Plonsky believed that cybernetic prostheses of the organs of sight and hearing can already be discussed at least speculatively.

Many experts held that cybernetics had also to be developed to prevent a build-up of the information barrier. This barrier could hamper the advance of science if no revolution, similar to that in the sphere of physical labour occurring over the last two centuries, would be carried out in the mental sphere. It is just for this reason that cybernetics was called the developer of artificial researchers, or the Big Brain, the generator and transmitter of information.

In 1976 Siphorov wrote that "thinking" machines with properties currently "impossible" will be developed. These machines, in his view, "will represent a qualitatively new form of the existence of matter, whose evolutionary laws will be different from the laws of evolution of present-day technology, on the one hand, and from those of the living nature, on the other" [8].

The search for ways to overcome the information barrier leads to attempts to discover new methods of communication. Thus, the British physicist John Bernal wrote as far back as 1958: "It is by no means impossible that man may succeed, by a combination of electronic devices reacting with brain cells, to communicate thoughts directly from one mind to another, without the use of language. This would probably mean that not only thoughts but also emotions and memories could be transmitted with the vividness of actual experience. Such a method of communication would enlarge immensely, in content and immediacy, the picture and the book. It would permit mankind to pass on from generation to generation the essentials of personal contributions and not only a few relics which is all we can do now"[9].

Ten years later, the American scientist and Nobel Prize winner Glenn Seaborg made the same suggestion in his article "Where is science taking us?": "... some day in the future it may be possible to program information directly into the human brain, or develop control systems through which a man's thought alone can remotely control a machine"[10].

Long-term forecasting is impossible without analysis of the development of science both currently and in the near future. And such an analysis depends on a close examination of the actual problems of the period of time being considered. Thus, predictions "work" not only for the future but also for the present day by contributing to more efficient scientific research, to improved planning and project development, to cost effectiveness, and, hence, to our progress in general.

References

1. Arthur C. Clarke. *Profiles of the Future. An Inquiry into the Limits of the Possible*. 1st ed. New York: Harper & Row, 1960, 233.
2. Beinhauer H.H. and E. Schmacke. *Fahrplan in die Zukunft. Digest internationaler Prognosen*. Dusseldorf: Droste Verlag, 1970.
3. Thomson G. *The Foreseeable Future*. Cambridge: Cambridge University Press, 1955, 161, 162.
4. Кузнецов Б. Г. *Наука, в 2000 году*. (Москва, 1969).
5. Kozmetsky, G. *Automation in 2001*. E.B. Konecci, M.W. Hunter II and R.F. Trapp, eds. *Space Age in Fiscal Year 2001*. Proceedings on the Fourth AAS Goddard Memorial Symposium 15-16, March 1966. An American Astronautical Society Publication, Washington, v. 10, 1967, 392.
6. Braines, S.N., *Future of Science. International Yearbook*, Moscow, 1968, 223-224.
7. Plonsky, A.F. In: *Future of Science. International Yearbook*. (in Russian), Moscow, 1976, 157.
8. Siphorov V. I. In: *Future of Science. International Yearbook*, Moscow, 1976, 157.
9. Bernal, I.D. *World Without War*. London: Routledge & Kegan Paul, 1958, 279.
10. Seaborg, G.T. Where is science taking us? In: *Future of Science. International Yearbook*, Moscow, 1970, 69.

About the Authors

Igor A. APOKIN, Cand. Sc. (Engineering), is a Senior Researcher at the Institute for the History of the Natural Sciences and Engineering under the USSR Academy of Sciences.

Academician Oleg M. BELOTSERKOVSKY is a deputy academician-secretary of the Mechanics and Control Processes Department at the USSR Academy of Sciences. He is the chairman of the Scientific Board on Cybernetics and the director of the Moscow Physical Engineering Institute.

Professor Boris V. BIRYUKOV, D. Sc. (Philosophy), is a deputy chairman of the Cybernetics Methodology Section of the Scientific Board on Cybernetics of the USSR Academy of Sciences.

Mikhail M. BOTVINNIK, D. Sc. (Engineering), heads a department at the Electrical Energy R & D Institute under the USSR Ministry for Power Engineering. He is an international grandmaster and is a former world chess Champion.

Andrey V. BRUSHLINSKY, D. Sc. (Psychology), is the director of Thinking-Psychology Studies at the Psychology Institute under the USSR Academy of Sciences.

Modest G. GAAZE-RAPOPORT, Cand. Sc. (Engineering), is a member of the Scientific Board on Cybernetics under the Presidium of the USSR Academy of Sciences. He specializes in the methodological problems of cybernetics,

Academician Victor M. GLUSHKOV (1921-1981), was a vice-president of the Ukrainian Academy of Sciences and directed the Cybernetics Institute under the Ukrainian Academy of Sciences. He was a hero of Socialist Labour and a winner of the Lenin and State Prizes.

I. GREKOVA (Professor Ekaterina S. VENTSEL) is a member of the USSR Writers Union, D. Sc. (Physics & Mathematics), and specializes in operations research and systems analysis.

Professor Yury M. KANYGIN, D. Sc. (Economy), heads the Laboratory for Economic and Computer Information Studies at the Cybernetics Institute under the Ukrainian Academy of Sciences.

Academician Andrey N. KOLMOGOROV is a hero of Socialist Labour, a winner of the State and Lenin prizes, a fellow of the US Academy of Sciences, a fellow of the Royal Society, UK, and the member of the Paris Academy of Sciences.

Igor M. MAKAROV is a Corresponding Member of the USSR Academy of Sciences. He is the chairman of the Scientific Board on Robotics under the USSR Academy of Sciences.

Victor D. PEKELIS is an essayist and is a member of the USSR Writers Union.

Academician Boris N. PETROV (1913-1980) was a vice-president of the USSR Academy of Sciences and headed the Intercosmos project. He was a hero of Socialist Labour and a State-prize winner.

Professor Sergey N. PLOTNIKOV, D. Sc. (Philosophy), heads the Social Research Department at the Culture Research Institute under the RSFSR Ministry for Culture.

Dmitry A. POSPELOV, D. Sc. (Engineering) is the head

of a Laboratory at the Computer Centre of the USSR Academy of Sciences.

Germogen S. POSPELOV is a corresponding member of the USSR Academy of Sciences, a deputy academician-secretary of the Mechanics and Control Processes Department at the USSR Academy of Sciences, and is the chairman of the Artificial Intelligence Research Board of the Systems Analysis Committee under the USSR Academy of Sciences.

Igor M. ROSSOKHOVATSKY is a science-fiction writer and a member of the USSR Writers Union.

Iosif S. SHKLOVSKY is a corresponding member of the USSR Academy of Sciences and heads the Astrophysics Department at the Space Research Institute under the USSR Academy of Sciences. He is a Lenin Prize winner, a fellow of the US Academy of Sciences, and a fellow of the Royal Society, UK.

Professor Georgy V. SKROTSKY, D. Sc. (Physics & Mathematics), is the head of the Macroscopic Quantum Physics Department at the Moscow Physical Engineering Institute.

Georgy L. SMOLYAN, Cand. Sc. (Philosophy), specializes in cybernetics methodology and philosophy.

Professor Filipp G. STAROS (1917-1979), D. Sc. (Engineering).

Anatoly A. STOGNY is a corresponding member of the Ukrainian Academy of Sciences and a staff member at the Cybernetics Institute under the Ukrainian Academy of Sciences.

Professor Viktor S. TYUKHTIN, D. Sc. (Philosophy), is the head of a research section at the Philosophy Institute under the USSR Academy of Sciences.

Academician Evgeny P. VELIKHOV is a vice-presi-